WORKSHOP MATHEMATICS

PART II.

WORKSHOP MATHEMATICS

PART II.

BY

FRANK CASTLE, M.I.Mech.E.

LATE OF THE MECHANICAL LABORATORY, ROYAL COLLEGE OF SCIENCE, SOUTH KENSINGTON;
LECTURER IN PRACTICAL MATHEMATICS, MACHINE CONSTRUCTION AND DRAWING,
BUILDING CONSTRUCTION AND ENGINEERING SCIENCE, AT THE
MUNICIPAL TECHNICAL INSTITUTE, EASTBOURNE

MACMILLAN AND CO., LIMITED
ST. MARTIN'S STREET, LONDON
1946

PRINTED IN GREAT BRITAIN

PREFACE

To perform his work intelligently, an artizan must have a knowledge of Elementary Mathematics. When he comes to appreciate this fact for himself the workman generally finds that even the arithmetic he learnt at school has left him, and that he remembers little more than four simple rules and the multiplication table. Teachers soon discover that though anxious to learn, a student of this kind does not wish to lose contact with the practical requirements of the workshop,— he is impatient of "pure" mathematics,—so the question arises how to teach him mathematics enough, by dealing with the calculations themselves which he is actually called upon to make at his work.

The plan which is found most successful is a compromise. It is useless to say that all students ought to learn the broad principles of mathematics first, and apply them afterwards. Experience has proved that most artizans will not attend classes where the authorities decide that this is the only course.

To meet the difficulty classes in Workshop Arithmetic, Workshop Calculations and Practical Mathematics, have grown up, and it is to provide for young workmen beginning to attend one of these classes that this little book has been prepared. It will form with Part I. an introduction to my larger volume on "Practical Mathematics" which has been received very favourably, and will, I trust, prove serviceable to a class of students who deserve every assistance.

A long experience in my own classes has convinced me that the solution of a large number of carefully graduated exercises of a practical kind is the best way to maintain the interest of the student. It will consequently be found that the most prominent characteristics of the present book, and also of Part I., is the subordination of rigid mathematical proof to the provision of numerous problems drawn from the student's everyday experience.

FRANK CASTLE.

At the end of this edition Miscellaneous Exercises have been added, arranged in sections, corresponding roughly to those adopted in the book. It is hoped that these may be found useful either for working simultaneously with the sections to which they refer, or as revision exercises. Some corrections to the answers have been made ; and this opportunity is taken to thank those teachers and students who have directed my attention to the need for them. Also in this edition a chapter on Numerical Trigonometry has been added. Numerous exercises are given, many of which may be solved either by drawing, or calculation, or by both combined ; and these should serve as a useful introduction to an important subject. For proofs of formulae, where such are used, reference may be made to my "Manual of Practical Mathematics" published by Messrs. Macmillan & Co., Ltd. Thanks are gratefully expressed to the Union of Lancashire and Cheshire Institutes [L.C.U.], the Union of Educational Institutions [U.E.I] and the National Union of Teachers [N U.T.] and other authorities for their permission to use questions from examination papers.

F. C.

CONTENTS.

WORKSHOP MATHEMATICS.

SECTION I.—LABOUR-SAVING METHODS.

CHAPTER I.

DUODECIMALS.

In the mensuration of both plane and solid figures, the somewhat tedious and troublesome arithmetical operations of multiplication, division, involution and evolution are continually required. To facilitate such computations, however, many labour-saving devices are used by practical men. By such means operations which otherwise would involve considerable labour, and consequent risk of error, are performed readily and in many cases almost mechanically.

In Part I. of this course the subject of Mensuration, as far as plane figures, has been considered, and before proceeding further it will be advantageous to describe some of these shortened methods which are in general use.

Amongst the many forms of labour-saving contrivances we can only refer to a few. Perhaps the most common is that of a carefully compiled table of numbers by means of which, knowing the weight or price of a single article, the weight or price of any number can at once be ascertained. Such tables constitute the so-called "**ready reckoners.**"

Also, in special cases where a large amount of multiplication, division, etc., has to be performed, one or other of the many

forms of **calculating machines** may be used. These are, however, far too expensive for general use. Hence, when it is
necessary for any practical purpose to multiply or divide one set
of numbers by another, contracted methods of multiplication, as
shown in Part I. p. 30, may be adopted ; or, in some cases, what
are called *duodecimals* may be used with advantage.

But in all cases probably the best and most trustworthy
method of performing the different arithmetical processes is by
means of *logarithms*.

Duodecimals.—When it is required to multiply two quantities together, in which both multiplier and multiplicand are
expressed in feet and inches, we may reduce the given quantities
to feet, and fractional parts of a foot, and obtain the product in
square feet by using either vulgar or decimal fractions. Or,
both the given terms may be expressed in inches, when the
product will be in square inches.

By the method of duodecimals, practically used by bricklayers,
painters, glaziers, and others engaged in the building trades, in
estimating their work, it is not necessary to reduce lengths, etc.,
to the same denomination. The process is in many respects
analagous to the multiplication of decimals.

The unit, one *foot*, is divided into 12 primes (1') ; the primes
are each divided into 12 seconds (1") ; and each second again
into 12 thirds (1''') ; and these are divided into 12 fourths (1^{iv}),
and so on. The word 'parts' is sometimes used instead of
'seconds.'

The divisions and subdivisions of the square foot are called
superficial primes, seconds, etc. ; and in the subdivision of cubes
the parts are called *cubic* primes, *cubic* seconds, and so on.

In the first place, then, the product of feet multiplied by feet
is called square feet. The product of primes and feet are superficial primes : thus, 1 prime $= \frac{1}{12}$ sq. ft., and 1 prime multiplied
by 1 foot $= \frac{1}{12} \times 1 = 1$ superficial prime. In a similar manner,
the product of feet and seconds are called superficial seconds.

The process of multiplication and the conversion of the result
to cubic measure may be shown by a simple example :

Ex. 1. (*a*) Find the product of 4 ft. 8 in. and 3 ft. 2 in. (*b*) Multiply the product by 10 ft. 2½ in.

Method.—(*a*) Write down the two given dimensions so that like quantities are immediately under each other.

Begin with the number denoting feet in the multiplier and the lowest dimension in the multiplicand, and carry one to the left for every 12 in each product. Next multiply by the inches; carry one as before and set down the result one place to the right of the former product; proceed in like manner with a third dimension when one is present.

$$\begin{array}{rrr} 3 \text{ ft.} & 2' & \\ 4 & 8 & \\ \hline 12 \text{ ft.} & 8' & \\ 2 & 1 & 4'' \\ \hline 14 \text{ ft.} & 9' & 4'' \end{array}$$

Thus, in the above example, multiplying by 4 we have the product of 3 ft. 2′ by 4 = 12 ft. 8′, as shown.

Next, multiplying by 8 we have $8 \times 2 = 16 = 12 + 4$. We set down the 4 one place to the right, and carry 1 to the next figure. Then $8 \times 3 = 24$ and 1 carried from the last figure makes $25 = 24 + 1$. So we set down 1 and carry 2 to the next place.

Adding these, the product is 14 sq. ft. + 9 superficial primes + 4 superficial seconds.

This may be converted into square feet and square inches as follows :

$$14 \text{ sq. ft.} + 9' + 4'' = 14 \text{ sq. ft.} + \left(\tfrac{9}{12} + \tfrac{4}{144}\right) \times 144 \text{ sq. in.}$$
$$= 14 \text{ sq. ft.} + \left(\tfrac{108}{144} + \tfrac{4}{144}\right) \times 144 \text{ sq. in.}$$
$$= 14 \text{ sq. ft.} + 112 \text{ sq. in.}$$

As already indicated in Part I., p. 113, the product of two given lengths, or linear dimensions, corresponds to the area of a rectangle, and is denoted by square feet, square inches, etc. In like manner, when the product is multiplied by a third length, called the altitude, the height, or the thickness, the result is expressed by cubic feet, cubic inches, etc., and corresponds to the volume of a given solid.

(*b*) We have now to multiply the product 14 sq. ft. 9′ 4″ by 10 ft. 2½ in.

Now 10 ft. 2½ in. = 10 ft. + $2\tfrac{6}{12}$ in. = 10 ft. 2′ 6″.

As before, we commence by multiplying by 10 ; thus, $10 \times 4 = 40$. Hence we carry 3 primes to the next figure and write down the remaining 4 seconds. Next,

$$10 \times 9 + 3 = 93 = (7 \times 12) + 9.$$

This gives 7 to be carried to the next figure, and the remainder 9 is written down. Finally, $10 \times 14 + 7 = 147$.

$$\begin{array}{rrrrr} 14 \text{ ft.} & 9' & 4'' & & \\ 10 & 2 & 6 & & \\ \hline 147 \text{ ft.} & 9' & 4'' & & \\ 2 & 5 & 6 & 8''' & \\ & 7 & 4 & 8 & 0^{iv} \\ \hline 150 \text{ ft.} & 10' & 3'' & 4''' & \end{array}$$

The remaining two products are found in like manner; and, on adding, the volume is found to be 150 cub. ft. 10 cub. primes + 3 cub. seconds + 4 cub. thirds, or

$$150 \text{ cub. ft.} + \left(\frac{10}{12} + \frac{3}{144} + \frac{4}{1728}\right) \times 1728 \text{ cub. in.}$$
$$= 150 \text{ cub. ft.} + 1480 \text{ cub. in.}$$

EXERCISES. I.

Find by duodecimals, and express in square feet, inches, etc., the areas of rectangles whose lengths and breadths are

1. 4 ft. 7 in. and 9 ft. 6 in. **2.** 17 ft. 8 in. and 11 ft. 3 in.

3. 2 ft. 3 in. and 5 ft. 7 in. **4.** 9 ft. 10 in. 5″ and 10 ft. 5 in. 6″.

Express in cubic feet, inches, etc., the volumes of solids whose lengths, breadths and altitudes are

5. 10 ft. 2½ in., 4 ft. 8 in., and 6 ft. 4 in.

6. 23 ft. 3 in., 15 ft. 6 in., and 18 ft. 7 in.

7. 3 ft. 5 in., 4 ft. 9 in., and 8 ft. 7 in.

8. 9 ft. 3 in., 11 ft. 5 in., and 3 ft. 2 in.

9. 2 ft. 9 in., 1 ft. 8 in., and 1 ft. 4 in.

10. 13 ft. 7 in., 9 ft. 3 in., and 2 ft. 5 in.

11. 4 ft. 2 in. 7 parts, 3 ft. 2 in. 3 parts, and 7 ft. 5 in.

12. 7 ft. 5 in. 7 parts, 4 ft. 2 in., and 3 ft. 4 in. 7 parts.

13. 4 ft. 7 in., 4 ft. 2 in. 5 parts, and 2 ft. 7 in. 6 parts.

14. 3 ft. 8 in. 4′, 1 ft. 7 in. 6′, and 1 ft. 4 in. 9′

15. The internal measurements of a wooden box without a lid are: Length, 4 ft. 5 in.; breadth, 3 ft. 7 in.; depth, 2 ft. 5 in. Find, preferably by the duodecimal method, (i) the volume of the box, (ii) the total internal area of the wood used. [N.U.T.]

16. Find, using duodecimals, the area of an oblong notice-board, 4 ft. 7½ in. long and 2 ft. 6 in. wide. [N.U.T.]

17. The breadth of an oblong floor is three-quarters of its length, the perimeter of the floor is 86 ft. 4 in. Find the area of the floor. [N.U.T.]

CHAPTER II.

LOGARITHMS.

MULTIPLICATION AND DIVISION BY LOGARITHMS.

Logarithms and Logarithmic Tables.—The two most important labour-saving methods are furnished by *logarithms* and the *slide-rule*. As it is necessary that both the student and the practical man should be able to use logarithmic tables with ease and facility, and as they may be used readily even by those who are not acquainted with the manner in which they are calculated, it is desirable before entering into any explanation as to the principles on which common and hyperbolic logarithms are based to consider how, by means of a table of logarithms, the arithmetical operations of multiplication, division, involution and evolution are performed. We shall also find that many problems which would be impossible by arithmetical processes are readily solved when logarithms are used. Again, in using a slide rule, a knowledge of the use of logarithms is of service, enabling the significance of its divisions to be more intelligible than would otherwise be the case.

Logarithms of numbers consist of an integral part called the **index** or **characteristic,** and a decimal part called the **mantissa.** If the reader will refer to Table III., he will find that opposite each of the numbers from 10 to 99 four figures are placed. These four figures are called the *mantissa*; the *characteristic*, which may be either positive or negative, has to be supplied when writing down the logarithm of any given number in a way to be presently described.

Where great accuracy is required, seven or more figures are to be found in the mantissa.

Logarithmic tables of all numbers from 1 to 100000 have been calculated with seven figures in the mantissa, but for all ordinary purposes, and where only approximate calculations are required, such a table as that shown in Table III., p. 164, and known as *four-figure logarithms*, is very convenient.

By means of the numbers 10 to 99, and (*a*) those at the top of the table, and (*b*) those in the difference column on the right, the logarithm of any number from 0 to 10000 can be written down.

In logarithms all numbers are expressed by the powers of some number called the *base*.

DEFINITION.—**The logarithm of a number to a given base is the index showing the power to which that base must be raised to give the number.**

Thus, if N denote any number and a a given base, then by raising a to some power x we can get N. This is expressed by the equation

$$N = a^x.$$

Any number can be used as the base, but, as we shall find, the system of logarithms in which the base is 10 is commonly used.

Thus, if the base be 2, then as $8 = 2^3$, 3 is the logarithm of 8 to the base 2. This can also be expressed by writing $\log_2 8 = 3$.

In a similar manner, if the base be 5, then 3 is the logarithm of 125 to the base 5;

$$\therefore \quad \log_5 125 = 3.$$

Also $64 = 2^6 = 4^3 = 8^2.$

Hence   6 is the log of 64 to the base 2 ;

            3 is the log of 64 to the base 4 ;

            2 is the log of 64 to the base 8, etc.;

$$\therefore \quad \log_2 64 = 6 \; ; \quad \log_4 64 = 3 \; ; \quad \log_8 64 = 2, \text{ etc.},$$

using in each case the abbreviation *log* for logarithm.

Logarithms to the Base 10.—It is most convenient to use 10 as the base for a system of logarithms. It is then only necessary to print in a table of such logarithms the decimal part or mantissa ; the characteristic can, we shall see, be determined by inspection. The tables are in this way less bulky than would otherwise be the case. When calculated to a base 10, logarithms are known as Common Logarithms.

$$Since \ N = 10^x;$$
$$\therefore \ \log_{10} N = x,$$

or by definition, substituting positive numbers for N,

As $\qquad\qquad 1 = 10^0; \quad \therefore \ \log \ 1 = 0.$

Also, $\qquad\quad 10 = 10^1; \quad \therefore \ \log \ 10 = 1.$

Again, $\qquad\quad 100 = 10^2; \quad \therefore \ \log 100 = 2,$ etc.

In the chapter on Indices (p. 113) we find that ·1, or $\frac{1}{10}$, can be written as 10^{-1}; also ·01, or $\frac{1}{100}$, can be written as 10^{-2}.

Hence $\qquad\qquad \log ·1 = \log \frac{1}{10} = -1,$

and $\qquad\qquad \log ·01 = -2,$ etc.

The *mantissa is always positive*, and instead of writing the negative sign in front of the characteristic, it is customary in logarithms to place it over the top; thus, log ·1 is not written -1 but as $\bar{1}$, and log ·01 = $\bar{2}$.

In the preceding logarithms we have only inserted the characteristic; the mantissa consists of a series of ciphers.

Thus, $\qquad\qquad \log \quad 1 = 0·0000,$

$\qquad\qquad\qquad \log \ 10 = 1·0000,$

$\qquad\qquad\qquad \log 100 = 2·0000,$ and so on.

As the logarithm of 1 is zero, and log 10 is 1, it is evident that the logarithms of all numbers between 1 and 10 will consist of a certain number of decimals.

Thus, $\log 2 = ·3010$ indicates, that if we raise 10 to the power ·3010 we shall obtain 2, or $10^{·3010} = 2$.

In a similar manner, $200 = 2 \times 100$ might be written as $10^2 \times 10^{·3010}$,

$$\therefore \ 200 = 10^{2·3010}.$$

Hence we write $\qquad \log 200 = 2·3010.$

The characteristic of a Logarithm.—It will be seen by reference to Table III. that the logarithms of numbers become larger as the numbers are larger.

Referring to Table III., opposite the number 47 we find the *mantissa* ·6721, and as 47 lies between 10 and 100 the characteristic is 1. Hence the log of 47 is 1·6721.

Again, the number 470 lies between 100 and 1000, and therefore the characteristic is in this case 2 ;

$$\therefore \ \log 470 = 2 \cdot 6721.$$

In a similar manner, the logarithms of 4700 and 47000 are $3 \cdot 6721$ and $4 \cdot 6721$ respectively; in each case the mantissa is the same, but the characteristic is different.

The rule by which the characteristic is found may be stated as follows : *The characteristic of any number greater than unity is positive, and is less by one than the number of figures to the left of the decimal point.*

It must also be borne in mind that the *characteristic of a number less than unity is negative, and is greater by one than the number of zeros which follow the decimal point.*

Ex. 1.   To write down log ·047.

Here one zero follows the decimal point, hence the characteristic is $\overline{2}$;

$$\therefore \ \log \cdot 047 = \overline{2} \cdot 6721.$$

Again, to obtain the log of ·00047.

As there are three zeros following the decimal point, the characteristic is $\overline{4}$, and

$$\therefore \ \log \cdot 00047 = \overline{4} \cdot 6721.$$

Similarly in the case of log ·47.   Here the rule will give $\overline{1}$ for the characteristic ;

$$\therefore \ \log \cdot 47 = \overline{1} \cdot 6721.$$

Other numbers should be taken from Table III., and the characteristic of the corresponding logarithm determined by inspection.   After a little practice the writing down of the logarithm of any number becomes quite easy.

Another method of determining the characteristic is to treat any given number as follows :

$$470 = 4 \cdot 7 \times 100 = 4 \cdot 7 \times 10^2.$$

Hence as before the characteristic is 2.

Similarly, $4700 = 4 \cdot 7 \times 10^3,$ $\cdot 47 = 4 \cdot 7 \times 10^{-1},$

$$\cdot 047 = 4 \cdot 7 \times 10^{-2}, \quad \cdot 0047 = 4 \cdot 7 \times 10^{-3}.$$

If all numbers are written in the above convenient form the characteristic is, as already indicated, the index of the multiplier 10.   If this method can be easily and readily applied by the student it will save the trouble of remembering rules.

Logarithmic Tables.—*To obtain the logarithm of a number consisting of four figures.*

The way to proceed is as follows:

Ex. 1. Find the log of 3768.

First look in Table III. for the number 37, then the next figure 6 is found at the top of table, so that the mantissa of

$$\log 376 = \cdot5752.$$

At the extreme right of the table will be seen a column of differences, as they are called ; thus, under the figure 8 is found the number 9. This must be added to the mantissa previously obtained.

Hence we have mantissa of $\log 376 = 5752$

$$\begin{array}{r}\text{Add difference,} \quad 9 \\ \hline\end{array}$$

Given mantissa for $\log 3768 = \overline{5761}$

Hence	$\log 3768 = 3\cdot5761,$
also	$\log \cdot003768 = \bar{3}\cdot5761,$
and	$\log \cdot3768 = \bar{1}\cdot5761,$ etc.

To find the number corresponding to a given logarithm or the antilogarithm of a number.

Ex. 2. Given the logarithm $2\cdot4725$, to find the number.

From Table IV. of antilogarithms,

Opposite the mantissa $\cdot472$ we have 2965. In the difference column under the number 5, and on the horizontal line 47, we have the figure 3.

Hence the corresponding mantissa $= 2968$, and the number required is $296\cdot8$.

If the given logarithm had been $\bar{2}\cdot4725$ the required number would be $\cdot02968$.

Multiplication by Logarithms.—*By adding the logarithms of two or more numbers together, we obtain the logarithm of their product, and the number corresponding to this logarithm, obtained from Table IV. of antilogarithms, is the product required.*

Ex. 1. Multiply $\cdot2885$ by $\cdot915$.

From Table III.,	$\log 288 =$	4594
	Diff. col. for 5,	8

$$\therefore \ \log \cdot2885 = \bar{1}\cdot4602$$

Also $\qquad \log \cdot915 = \bar{1}\cdot9614$

$\therefore$ logarithm of product $= \bar{1}\cdot4602 + \bar{1}\cdot9614 = \bar{1}\cdot4216.$

From Table IV.,   antilog 421 = 2636

Diff. col. for 6,   4

∴ antilog 4216 = 2640

The negative characteristic indicates that the product is a decimal.
Hence number corresponding to $\bar{1}$·4216 = ·264 ;

∴ ·2885 × ·0915 = ·264.

In adding the two logarithms we commence with the mantissa
and obtain 4216 with 1 to carry; next adding the two negative
characteristics we have $\bar{2}$ + 1 = $\bar{1}$.

EXERCISES. II.

Multiply

1. 709·3 by 1·007.   **2.** 18·07 by ·0651.   **3.** 23·26 by 2·087.

4. 46·237 by 18·45.   **5.** 30·98 by ·00258.   **6.** 51·47 by 20·7.

7. 321·4 by 3·063.   **8.** 70·93 by 4·051.   **9.** 85·61 by ·07561.

10. (i) 6·709 by 3·604 ; (ii) ·000215 by 3490000.

Multiply together

11. 3·54, ·026, and 1·34.   **12.** $\frac{3}{16}$, ·07653, and 5·007.

13. ·05, ·0156, and 20·01.   **14.** 1·102, 27·01, and 5·002.

Multiply the following :

15. 28·31 by ·00894.   **16.** 11·82 by ·003961.   **17.** ·5684 by 893.

18. ·03571 by ·2568.   **19.** 27·85 by ·08603.   **20.** ·3948 by $\frac{54}{395}$.

21. 13·02 by ·6982.   **22.** 13·73 by ·006507.   **23.** 79·35 by 2·315.

24. ·621 by ·026.   **25.** (i) ·05849 by ·726 ; (ii) 17·28 by 14·4.

26. (i) 12·75 by ·0684 ; (ii) ·01019 by 23·04.   **27.** 14·95 by ·00734.

28. 420·3 by 2·317.   **29.** 5·617 by ·01738.   **30.** ·01342 by ·0055.

31. Find the numerical value of $a \times b$ when

(i) $a = 3·05$, $b = ·25$.   (ii) $a = ·32$, $b = ·231$.

(iii) $a = 76·05$, $b = 1·0305$.   (iv) $a = 125000$, $b = ·00005$.

Division by Logarithms.—*The logarithm of a quotient is
obtained by subtracting the logarithm of the divisor from the
logarithm of the dividend; the number corresponding to this
logarithm, found on reference to the table of antilogarithms, is
the number required.*

Using this rule for division, it is an easy matter to write
down the logarithm of a number less than unity, and to verify
the rule given on p. 18.

Thus, $\log \cdot 047 = \bar{2} \cdot 6721$.

This may be verified by noting that $\cdot 047 = \dfrac{4 \cdot 7}{100}$;

$$\therefore \ \log \cdot 047 = \log \frac{4 \cdot 7}{100} = \log 4 \cdot 7 - \log 100 = \cdot 6721 - 2 = \bar{2} \cdot 6721.$$

In a similar manner $\cdot 47 = \dfrac{4 \cdot 7}{10}$;

$$\therefore \ \log \cdot 47 = \log \frac{4 \cdot 7}{10} = \log 4 \cdot 7 - \log 10 = \cdot 6721 - 1 = \bar{1} \cdot 6721.$$

Ex. 1. Divide $3 \cdot 048$ by $\cdot 00525$.

From Table III., $\qquad\qquad \log 304 = \quad 4829$

$\qquad\qquad\qquad$ Diff. col. for 8, $\qquad 11$

$\qquad\qquad\qquad \therefore \ \log 3 \cdot 048 = \quad \cdot 4840$ ....(i)

Also $\qquad\qquad\qquad\quad \log \cdot 00525 = \bar{3} \cdot 7202$ ....(ii)

$\qquad\quad$ Subtracting (ii) from (i), $2 \cdot 7638$

From Table IV., $\qquad\quad$ antilog $763 = 5794$

$\qquad\qquad\qquad\quad$ Diff. col. for 8, $\quad 11$

$\qquad\quad \therefore \ $ antilog of $7638 = 5805$

Hence $\qquad\qquad\qquad \log 2 \cdot 7638 = 580 \cdot 5$;

$\qquad\quad \therefore \ 3 \cdot 048 \div \cdot 00525 = 580 \cdot 5.$

EXERCISES. III.

Divide

1. $\cdot 006362$ by $2 \cdot 052$.
2. $99 \cdot 94$ by 2890.
3. $42 \cdot 547$ by $\cdot 00542$.
4. 548 by $\cdot 0137$.
5. $\cdot 414$ by $34 \cdot 5$.
6. $15 \cdot 17$ by $347 \cdot 2$.
7. $\cdot 1538$ by $2 \cdot 17$.
8. $907 \cdot 9$ by $17 \cdot 03$.
9. $10 \cdot 83$ by $\cdot 05309$.
10. $360 \cdot 2$ by $898 \cdot 9$.
11. $\cdot 34935$ by $\cdot 000137$.
12. $\cdot 05344$ by $83 \cdot 5$.
13. $4 \cdot 32$ by $\cdot 00036$.
14. $\cdot 00729$ by $\cdot 2735$.
15. $157 \cdot 3$ by 3405.
16. $8 \cdot 312$ by $23 \cdot 05$.
17. $4 \cdot 736$ by $\cdot 0435$.
18. $\cdot 2098$ by $36 \cdot 15$.
19. $\cdot 0009481$ by $\cdot 0157$.
20. $\frac{5 \, 1}{6 \, 4}$ by $7 \frac{7}{16}$.
21. $16 \cdot 25$ by $4 \cdot 35$.
22. (i) $\cdot 01$ by $\cdot 85$; (ii) $\cdot 01342$ by $\cdot 0055$.
23. $\cdot 5$ by $\cdot 0065$.
24. $\cdot 0004692$ by $\cdot 000365$.
25. The product of $\cdot 0047$, $\cdot 00035$, and $\cdot 00918$ by $\cdot 018$.

MISCELLANEOUS EXERCISES. IV.

Divide

1. (i) 17·28 by 14·4 ;   (ii) ·008827 by ·080325.
2. (i) 59·43 by ·047 ;   (ii) 27·53 by ·0374.
3. (i) 23·41 by 798·6 ;   (ii) 7·448 by 48·05.
4. (i) 94·78 by 2·847 ;   (ii) 2·016 by ·071.
5. (i) 1·013 by 3·375 ;   (ii) 27·53 by ·0374.
6. (i) 13·75 by ·0125 ;   (ii) 226·1 by ·008354.
7. (i) 17·25 by ·0023 ;   (ii) 16·25 by 4·35.
8. (i) ·0123 by ·85 ;   (ii) ·5 by ·0065.
9. ·0004692 by ·000365.
10. If $x = \dfrac{20000 \times 240}{1440000 \times 3\cdot1416}$, find the numerical value of x.
11. Calculate $a \times b \div c$,
    (i) When $a = 619\cdot3$, $b = \cdot117$,   and $c = 1\cdot43$.
    (ii) When $a = 6\cdot234$, $b = \cdot05473$, and $c = 756\cdot3$.
    (iii) When $a = 10$, $b = \cdot01342$, and $c = \cdot0055$.
12. How many portions ·07 inches long can be cut from a rod 12 inches long ?
13. Calculate the value of $a \times b$ and $a \div b$ when
    (i) $a = 201\cdot43$, $b = 3\cdot128$.   (ii) $a = 420\cdot3$, $b = 2\cdot317$.
    (iii) $a = \cdot008827$, $b = \cdot000235$.   (iv) $a = \cdot01342$, $b = \cdot0055$.
    (v) $a = 210\cdot15$, $b = 4\cdot634$.   (vi) $a = 27\cdot53$, $b = \cdot0374$.
    (vii) $a = 721\cdot4$, $b = 21\cdot9$.

Summary.

The **logarithm** of *a number* (abbreviated to log.) *to a given base is the index of the power to which that base must be raised to give the number.* Thus, if the base be 10, the log. of 100 = 2, since $10^2 = 100$.

Two systems.—There are two systems of logs in general use ; these are known as *common* in which the base is 10, and *Napierian,* or (as they are often called) *hyperbolic,* in which the base is 2·71828.... This base is usually denoted by the letter *e*.

Mantissa and Characteristic.—The log. of a number consists of two parts called the mantissa and the characteristic ; the former may be obtained from Table III., the latter is determined by inspection.

Multiplication.—Add together the logs. of the numbers, and find the number whose antilog. is their sum ; this number is the product required.

Division.—Subtract the log. of the divisor from the log. of the dividend and find the number whose antilog. is the difference ; this will give the quotient required.

CHAPTER III.

INVOLUTION AND EVOLUTION BY LOGARITHMS.
COMMON AND NAPIERIAN LOGARITHMS.

Involution by Logarithms.—*To obtain the power of a number multiply the logarithm of the number by the index representing the power required; the product is the logarithm of the number required.*

Ex. 1. Calculate the value of $(0 \cdot 07)^3$.

The process is as follows : Write down the log. of the number as shown ; multiply by the index (3), and obtain for the mantissa $\cdot 5353$ and the characteristic $\overline{4}$. This usually presents some difficulty to a beginner. To obtain the characteristic we say $3 \times 8 = 24$, plus 1 carried from last figure, gives 25, and we write down 5 ; next, $3 \times (-2) = -6$ and -6 added to $+2$ carried from previous figure, gives -4, which, as already described, is written $\overline{4}$.

$$\log \cdot 07 = \overline{2} \cdot 8451$$
$$\underline{\phantom{\log \cdot 07 = \overline{2} \cdot 8}3}$$
$$\log (0 \cdot 07)^3 = \overline{4} \cdot 5353$$

$$\therefore \quad \log (0 \cdot 07)^3 = 3 \times \overline{2} \cdot 8451$$
$$= \overline{4} \cdot 5353.$$

Referring to table of antilogarithms—

$$\begin{array}{lr} \text{Corresponding to 535 we find} & \mathbf{3428} \\ \text{Diff. col. for 3 we find} & \underline{2} \\ & 3430 \end{array}$$

Hence $\log \overline{4} \cdot 5353$ corresponds to the number $\cdot 000343$.

$$\therefore \quad \cdot 07^3 = \cdot 000343.$$

Contracted multiplication may with advantage be used when the index consists of three or more figures.

Ex. 2.   Calculate the value of $(9)^{3.76}$.

$$\log 9 = .9542 ;$$
$$\therefore \quad .9542$$
$$673$$
$$\overline{2.8626}$$
$$6679\tfrac{4}{}$$
$$5725\tfrac{2}{}$$
$$\overline{3.5877}$$

$$\text{antilog } 587 = 3864$$
$$\text{Diff. col. for } 7 = \underline{\quad 6}$$
$$\therefore \quad \text{antilog } 5877 = 3870$$

Hence
$$(9)^{3.76} = 3870.$$

When the index of a number not only consists of several figures, but the number itself is less than unity, so that the characteristic of the logarithm of the number is negative, it is necessary to convert the whole logarithm into a negative number before proceeding to multiply by the index.

Ex. 3.   Calculate $(.578)^{-3.76}$.

$$\log .578 = \bar{1}.7619, \text{ or } -1 + .7619 = -.2381.$$

The product of $-.2381$ and -3.76 is $.8952$.

$$\text{antilog } 8952 = 7856 ;$$
$$\therefore \quad (.578)^{-3.76} = 7.856.$$

When the mantissa of a logarithm is positive, and the index a negative number, the resulting product is negative. When this occurs the mantissa must be made positive before reference is made to Table IV.

Ex. 4.   Calculate the value of $(8.4)^{-1.97}$.

$$\log 8.4 = .9243.$$
$$-1.97 \times .9243 = -1.8208.$$

As the mantissa $.8208$ is negative, it must be made positive, *i.e.*,

$$-.8208 = \bar{1}.1792.$$

Hence,
$$-1.8208 = \bar{2}.1792.$$
$$\text{antilog } 1792 = 1511 ;$$
$$\therefore \quad (8.4)^{-1.97} = .01511.$$

This may be verified, if necessary, by writing $(8.4)^{-1.97}$ in its equivalent form, $\dfrac{1}{(8.4)^{1.97}}$.

Evolution by Logarithms.—*Divide the logarithm of the number, the root of which is required, by the number which indicates the root.*

No difficulty will be experienced when the characteristic and mantissa are both positive. But, although the characteristic of the logarithm may be negative, the mantissa remains positive. Hence the characteristic, when negative, usually requires a little alteration in form before dividing by the number, in order to make such logarithm exactly divisible by the number.

The methods adopted can best be shown by examples.

Ex. 1. Find the cube root of 475.

From Table III., mantissa of $\log 475 = 6767$;

$$\therefore \quad \log 475 = 2 \cdot 6767.$$

To obtain the cube root it is necessary to divide the logarithm by 3, and we obtain

$$\frac{2 \cdot 6767}{3} = \cdot 8923.$$

From Table IV., p. 167, we get

$$\text{antilog } 892 = 7798$$
$$\text{Diff. col. for 3,} \qquad 5$$
$$\therefore \quad \text{antilog } 8923 = 7803$$

Hence $\qquad\qquad \sqrt[3]{475} = 7 \cdot 803.$

When the given number is less than unity, the characteristic of its logarithm is negative, and a slight adjustment must be made before the division is performed.

Ex. 2. Find the value of $\sqrt[3]{\cdot 475}$.

$$\log \cdot 475 = \bar{1} \cdot 6767.$$

To obtain the cube root it is necessary to divide $\bar{1} \cdot 6767$ by 3 ; before doing so the negative characteristic is, by adding -2, made into $\bar{3}$, so as to be exactly divisible by 3. Or, $+2$ is added to the mantissa, thus $\bar{1} \cdot 6767$ becomes $\bar{3} + 2 \cdot 6767$.

Hence $\qquad \frac{1}{3}(\bar{3} + 2 \cdot 6767) = \bar{1} \cdot 8923.$

As in the preceding example, the corresponding antilog is 7803 ;

$$\therefore \quad \sqrt[3]{\cdot 475} = \cdot 7803.$$

The adjustment indicated in the preceding example should be performed mentally, although at the outset the beginner may find it advisable to write down the numbers as shown in the example above.

In dividing a logarithm by a given number it is necessary, when the divisor is greater than the first term in the mantissa, to prefix a cipher.

Ex. 3.   Find the fifth root of 3.

$$\log 3 = \cdot 4771,$$

and

$$\tfrac{1}{5}(\cdot 4771) = \cdot 0954.$$

$$\text{antilog } 0954 = 1246 ;$$

$$\therefore\ 3^{\frac{1}{5}} = 1 \cdot 246.$$

In this example since the divisor 5 is greater than the first term 4 in the mantissa, a cipher is prefixed. Then by ordinary simple division we have 5 into 47 gives 9 ; the remaining two figures 5 and 4 are obtained in a similar manner.

Ex. 4.   Find the 4th root of 0·007 or $(\cdot 007)^{\frac{1}{4}}$.

$$\log \cdot 007 = \bar{3} \cdot 8451.$$

$$\tfrac{1}{4}(\bar{3} \cdot 8451) = \tfrac{1}{4}(\bar{4} + 1 \cdot 8451)$$

$$= \bar{1} \cdot 46127$$

$$\therefore\ \log(\cdot 007)^{\frac{1}{4}} = \bar{1} \cdot 4613.$$

Corresponding to the mantissa 461 we find the antilogarithm $= 2891$
Diff. col. for $3 = \dfrac{2}{2893}$

$\therefore$ the antilogarithm corresponding to the logarithm $\bar{1}\cdot 4613$ is 2893.
Hence $(0\cdot 007)^{\frac{1}{4}} = \cdot 2893.$

Ex. 5.   Find the 7th root and the 7th power of 0·9306.

$$\log \cdot 9306 = \bar{1} \cdot 9688,$$

$$\log \text{ of } 7^{\text{th}} \text{ root} = \tfrac{1}{7}(\bar{7} + 6 \cdot 9688) = \bar{1} \cdot 9955.$$

Referring to table of antilogarithms, we find

$$\text{antilogarithm of } 995 = 9886$$

$$\text{Diff. col. for 5,} \quad \underline{11}$$

$$\therefore\ \text{antilogarithm of } \cdot 9955 = 9897$$

The characteristic $\bar{1}$ indicates that the number is less than unity.
Hence   7th root $= \cdot 9897.$
Let x denote the 7th power of ·9306.
Then $x = (0\cdot 9306)^7.$

$$\therefore\ \log x = 7 \log \cdot 9306$$

$$= 7 \times \bar{1} \cdot 9688 = \bar{1} \cdot 7816.$$

$$\text{antilog } 781 = 6039$$

$$\text{Diff. col. for 6,} \quad \underline{8}$$

$$\phantom{\text{Diff. col. for 6,} \quad} 6047$$

Hence $x = \cdot 6047.$

Ex 6. A square field has an area of 2 acres. What is the length of a path diagonally across it?

Let $ABCD$ (Fig. 1) represent the field. All the sides being equal, the length of each is

$$\sqrt{4840 \times 2} = \sqrt{9680}.$$

$$\log 9680 = 3 \cdot 9859 ;$$

$$\therefore \ \log \sqrt{9680} = \tfrac{1}{2}(3 \cdot 9859) = 1 \cdot 9929.$$

antilog $9929 = 9837$.

Hence $AB = 98 \cdot 37$ yards.

As ABC is a right-angled triangle, the square on AC is equal to the sum of the squares on AB and BC ;

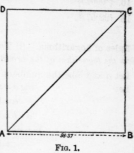

Fig. 1.

$$\therefore \ AC = \sqrt{AB^2 + BC^2} = \sqrt{2 \times (98 \cdot 37)^2}.$$

$$2 \log 98 \cdot 37 = 3 \cdot 9858$$

$$\log 2 = \ \cdot 3010$$

$$2 \overline{)4 \cdot 2868}$$

$$2 \cdot 1434$$

antilog $1434 = 1391$;

$$\therefore \ AC = 139 \cdot 1 \text{ yards.}$$

EXERCISES. V.

1. Find the cube root of ·00006706.
2. Find the fifth root of ·03786.
3. Find the cube root of (i) 27·27, (ii) ·08765.
4. Find the square root of 253400.
5. Find the cube root of 8·742.
6. Find the cube root of ·0006147.

Find the numerical values of the following :

7. $\left(\dfrac{\cdot 01607}{\cdot 00881}\right)^{\frac{1}{4}}.$

8. (i) $\left(\dfrac{3147}{27 \cdot 64}\right)^{\frac{1}{4}}$; (ii) $\left(\dfrac{\cdot 0275}{\sqrt{\cdot 0176}}\right)^{\frac{1}{4}}.$

9. $\dfrac{(3 \cdot 1416)^{12}}{(2 \cdot 1782)^{20}}.$

10. $\dfrac{42 \times (\cdot 0016)^{\frac{7}{4}}}{\sqrt[3]{108}}.$

11. $\dfrac{(42 \cdot 67)^{12} \times (\cdot 0765)^{10}}{1 \cdot 147 \times (194 \cdot 3)^4}.$

12. $(32 \cdot 16)^{\frac{2}{7}}.$

13. (i) $(2 \cdot 07)^3$; (ii) $(32 \cdot 76)^{\frac{1}{2}}$; (iii) $(\cdot 6944)^{\frac{3}{2}}.$

14. $(10)^{\frac{3}{5}}.$

15. Find the fifth root of ·04633.

W.M. II.

Find the numerical values of the following :

16. $(\cdot 00645)^{\frac{2}{3}}$.

17. $\sqrt[4]{\cdot 086} \times 39 \cdot 864$.

18. $(22 \cdot 07)^{\frac{3}{5}}$.

19. $(1 \cdot 56)^{1 \cdot 5} \times (1 \cdot 5)^2 \times (1 \cdot 56)^{2 \cdot 5}$.

Rules of Logarithms.—(i) *The sum of the logarithms of two numbers gives the logarithm of the product of these numbers.*

Let a and b be the numbers.

Let $\qquad \log a = x$ and $\log b = y$;

$$\therefore \ a = 10^x, \ b = 10^y.$$

$$a \times b = 10^{x+y},$$

or $\qquad \log_{10} ab = x + y$

$$= \log a + \log b.$$

(ii) *The logarithm of one number subtracted from the logarithm of another gives the logarithm of the quotient which is obtained by dividing the latter number by the former.*

As before let a and b be the two numbers.

Let $\qquad \log a = x$ and $\log b = y$;

$$\therefore \ a = 10^x, \ b = 10^y.$$

Hence $\qquad \dfrac{a}{b} = \dfrac{10^x}{10^y} = 10^{x-y},$

or $\qquad \log_{10} \dfrac{a}{b} = x - y$

$$= \log a - \log b.$$

(iii) *The logarithm of the power of a number is the product of the logarithm of the number by the index representing the power of the number.*

Let $\qquad \log a = x.$

Then $\qquad a = 10^x.$

And $\qquad a^n = (10^x)^n$;

$$\therefore \ \log_{10} a^n = nx = n \log a.$$

The system of logarithms employed by the discoverer of logarithms, Napier, and called the **Napierian** or **Hyperbolic system**, is much used. The base of this system is denoted by the symbol e, and is the number which is the sum of the series.

$$2 + \frac{1}{2} + \frac{1}{2 \times 3} + \frac{1}{2 \times 3 \times 4} + \dots.$$

This sum to five figures is $2 \cdot 7183$.

Transformation of Logarithms.—A system of logarithms calculated to a base a may be transformed into another system in which the base is b.

Thus let N be a number; its logarithm in the first system we may denote by x, and in the second system by y.

Then
$$N = a^x = b^y;$$
$$\therefore \; a^x = b^y;$$
$$\therefore \; b = a^{\frac{x}{y}}.$$

Or
$$\frac{x}{y} = \log_a b,$$

and
$$\frac{y}{x} = \frac{1}{\log_a b}.$$

Hence, if the logarithm of any number in the system in which the base is a be multiplied by $\dfrac{1}{\log_a b}$, we obtain the logarithm of the number in the system in which the base is b.

The common logarithms, or, as they are usually called simply logarithms, have been calculated from the Napierian logarithms. Let l and L be the logarithms of the same number in the common and Napierian systems respectively, then

$$l = \frac{1}{\log_e 10} L,$$

$$\log_e 10 = 2\cdot30258509,$$

and
$$\frac{1}{2\cdot30258509} = \cdot43429448.$$

Hence, the common logarithm of a number may be obtained by multiplying the Napierian logarithm of the same number by $\cdot4343\ldots$.

To convert common into Napierian logarithms we multiply by $2\cdot3026$ instead of the more accurate number $2\cdot30258509$.

Ex. 1. Find the hyperbolic logarithm of $8\cdot43$.

From Table III, p. 165, $\log 8\cdot43 = \cdot9258$;

$$\therefore \; \log_e 8\cdot43 = \cdot9258 \times 2\cdot3026$$
$$= 2\cdot1317.$$

MISCELLANEOUS EXERCISES. VI.

Find the value of

1. $\dfrac{1\cdot265 \times \cdot00271}{2\cdot382 \times 10\cdot71}$.

2. $\dfrac{70\cdot25 \times \cdot6796}{21000 \times \cdot01825}$.

3. Explain how logarithms are used for calculating products, quotients, powers, and roots of numerical quantities.

4. Calculate the value of $\cdot285 \times \cdot002 \times 1\cdot8 \div (\cdot009 \times \cdot038)$,

5. $\dfrac{(2\cdot05)^2 \times 2\cdot24}{\cdot0041}$.

6. $(\cdot05)^3 \times (1\cdot04)^2$.

7. Find the square root of 15.

8. Write down the logarithms of 544000, 544, and $\cdot0000544$.

9. Find the value of $\dfrac{(24\cdot76)^{\frac{2}{7}}}{(\cdot0045)^{\frac{3}{2}}}$.

10. Find the fifth root of $\cdot003463$.

11. Find a fourth proportional to $\cdot5468$, $7\cdot63$, and $762\cdot9$.

12. Divide $\overline{1}4\cdot3268$ by 9.

Find the numerical value of

13. $\left(\dfrac{\cdot03214}{\cdot01762}\right)^{\frac{1}{4}}$.

14. $\dfrac{(\cdot0476)^3}{(3\cdot005)^{\frac{1}{4}}}$.

15. Find the value of $\dfrac{\left(\dfrac{125}{123}\right)^{10}}{(\cdot0043)^{\frac{2}{5}}}$.

16. Find the fifth root of $14\cdot52$.

17. Find the square root of $\cdot00048$.

18. What is the value of $8^{3\cdot6}$?

19. Find the value of $\dfrac{a^{\frac{1}{2}} \times b^{1\cdot7}}{c}$ when $a = 35$, $b = 12$, $c = 13$.

20. Find the value of $\left(\dfrac{(\cdot21)^{\frac{1}{2}} \times (\cdot21)^{\frac{1}{3}} \times (\cdot21)^{\frac{3}{4}} \times 365^2}{(\cdot00416)^2 \times (\cdot3125)^3 \times \sqrt[4]{365}}\right) \times \dfrac{1}{10^6}$.

21. $\dfrac{(42\cdot66)^{12}}{1\cdot147} \times \dfrac{(\cdot0765)^{10}}{194\cdot3 \times 10^3}$.

22. $\sqrt{4^{\frac{1}{3}} + 5^{\frac{1}{3}}}$.

23. Find the fourth proportional to $(1\cdot027)^{\frac{1}{2}}$, $(2\cdot546)^{\frac{1}{3}}$, $(31\cdot027)^2$.

24. (i) Prove that $\log(3^5 \times 4^6) = 5 \log 3 + 6 \log 4$; (ii) find the value of $(\cdot0874)^{\frac{1}{5}}$.

25. Multiply $\cdot076$ by $\cdot0007$, and divide the product by $\cdot000019$.

26. Find the fifth root of ·00374.

27. Find a mean proportional to

$$\sqrt{4 \cdot 756} \quad \text{and} \quad \sqrt[3]{(\cdot 0078)^2}.$$

Find the value of

28. $\left(\dfrac{\cdot 004}{\cdot 02}\right)^3.$

29. $\dfrac{(19 \cdot 4)^3 \times (\cdot 0375)^{\frac{1}{3}}}{(\cdot 72)^{\frac{1}{5}} \times \sqrt{3607}}.$

30. Find the quotient of ·08643 divided by $(3 \cdot 4276)^{\frac{1}{3}}$.

Find the value of

31. $\dfrac{a \times b}{c}$, when $a = 1 \cdot 986$, $b = \cdot 1188$, an $c = \cdot 5046$.

32. $a^{\frac{3}{2}} \div b$, when $a = 12 \cdot 45$, $b = \cdot 00740$.

33. $a \times b \div c^3$, when $a = 8352$, $b = 3 \cdot 69$, $c = 30 \cdot 57$.

34. Find the value of

$$\frac{256 \cdot 5}{\cdot 045} \{(1 \cdot 045)^{14} - 1\}.$$

35. Find the value of x, when $10^{\frac{1}{x}} = 2 \cdot 45$.

36. If

$$y = \frac{32 W l r^2}{\pi d^4},$$

calculate the value of y, when $W = 100$, $l = 80$, $2r = 2 \cdot 55$, $\pi = 3 \cdot 142$, $d = \cdot 25$.

37. Calculate $ab \times cd$ and $ab \div cd$, when

    (i) $a = 35 \cdot 125$, $b = \cdot 3397$, $c = 10500$, $d = \cdot 009126$.

    (ii) $a = \cdot 6325$, $b = \cdot 001355$, $c = 1 \cdot 191$, $d = 5 \cdot 355$.

    (iii) $a = 1 \cdot 265$, $b = \cdot 01628$, $c = 2 \cdot 283$, $d = 64 \cdot 28$.

38. Calculate (i) $a^{\frac{1}{3}} \times b^{\frac{3}{4}} \div c^{\frac{1}{2}}$;   (ii) $a^{\frac{1}{3}} \times b^{\frac{3}{4}} \times c^{\frac{1}{2}}$;

when $a = 15 \cdot 6$, $b = \cdot 0045$, $c = \cdot 00065$.

39. Find the value of

$$a^{\frac{2}{3}} b^{\frac{5}{6}} (a + b)^{-\frac{7}{3}} (a - b)^{\frac{1}{5}},$$

if $a = 3 \cdot 142$, $b = 2 \cdot 718$.

40. If

$$V = \sqrt[3]{\frac{H \times C}{D^{\frac{2}{3}}}},$$

    (i) Calculate the value of V, when $C = 232 \cdot 4$, $D = 14860$, and $H = 16150$.

    (ii) When $C = 157 \cdot 3$, $D = 2500$, and $H = 12980$.

    (iii) When $C = 258 \cdot 6$, $D = 4720$, $H = 1788$.

Find the values of

41. (a) $3\cdot142 \times 5\cdot268^2$; (b) $9\cdot278 \div 10\cdot76$; (c) $\sqrt[3]{536\cdot9}$. [U.E.I.]

42. (a) $\dfrac{271\cdot8 \times 0\cdot009278}{10\cdot43}$; (b) $(0\cdot8241)^3$; (c) $\sqrt{1527}$. [U.E.I.]

43. (a) $15\cdot97 \times 0\cdot8642 \div 0\cdot02561$; (b) $(1\cdot62)^{\frac{3}{2}}$; (c) $\sqrt[4]{25\cdot76}$;
(d) $(0\cdot45)^3$; (e) $(12\cdot7)^3$. [U.E.I.]

44. $\sqrt{435\cdot8}$; $(4\cdot358)^2$; $(8\cdot241 \times 2\cdot661) \div (2\cdot061 \times 3\cdot116)$. [L.C.U.]

45. $\dfrac{0\cdot7854 \times (11\cdot32)^2 \times 784 \times 273}{13\cdot96 \times 760 \times 302}$. [L.C.U.]

46. $(7\cdot624)^{2\cdot3}$; $(3950)^{-3}$, $x^{0\cdot54} = 2\cdot609$. [N.U.T.]

47. $\dfrac{2\pi k(t_2 - t_1)}{\log r_2 - \log r_1}$, when $k = 0\cdot85$, $t_1 = 75\cdot8$, $t_2 = 96\cdot4$, $r_1 = 1\cdot5$, $r_2 = 2\cdot05$. [N.U.T.]

48. If $G = \sqrt{\dfrac{(3D)^5 \times H}{L}}$, find D when $G = 84\cdot8$, $L = 33\cdot33$, $H = 1\cdot46$. [N.U.T.]

49. Solve $(500)^{x+1} = (684)^{x-1}$. [N.U.T.]

50. Solve the equations :
  (a) $5\cdot2 V^{1\cdot4} = 18\cdot7$; (b) $2\cdot718^{0\cdot6x} = 92\cdot56$. [U.E.I.]

51. Evaluate $\sqrt[3]{5\cdot888} \times 3\cdot142 \div 2\cdot9$. [L.C.U.]

Summary.

Involution.—To raise a number to a given power, multiply the log. of the number by the index of the power, and find the number the antilog. of which is the product.

Evolution.—Divide the log. of the number by the index of the root required (first making, if necessary, the requisite adjustment in the characteristic). The quotient is the antilog. of the root.

Napierian logarithms.—Logarithms in which the base is denoted by e, where $e = 2\cdot7182818...$, are called Napierian logarithms.

Common logarithms.—Logarithms calculated to the base 10 are called common logarithms. *Common logarithms* may be converted into *Napierian* or *hyperbolic* by multiplying by $2\cdot3026$. Napierian logarithms may be converted into common logarithms by multiplying by $\cdot4343$.

CHAPTER IV.

THE SLIDE RULE.

Slide Rule.—It will already be clear to the reader who has followed the section dealing with logarithms, that by their use the multiplication of two or more numbers is effected by adding the logarithms of the factors, and their division by the subtraction of the logarithms of the factors. Or, shortly, by the use of logarithms multiplication is replaced by addition, and division by subtraction.

Hence, if instead of the equal divisions of a scale (Fig. 2), unequal divisions corresponding to the logarithms were employed, then, when performed graphically, multiplication will correspond to addition and division to subtraction.

It is an easy matter to add together two linear dimensions by means of an ordinary scale or rule. Thus, to add 2 and 3 units together. Assume the scale B (Fig. 2) to slide along the edge

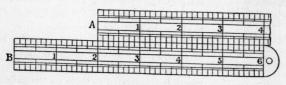

FIG. 2.

of the scale A, then the addition of the numbers 2 and 3 is made when the 2 on B is coincident with 0 on A; the addition of the two numbers is found to be 5 opposite the number 3 on the scale A.

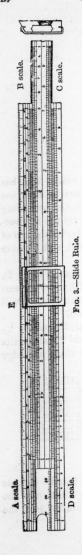

B scale.

C scale.

A scale.

D scale.

E

Fig. 3.—Slide Rule.

If the scales on A and B are not divided in the proportion of the numbers, but of the logarithms of the numbers, then with this system of graphic logarithms, by sliding one scale along the other in the manner described, addition would be performed, but, as the scales are logarithmic, the result would correspond to the product of the numbers added.

Similarly, the number corresponding to the difference would be a quotient.

Construction of Slide Rule.—As already stated the object of the slide rule is to perform *arithmetical calculations* in a simple manner.

There is a great saving of time and labour effected by its use, as it solves at sight all questions depending on ratio.

It consists of a fixed part or rule containing a groove in which a smaller rule slides.

Reference to Fig. 3 shows that the upper part of the rule contains two scales exactly alike, while the lower part of the rule contains only one scale, its length being double that of the upper one. As the upper part contains two scales, it will be convenient to refer to the division 1 in the centre of the rule, shown at E, as the *left-hand* 1, the other to the right of it as the *right-hand* 1.

There are two scales on the smaller rule or *slide*, as we may call it, at B; and at C one double the length. Hence, the scales on the slide correspond to those on the rule.

It will be convenient to refer to the four scales by the letters A, B, C, D, as shown in Fig. 3.

If an examination of a slide rule be made it will be found to consist of a fixed part or frame, a slide, and, in addition, in the slide rule, there is also an additional movable frame or thin metal *cursor*, held in position on the face of the rule by sliding in two grooves. This is shown both at E and in the end view. Although it slides freely along the instrument, any shake which might otherwise occur is prevented by a small steel spring placed at the upper part of the carrier.

The principle of action is the same in all slide rules, although the arrangement of the lines depends upon the purpose to which the rule is to be applied. The modified form of the slide rule, of the kind which we propose to explain, is one of the most accurate instruments of the kind that can be obtained. The instrument, with the exception of the cursor E, is usually made of boxwood or mahogany. The wood is faced with white material, the black division lines showing more clearly on the white background.

Graduation of Slide Rules.—In Fig. 3, which shows a slide rule, it will be seen that the distance apart of the divisions are by no means equal. The divisions and subdivisions are not equidistant as in an ordinary scale, but are logarithms of the numbers, and are set off from the left or commencing unit.

In studying Indices we find, p. 112, that

if 10^3 be multiplied by 10^4 the result is 10^{3+4} or 10^7.

From the definition of a logarithm,

$$2 \text{ is the logarithm of } 100, \text{ since } 10^2 = 100.$$

Or, as 10 raised to the power 2 gives 100, the logarithm of 100 is 2.

In a similar manner if 10 be raised to a power ·4771, we obtain the result 3 ; $\therefore$ log 3 = ·4771.

Also, since $10^{·3010} = 2$; $\therefore$ log 2 = ·3010.

Hence ·7781 is the log of $6 = 10^{·3010 + ·4771}$.

Again $$\frac{10^5}{10^2} = 10^{5-2} = 10^3.$$

So also $$\frac{10^{·7781}}{10^{·3010}} = 10^{·7781 - ·3010} = 10^{·4771}.$$

Or more simply, to divide 6 by 2.

$$\log 6 - \log 2 = ·7781 - ·3010$$
$$= ·4771 ;$$

and ·4771 is the log of 3.

Hence $$\frac{6}{2} = 3.$$

Simple exercises similar to the above will be found very useful as a first step, and such practice will enable the student to deal with the numbers with certainty and ease. It is an excellent exercise to make a slide rule, using two strips of cardboard or thick paper.

Assuming any length, such as from 1 to E, scale A, to be 10 inches long and to be divided into 10 parts, then the distance from 1 of any intermediate number from 1 to 10 is made proportional to its logarithm.

To find the position of the 2nd division, since $\log 2 = ·301$, ·301 parts, or 3·01 inches from 1, would indicate its position.

In like manner the 3rd division would be ·477 parts, or 4·7 inches; the 4th, ·602 parts, or 6·02 inches; the 5th, 6·99 inches, etc.

Denoting the distance of any division from point 1 by x, if l denote the length of the scale from 1 to E, and L the logarithm of the number indicating the division required, then

$$x = l \cdot L.$$

When the upper scale A is set out, the scales B and C on the slide and the scale D may be similarly marked from it.

The excellence of any slide rule depends upon the skill with which these division lines have been constructed, so that they are as accurate as it is possible to make them, and in dealing with a carefully made slide rule we deal with the *effect* of a considerable amount of labour and thought which have been expended in its construction.

Although a knowledge of logarithms is not essential before a slide rule is used, any more than it is necessary that a man should be able to make a watch before he is allowed to use one, or that he should understand the nature of an electric current before using an electric bell, it is much better to clearly understand the principles underlying the construction of any instrument.

Multiplication.—In (Fig. 3) putting the units' figure of the slide opposite the 2 on the fixed scale A, we get registered the products of all the numbers on the slide and 2 above. Thus $2 \times 1 = 2$, $2 \times 2 = 4$, $2 \times 3 = 6$, etc. The units' figure may denote 1, or 10, or 100, etc.; thus the products may be read off as $2 \times 10 = 20$, $2 \times 20 = 40$, or $2 \times 100 = 200$, etc.

Or we may use the lower scale *D* of the rule and scale *C* of the slide. Always make 1 of the slide coincide with either of the factors on the scale, and the product will be found on the scale opposite to the other factor read on the slide. If the product cannot be found when the left-hand 1 is used, the right-hand 1 must be employed.

Facility in using the rule can only be obtained by practice, and as soon as the principle is understood the so-called rules are not of much use.

From any table of areas and circumference of circles, examples for practice can be obtained, or the examples given on pp. 33 and 41 may be used for the same purpose, so that it is not necessary to give such at this stage.

Ex. 1. Multiply 12·8 by 4.

Setting the 1 on the slide to 12·8 on the rule, then opposite 4 on slide is the number 51·2.

Ex. 2. The diameter of a circle is 2·5 inches, find its circumference (p. 30).

Set 1 on slide against 2·5 on scale; then *A* opposite 3·14 (which is marked on slide), is the circumference, 7·85 inches.

Division.—Set the divisor on *B* under the dividend on *A*, and read the quotient on *A* over the index of *B*; *or*, set the divisor on *C* over the dividend on *D*, and read the quotient on *D* under the units' figure of *C*.

Ex. 1. Divide 9 by 4.

Set the 4 on scale *B* opposite 9 on scale *A*; then coincident with 1 is the answer 2·25.

Ex. 2. Divide 9·5 by 2·5.

Set 2·5 on scale *C* coincident with the division 9·5 on *D*, then coincident with 1 on *C* is the answer 3·8 on *D*.

Ex. 3. The circumference of a circle is 29·53 inches, find the diameter.

Set 3·14 on slide opposite 29·53; coincident with 1, we read 9·4, the answer required.

Involution.—On inspection, the numbers on the upper scale *A* are seen to be the squares of the numbers on the lower scale.

To obtain the square of a fractional number some difficulty would be experienced in noting the coincidence of divisions on *A*

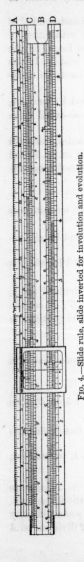

Fig. 4.—Slide rule, slide inverted for involution and evolution.

and *D*, separated as they are by the slide, in this case we can make use of the *cursor*, thus :

Set the cursor to coincide with the given number on the scale *D*, and, by its means, read off the square of the number on scale *A*. In this manner, the fourth, or any even power, can be obtained.

Square Root.—In extracting square roots the above process is reversed.

The number, the root of which is required, is found on the scale *A*, and its root is, as before, found directly below. The cursor enables the coincidence of the two divisions denoting the number and its root to be readily obtained.

As shown on p. 36, the area of a circle is $3 \cdot 1416 \times r^2$, or $\cdot 7854 d^2$, where *r* is the radius and *d* the diameter of the given circle. Conversely, if the area of a circle is given, the diameter can be obtained from :

$$\text{diameter} = \sqrt{\frac{\text{area}}{\cdot 7854}}.$$

Ex. 1. Find area of a circle 3″ diameter.

The mark on the cursor is set to the 3 on the lower scale ; the upper mark over the top scale registers 9. Then moving the slide to the right until the 1 coincides with the mark, we have coincident with ·7854 (which is marked on the scale) the required area 7·01 square inches.

Ex. 2. Find area of a circle 2·5″ diameter.

The square of 2·5 is seen to be 6·25, and multiplied by ·7854 the area is 4·9 square inches.

Practice in Use of Slide Rule.—Practice in the use of the slide-rule is obtained by getting the powers and roots of various numbers, by determining areas of circles from given diameters, and conversely, diameters from given areas. The circumferences and diameters may be treated in like manner. All results when obtained may be verified by calculation, or from tables.

To obtain the cube of a number.--Bring the right-hand 1 of scale C to the given number on D. Then over the same number on the scale B read off the required cube on A.

Instead of the above plan the slide may be inverted (Fig. 4), keeping the same face upwards. The scale B will now move along scale D. Put in coincidence on the scales B and D the two marks indicating the number the cube of which is required, then opposite the right-hand 1 on the slide the cube required will be found on scale A.

Cube Root.—As in the case of finding the cube of a number, two methods may be used to obtain the cube root of a number.

First Method.—Move the slide to the right or left until under the given cube on A is found on B a number identical with a number which is simultaneously found on the D scale coincident with the 1 on scale C.

Second Method.—The inverted slide is used. This is placed with the 1 of the slide coincident with the number the cube root of which is required. Then find what number on the scale D coincides with the same number on the inverted scale of B; this number is the cube root required.

It will be found advisable to obtain the cube roots of easy numbers before proceeding to more difficult cases.

Ex. 1. Find the cube root of 64.

Move the slide from right to left, and it will be found that 4 on scale B coincides with 64 on scale A, simultaneously with 4 on D and 1 on C. Hence 4 is the cube root required.

Invert the slide, keeping the same face uppermost. Set 1 on C, inverted to 64 on scale A, the division on B which coincides with D is 4. Hence 4 is the cube root.

EXERCISES. VII.

1. Find the areas of circles the diameters of which are 2, 3, 4, 6, 2·3, 3·2, 4·2, and 6·2 inches respectively.

2. Find the area of an air-pump bucket if its area is $\frac{1}{5}$ that of a cylinder of 63 inches diameter.

3. Find the diameter of a cylinder, the area being 20 square inches.

4. Write down the square and cube roots of the numbers 1, 2, 3, ... 10 inclusive.

SECTION II.—MENSURATION.

CHAPTER V.

CIRCUMFERENCE OF A CIRCLE AND AN ELLIPSE LENGTH OF A CIRCULAR ARC.

In Part I. of this course of work a portion of the subject of the mensuration of plane figures has been considered, and, in continuation, we may with advantage deal with the mensuration of certain plane figures in which the periphery consists of curved instead of straight lines.

Circumference of a Circle.—The number of times that the length of the circumference of a circle contains the length of the diameter of a circle cannot be expressed exactly, but it is very nearly 3·14159265. The number 3·1416 is used for convenience and is sufficiently exact for nearly all purposes. This number is denoted by the Greek letter π.

An approximate value of π, sufficiently exact for all practical purposes, and very convenient when four-figure logarithms are used, is $3\frac{1}{7}$ or 3·142. Thus, $\pi = 3\cdot14159265 = \frac{22}{7}$ within $\frac{1}{20}$ per cent.

That the length of the circumference of a circle is πd or $2\pi r$ where d is the length of the diameter and r the radius, may be shown in several ways. Two simple experimental methods will be sufficient in this place.

1. *By rolling a disc of metal or wood on any convenient scale.* Make a mark on the circumference of the disc. Put the mark coincident with a scale division. Slowly roll the disc along the scale until the mark is again coincident with the scale, and note

carefully the distance in scale divisions moved through. Then by applying the scale to the disc obtain the diameter.

Simple division will then show that the length of the circumference is $3\frac{1}{7}$ times that of the diameter.

2. Or, *wrap a piece of thin paper round the disc*, and mark, by two points, the line along which the edges overlap; unroll the paper, and its length when measured will be found to be $3\frac{1}{7}$ times that of the diameter.

Length of a Circular Arc.—Let ABC (Fig. 5) be a circular

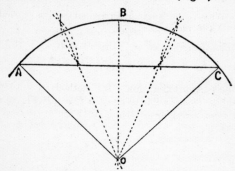

Fig. 5.—Length of a circular arc.

arc, it is required to find the centre of the circle of which ABC is a portion.

With A and B as centres and any convenient radius, describe intersecting arcs as shown; a line drawn through the intersections also passes through the centre of the circle of which ABC is a portion. The point of intersection O of the two lines obtained in this manner is the centre of the circle required.

Join O to A and C. Let the length of the radius be denoted by r, and the angle AOC by θ.

Then the measure in **radians*** of the angle $\theta = \dfrac{\text{arc } AC}{r}$;

$$\therefore \text{ arc } AC = r\theta.$$

Thus, when θ and the radius of the circle are known the length of the arc can be calculated.

* See Part I., p. 103; also Table I., p. 163.

If the angle is given in degrees, then as the number of degrees in a circle is 360, the length of the arc will have the same ratio to the circumference of the circle as the number of degrees in the angle has to 360 degrees.

If N denote the number of degrees in the given angle, then

$$\frac{\text{length of arc}}{2\pi r} = \frac{N}{360},$$

or, $$\text{length of arc} = \frac{N}{360} \times 2\pi r.$$

Ex. 1.   What is the length of an arc subtending an angle of 45° in a circle of 4 ft. radius ?

$$\text{Length of arc} = \frac{45}{360} \times 2\pi \times 4 = \pi \text{ ft.}$$

$$= 3\cdot1416 \text{ ft.}$$

Rankine's Approximation.—By methods due to the late Prof. Rankine it is possible to *set off a line AT* (Fig. 6) *equal in length to a given circular arc AB.*

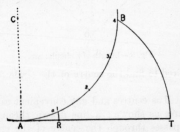

Fig. 6.—Rankine's approximation.

Obtain the centre C as described on p. 31.   Join A to C, and at A draw AT touching the arc and perpendicular to AC, then AT is a *tangent* to the arc at A.

Divide the arc AB into four equal parts as shown.   With the distance from A to the division 1 as radius, and with centre A, describe an arc cutting the tangent at R.   With centre R, radius RB, describe a second arc cutting the tangent at T.   Then

$$AT = \text{arc } AB \text{ (approximately).}$$

The angle subtended at the centre by the arc BA should not exceed 90°. The error introduced consists in the line being a little shorter than the corresponding arc; the amount of difference is about 1 in 900 for an arc which subtends an angle of 60°.

Ellipse.—It is only possible to obtain a rough approximation to the length of the circumference, or perimeter, of an ellipse. Perhaps the best rule is:

Length of circumference of an ellipse $=(a+b)\pi$,

where a denotes the semi-major axis OA, or OA' (Fig. 7), and

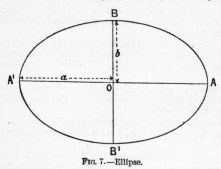

Fig. 7.—Ellipse.

b denotes the semi-minor axis OB or OB'. Or,

The circumference of an ellipse is half the sum of the major and minor axes multiplied by π.

Ex. 1. The major axis of an ellipse is 16 inches, the minor axis 10 inches: find the circumference.

Here $\qquad a=8$, $b=5$, and $a+b=13$;

$\qquad\therefore$ circumference $=13\times\pi=40\cdot84$ inches.

EXERCISES. VIII.

1. The circumference of a circle is 144·513 inches; find the diameter.

2. The diameter of a circle is 48·25 inches; find the circumference.

3. The wheels of a locomotive are 2 ft. 6 in. apart, what is the difference of the lengths of the paths of the wheels when the inner wheel is describing a circle 100 yards radius?

4. The earth's equatorial and polar axes being 7926 and 7899 miles respectively, what is the meridional circumference of the earth?

5. The minute hand of a clock is 6 feet long; what distance will its extremity move over in 36 minutes?

6. A carriage wheel is 2 ft. $7\frac{1}{2}$ in. in diameter; how many turns does it make in a distance of 7 miles 1331 yards?

7. The circumference of a wheel is 20 feet; how many turns will it make in rolling over 100 miles? Find the diameter of the wheel.

8. A rope is wrapped on a roller 1 ft. diameter; how many coils will be required to reach to the bottom of a well 200 ft. deep? What number of coils will be required if the rope is 1 inch thick?

9. How many iron railings will be required to fence a circular plot of ground 21 yards in diameter, the distance between each pair of rails being 6 inches?

10. If the circumference of the fore-wheel of a carriage be 54 inches and that of the hind-wheel 66 inches, how many more turns will be made by the fore-wheel than by the hind-wheel in a distance of 3 miles?

11. The wheel of a locomotive, 5 ft. in diameter, made 10,000 revolutions in a distance of 24 miles; what distance was lost due to the slipping of the wheels?

12. A wheel makes 1028 revolutions in passing over a distance of 2 miles 4 fur. 9 pls. 5 yds. 6 in.; what is the circumference of the wheel?

13. How many revolutions per minute would a wheel 56 in. diameter have to make in order to travel at 30 miles an hour?

14. The circumferences of two wheels differ by a foot, and one turns as often in going 6 furlongs as the other in going 7 furlongs; find the diameter of each wheel.

15. The hind and front wheels of a carriage have circumferences 14 and 16 ft. respectively; how far has the carriage advanced when the smaller wheel has made 51 revolutions more than the larger one?

16. Find the circumference of an ellipse, its axes being 16 and 12 inches.

17. A shaft is 100 feet deep; how many coils of rope will be required to reach the bottom, the roller on which they are wrapped being 11 inches in diameter, the rope 1 inch diameter?

18. If the outer diameter of a spiral spring is $2\frac{5}{8}$ inches and the inner diameter $2\frac{3}{8}$ inches, what is the length of wire in the spring assuming ten coils of the spring close to each other, and the length of the coils measured parallel to the axis to be 9 inches?

19. If the number of teeth in a spur wheel is 120, the pitch (distance from centre of one tooth to the centre of the next) $1\frac{1}{4}$ inches, find the diameter of the pitch circle. What would be the diameter when the number of teeth is 30?

20. The greater and lesser diameters of an elliptical man-hole door are 2 ft. 9 in. and 2 ft. 6 in. respectively ; find its periphery.

21. The dimensions of an oval door are 12 and 9 inches ; what is the circumference ?

22. Find the lateral surface of an oval cylinder, the diameters being 34 and 30 inches respectively, and the height 12 inches.

23. Find the number of degrees in that arc of a circle which is equal in length to the radius of the circle.

24. Through what angle must a rail 20 ft. long be bent to fit a curve of half a mile radius ?

25. The radius of a circle is 10 inches, and the angle subtended by an arc at the centre is 72° ; find the length of the arc.

26. The diameter of a circle is 1050 links ; what is the number of radians in an arc of 120 links ?

27. Find the length of that part of a circular railway-curve which subtends an angle of $22\frac{1}{2}$° to a radius of a mile.

28. What is the earth's diameter if the length of a degree of the earth's meridian be 69·1 miles ?

29. What is the length of a circular arc subtending an angle of 17° 16′ when the radius of the circle is 15 inches ?

30. A circle is 10 ft. in diameter ; how many degrees are there in an arc of it 16 ft. long ?

31. Find the distance in miles between any two places on the equator which differ in longitude by 6° 18′, assuming the earth's equatorial diameter to be 7926 miles.

32. Two places on the earth's equator are 300 miles apart ; what is their difference in longitude ?

33. A pendulum swings through an angle of 30° ; the end describes an arc of $13\frac{2}{21}$ inches ; find the length of the pendulum.

Summary.

Circumference of a circle $= \pi \times (\text{diameter}) = 2\pi (\text{radius})$ where π denotes 3·1416 or $3·142 = \frac{22}{7}$ approximately.

Length of an arc of a circle.—The length of an arc of a circle of radius r is $r\theta$; or $\dfrac{N}{360} \times 2\pi r$ where θ is the radian measure and N the number of degrees in the angle subtended by the arc at the centre of the circle.

Circumference of an ellipse.—The circumference of an ellipse is approximately $\pi (a+b)$ where $2a$ and $2b$ denote the major and minor axes respectively.

CHAPTER VI.

AREA OF A CIRCLE AND ELLIPSE. AREA OF A SECTOR OF A CIRCLE. AREA OF AN ANNULUS.

Area of a Circle.—If a regular polygon be inscribed in a circle, a series of triangles are formed by joining the angular points of the polygon to the centre of the circle.

The area of each little triangle is one-half the product of its base and the perpendicular let fall from the centre of the circle on the base of the triangle.

The length of the base may be denoted by a; the length of the perpendicular by p; and the radius of the circle by r. The area of the polygon will be $\frac{1}{2}p(a+a+...)$ or $\frac{1}{2}p\Sigma a$. The symbol Σ, which denotes "the sum of," is very convenient, and the form $\frac{1}{2}p\Sigma a$ simply means the product of $\frac{1}{2}p$, and the sum of all the terms each of which is represented by the letter a.

As the number of sides in the polygon is increased, its area becomes nearer and nearer that of the circle, and when the number of sides is indefinitely increased, the perimeter (or sum of the sides) of the polygon becomes equal to the circumference of the circle $=2\pi r$; the perpendicular referred to above also becomes the radius of the circle.

Hence the area of a circle $=\frac{1}{2}(2\pi r \times r)=\pi r^2$.

By dividing a circle into a large number of sectors, the bases may be made to differ as little as possible from straight lines. Each of the sectors forming the lower half of the circumference could be placed, along a horizontal line AB (Fig. 8). A corresponding number of sectors from the upper half of the circumference could be placed along the upper line CD, completing the parallelogram $ABCD$. The length of the base AB

will then be half the length of the circumference of the circle and the height of the parallelogram is equal to the radius of the circle, r.

$$\therefore \quad \text{Area of parallelogram} = AB \times r = r \times \pi r = \pi r^2.$$

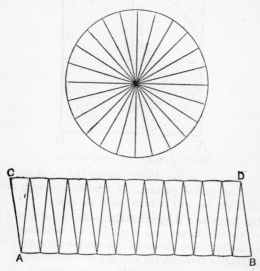

FIG. 8.—Area of a circle.

If a thin circular disc of wood be divided into narrow sectors, and a strip of tape glued to the circumference; then, when the tape is straightened the sectors will stand upon it as a series of triangles. By cutting the tape in halves the two portions may be fitted together as in Fig. 8.

Experimental Method.—A good experimental method where a balance is available is to draw two circles on a sheet of cardboard and to circumscribe one of the circles by a square $ABCD$ as shown in Fig. 9. By drawing two lines at right angles and passing through the centre of the circle, the square is divided into four equal squares, the length of a side of each of the squares being r.

Make $EM = \frac{1}{7}$ of ED.

Draw MN parallel to AD.

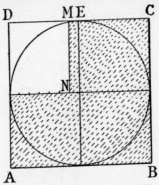

FIG. 9.—Area of a circle experimentally.

Then the area of the shaded figure $= 3\frac{1}{7}r^2$. Cut out a circle and also the shaded portion. If this be done with care the weights of the two will be found to be the same.

Using Rankine's Approximation.—As the area of a circle can be expressed in the form $\pi r \times r$, i.e. *half the circumference of a circle multiplied by the radius*, we can use the approximation due to Rankine to obtain the area of a circle graphically.

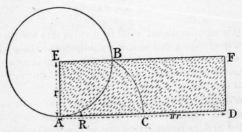

FIG. 10.—Area of a circle obtained graphically.

Thus, as shown in Fig. 10, make $AC =$ quadrant AB (p. 32). Produce AC to D, making $CD = AC$.

Then $AD = \pi r$.

Complete the rectangle $ADFE$ making its adjacent sides AD and DF equal to πr and r respectively.

Then, area of the circle is equal to the area of the rectangle

$$\therefore \ ADFE = \pi r \times r = \pi r^2.$$

If d denote the diameter of a circle, then as $d = 2r$,

$$\pi r^2 = \pi \left(\frac{d}{2}\right)^2 = \frac{\pi}{4} d^2.$$

In many cases it is convenient to use $\frac{\pi}{4} d^2$, instead of its equivalent πr^2.

Ex. 1. If the diameter of a piston is 30 inches (Fig. 11), find the total pressure on the piston. Pressure of steam $= 100$ lbs. per sq. in.

Area $= \frac{\pi}{4} \times 30^2 = 706 \cdot 86$ sq. in.

$\therefore$ total pressure on piston
$= 100 \times 706 \cdot 86 = 70686$ lbs.

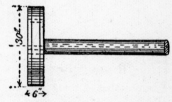

Fig. 11.— Piston and piston rod.

Ex. 2. The diameter of the safety-valve in a boiler is 3 inches; find the total pressure tending to raise the valve when the pressure of the steam is 120 lbs. per sq. in.

Area of valve $= \frac{\pi}{4} \times 3^2 = 7 \cdot 07$ sq. in.

$\therefore$ total pressure $= 7 \cdot 07 \times 120 = 848 \cdot 4$ lbs.

Area of Sector of a Circle.—*To find the area of the sector AE* (Fig. 12) *the angle θ being known.*

As the whole circle consists of 360 degrees, or 2π radians, the area of the sector will be the same fractional part of the whole area that the angle θ is of 360°, or of 2π.

Denoting the angle in degrees by N, then

area of sector $= \dfrac{N}{360} \pi r^2 = \dfrac{\theta}{2\pi} \pi r^2 = \dfrac{\theta r^2}{2}.$

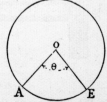

Fig. 12.—Area of sector of a circle.

Ex. 1. Find the area of the sector of a circle containing an angle of 42°, the radius of the circle being 15 feet ;

$$\text{area of circle} = \pi \times 15^2 ;$$

$$\text{area of sector} = \tfrac{42}{360}\pi \times 15^2 = 82\cdot47 \text{ square feet.}$$

Ex. 2. The length of the diameter of a circle is 25 feet, find the area of a sector in the circle, the length of the arc being 13·09 feet.

The area of the sector will be the same fraction of the whole area that 13·09 is of the circumference ;

$$\therefore \frac{13\cdot09}{25 \times \pi} \times \frac{\pi}{4} \times 25^2 = 81\cdot81 \text{ square feet.}$$

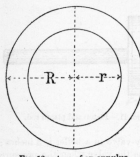

FIG. 13.—Area of an annulus.

Area of an Annulus.—If R (Fig. 13) denote the radius of the outer circle, and r the radius of the inner ; the area of the annulus is the difference of the two areas ;

$$= \pi R^2 - \pi r^2$$

$$= \pi(R^2 - r^2) = \pi(R+r)(R-r) ;$$

∴ *multiply the sum and difference of the two radii by $3\tfrac{1}{7}$ to obtain the area of an annulus.*

Ex. 1. Calculate the effective pressure on a piston 36 inches diameter (Fig. 14) ; the diameter of piston rod = 6 inches ; and the pressure of steam = 160 lbs. per sq. in.

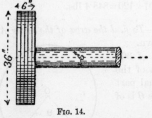

FIG. 14.

Area on one side of the piston

$$= \frac{\pi}{4}(36)^2 = 1017\cdot9,$$

total pressure

$$= 1017\cdot9 \times 160 ;$$

area of the other side

$$= \frac{\pi}{4}(36^2 - 6^2) = 989\cdot63 ;$$

$$\therefore \text{ total pressure} = 989\cdot63 \times 160,$$

or the difference in the total pressures on the two sides of the piston is $160(1017\cdot9 - 989\cdot63) = 4523\cdot2$ lbs.

Area of an Ellipse.—Denoting the two axes AA and BB' of an ellipse (Fig. 15) by $2a$ and $2b$, it is easy to illustrate by using an experimental method similar to that adopted in finding the area of a circle that the *area of an ellipse* $= \pi \times a \times b$.

Draw on a sheet of cardboard two ellipses, the axes of which are $2a$ and $2b$, circumscribe one of them by a rectangle, and draw the two axes AA and BB'. Make $BM = \frac{1}{7}BD$, and draw MN parallel to ED.

The area of each of the three rectangles is $a \times b$, and as $BMNO$ is $\frac{1}{7}ab$, the area of the shaded portion is $3\frac{1}{7}ab$.

If this area be cut out carefully and placed in one pan of a balance, while an ellipse of the same size, and cut out of the same material, be placed in the other pan, the two will be found to balance.

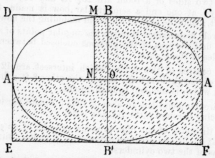

Fig. 15.—Area of an ellipse obtained experimentally.

Another method of obtaining the area of an ellipse is to draw the ellipse on squared paper. Count the enclosed squares, also estimate as accurately as possible, as shown on p. 44, the total area of the squares partially cut by the profile of the figure. By adding the two together, the area can be found.

EXERCISES. IX.

1. What is the diameter of a circular valve containing 227 square inches?

2. Find the diameter of a circle containing 20 square inches.

3. The area of a piston is 4536 square inches; find the diameter of the piston-rod, which is $\frac{1}{8}$ that of the piston.

4. Find the area of the rubbing-surface in a steam-cylinder 91½ inches in diameter, the stroke of the piston being 6 ft. 8 in.

5. A circular plot of land contains 6 ac. 1 r. 38 p. 16½ yds. ; what is its diameter ?

6. Find the diameter of a circle when the area in square inches is (i) 7, (ii) ·0000126, (iii) ·0003142, (iv) ·0314.

7. Find the area of a circle when its diameter in inches is (i) ·064, (ii) ·109, (iii) 3·3.

8. A pond 25 ft. diameter is surrounded by a path 5 ft. wide ; find the cost of making the path at 1s. 1½d. per square yard.

9. The perimeter of a circle is the same as that of a triangle, the sides of which are 13, 14, and 15 ft. ; find the area of the circle.

10. If the two perpendicular sides of a right-angled triangle are 70 and 98 ft. respectively, find the area of a circle described on the hypothenuse as a diameter.

11. The two sides of a room are 25¼ ft. and 14½ ft. in length respectively ; at one end a semicircular bow is made, the radius being 10½ ft. ; find the area of the room including the bow.

12. A circle is described through the angular points of a square of 6 ft. side ; find the area of the portions enclosed between the circle and the sides of the square.

13. The centres of two circles which intersect are 12 ft. apart ; the radius of one circle is 9 ft., that of the other 8 ft. ; find the area of the part which is common to both circles.

14. A circular pond has an area of 1963·5 square yards ; find the cost of fencing it round at 3s. 6d. per yard.

15. The diameter of the high-pressure cylinder of an engine is 36 inches, that of the low-pressure cylinder is 70 inches ; find the ratio of the areas of the two cylinders.

16. A sector contains 42°, the radius of the circle is 15 ft. ; find the area of the sector.

17. The length of the arc of a sector of a given circle is 16 ft., and the angle ⅓ of a right angle ; find the area of the sector. Find also the length of the arc subtending the same angle in a circle whose radius is four times that of the given circle.

18. The diameter of a circle is 5 ft. ; find the area of a sector which contains 18°.

19. Find the area of the sector of the end of a boiler supported by a gusset-stay, the radius of the boiler being 42 inches, length of arc 25 inches.

20. A sector of a circle contains 270° ; find its area when the radius of the circle is 25 ft.

21. The radius of a circle is 8 ft. ; find the area of a sector of the circle, the angle of which is 36°.

22. Find the radius of a circle such that the area of a sector corresponding to an angle of 90° may be 181·16 sq. ft.

23. Find the area of the annulus enclosed between two circles, the outer 9 inches and the inner 8 inches diameter.

24. The inner and outer diameters of an annulus are 9½ and 10 inches respectively ; find the area of the annulus.

25. The area of a piston is 5944·7 square inches; what is the diameter of the air-pump, which is one-half that of the piston?

26. The diameters of the piston and air-pump of an engine are as 2 : 1·2 ; find the diameter of the air-pump when the area of the piston is 1134·1 square inches.

27. What is the area of an elliptical plot of ground, the greater and lesser diameters being 200 and 150 feet respectively?

28. The major axis of an ellipse is 60 yds., the minor axis 40 yds. ; find its periphery and area.

29. What is the circumference and area of an ellipse when the major and minor axes are 16 and 12 ft. respectively ?

30. Find the area of an ellipse when the two axes are 70 ft. and 50 ft.

31. The greater and lesser diameters of an oval man-hole door are 24 and 18 inches respectively ; what is its area ?

32. A rectangular pond, 84 ft. long, 60 ft. wide, was lengthened by a semicircular extension at one end. What was then the area of the water surface? [L.C.U.]

33. If the angle at the centre of a circle of 3·6 in. radius is 67°, what is the length of the arc ? [L.C.U.]

Summary.

Area of a Circle $= \pi r^2 = \frac{\pi}{4} d^2$ where r and d denote the radius and diameter respectively.

Area of Sector of a Circle $= \frac{\theta}{2} r^2$, where θ is the angle in radians subtended at the centre.

Area of an Annulus $= \pi (R^2 - r^2)$, or, to find its area subtract the square of the smaller radius from the square of the greater and multiply the difference by π.

Area of an Ellipse $= \pi \times ab =$ product of its semi-axes multiplied by π.

CHAPTER VII.

AREAS OF IRREGULAR FIGURES. TRAPEZOIDAL AND SIMPSON'S RULES. PLANIMETERS. CENTRE OF GRAVITY.

Areas obtained by the Use of Squared Paper.—The areas of irregular figures may be estimated by drawing the figures on squared paper, and counting the squares enclosed by the periphery of the figure.

As an introduction to this method it may be advisable to commence with such simple regular geometrical figures as the rectangle, parallelogram, etc. (Fig. 16).

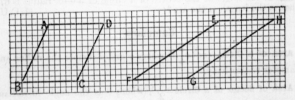

Fig. 16.—Parallelograms on equal bases and between the same parallels are equal.

When any figure is drawn upon squared paper there will usually be a number of complete squares enclosed by the periphery, and a number of squares cut by it. This is evident from Fig. 17, where the periphery ACB cuts a number of squares and also encloses a number of complete squares. To estimate the value of any square cut by the profile or periphery of the figure, it is convenient to neglect any square which is obviously less than one-half, and to reckon as a whole square any one cut which is equal to, or greater than, one-half.

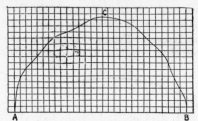

FIG. 17.—Area of an irregular figure.

One defect of this method of estimating areas is that large errors are likely to occur when portions of the periphery of the figure are nearly parallel to the lines of ruling. This may readily be seen by drawing parallelograms, or any simple geometrical figures, the bases of the figures making different angles with the lines, and comparing the results so obtained.

When the periphery of an irregular figure *ABCDEF* (Fig. 18) consists of a series of straight lines the area may be obtained by dividing the figure into a number of triangles, and the area of each triangle may be obtained separately. The sum of the areas of all the triangles into which the figure has been divided will give the area of the irregular figure.

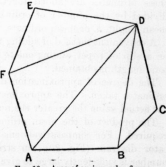

FIG. 18.—Area of an irregular figure.

When the ordinates of an irregular figure, in which one or more of the boundaries may consist of curved lines, are given it would be necessary in the graphical method just described either to set out the ordinates on squared paper or to draw these to some convenient scale, joining the extremities of the ordinates by an approximate curved line. In this process errors are likely to be introduced. Hence, several methods of finding the area of an irregular figure which depend only on calculation are used. Of these we may notice three in common use. The one known as *Simpson's Rule* is the most accurate.

Area of an Irregular Figure.—A common method of estimating the area of an irregular figure, such as *GFED*, Fig. 19,

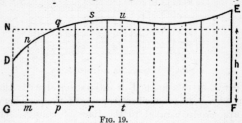

Fig. 19.

in which one of the boundaries is a curved line, is to divide the base *GF* into a number of equal parts, and at the centre of each of the equal parts to erect ordinates as shown. The length of each ordinate, *mn*, *pq*, *rs*, etc., from the base *GF* to the point where the vertical cuts the curve, is carefully measured, and all these ordinates are added together. The sum so obtained, divided by the number of ordinates, gives approximat ly the mean height, *h*, or mean ordinate, *GN*.

A convenient method of adding the ordinates is to mark them on a slip of paper, adding one to the end of the other until the total length is obtained.

The degree of approximation depends upon the number of ordinates taken. The approximation more closely approaches the actual value the greater the number of ordinates used.

The product of the mean ordinate and the base is the area required. For comparatively small diagrams, such as an indicator diagram (Fig. 20), ten strips are usually taken. This number is sufficiently large to give a fair average, and, moreover, dividing by 10 can be effected by merely shifting the decimal point.

The length of *GF*, Fig. 20, may correspond on a reduced scale to the travel of the piston in a cylinder, and the ordinates of the curve represent, to a known scale, the pressure per square inch of the steam in the cylinder at the various points of the stroke.

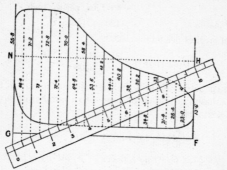

FIG. 20.—Area of an indicator diagram.

Hence, the mean height GN indicates the mean pressure P of the steam, in pounds per sq. inch, throughout the stroke (the stroke being the term applied to the distance moved through by the piston in moving from its extreme position at one end of the cylinder to a corresponding position at the other end).

If A denote the area of the piston in square inches, then the total force exerted by the steam on the piston is $P \times A$, and the work done by this force in acting through a length of stroke L is $P \times A \times L$. If N denote the number of strokes per minute, the work done per minute by the steam $= PALN$.

But the unit of power used by engineers, and called a Horse-power, is 33000 ft. lbs. per minute.

Hence, Horse-power of the engine $= \dfrac{P \times L \times A \times N}{33000}$.

Ex. 1. In Fig. 20 the indicator card of an engine is shown; the diameter of the piston is $23\frac{1}{8}$ inches, length of stroke 3 ft., and revolutions 100 per minute; find the mean pressure of the steam, also the horse-power of the engine.

Adding together the ten ordinates shown by dotted lines, we have

$$66 \cdot 6 + 73 \cdot 0 + 72 \cdot 4 + 64 \cdot 8 + 53 \cdot 6 + 44 \cdot 4 + 38 \cdot 0 + 34 \cdot 8 + 31 \cdot 4 + 23 \cdot 0$$

$$= 502.$$

As there are 10 ordinates,

$$\therefore \text{ mean pressure} = \frac{502}{10}$$

$$= 50 \cdot 2 \text{ lbs. per sq. inch.}$$

Area of piston $= 420$ sq. inches;

Number of strokes per minute $= 200$.

$$\therefore \text{ Horse-power} = \frac{50 \cdot 2 \times 3 \times 420 \times 200}{33000} = 383 \cdot 3.$$

The Trapezoidal Rule is another method to obtain the mean ordinate h, having divided the base into a number of equal parts, say 6 (Fig. 21), then :

$$h = \frac{s}{6} \{ \tfrac{1}{2}(h_1 + h_7) + h_2 + h_3 + h_4 + h_5 + h_6 \}.$$

Divide the base into any number of equal parts; add half the sum of the end ordinates to the sum of all the others. Multiply the result by the common interval s to obtain the area: divide by the number of spaces into which the figure is divided to obtain the mean ordinate.

Mean ordinate × length = area of figure.

It will be found very instructive to calculate by means of this rule the areas in the following examples, and compare the results obtained with the more accurate values as found by the application of Simpson's rule.

Simpson's Rule.—By means of what is called Simpson's rule,

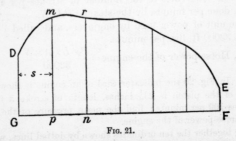

FIG. 21.

the area of an irregular figure *GFED* (Fig. 21) can be ascertained more accurately than by the trapezoidal method.

The base GF is divided into an even number of equal parts. This ensures that the number of ordinates is an odd number, 3, 5, 7, 9, etc. In Fig. 21 the base GF is divided into 6 equal parts, and the number of ordinates is therefore 7.

Denoting, as before, the lengths of the ordinates GD, pm, nr, etc., by h_1, h_2, $h_3 \ldots h_7$; then, if s denotes the common distance or space between the ordinates, we have

$$\text{Area of } GFED = \frac{s}{3}\{h_1 + h_7 + 4(h_2 + h_4 + h_6) + 2(h_3 + h_5)\}$$

$$= \frac{s}{3}(A + 4B + 2C)$$

where A denotes the sum of the first and last ordinates.

    " B "   "   even ordinates.

    " C "   "   odd ordinates.

$\therefore$ *Add together the extreme ordinates, four times the sum of the even ordinates, and twice the sum of the odd ordinates* (omitting the first and the last). *Multiply the result by one-third the common interval between two consecutive ordinates.*

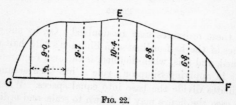

FIG. 22.

The end ordinates at G and F may both be zero, the curve commencing from the line GF (Fig. 22). In this case A is zero, and the formula for the area becomes

$$\frac{s}{3}(0 + 4B + 2C).$$

Or, using the given values in Fig. 22, where the length of the ordinates are expressed in feet, we have

$$\text{area} = \frac{6}{3}\{0 + 4(9 \cdot 0 + 10 \cdot 4 + 6 \cdot 8) + 2(9 \cdot 7 + 8 \cdot 8)\}$$

$$= 2(104 \cdot 8 + 37) = 283 \cdot 6 \text{ sq. ft.}$$

In certain cases the given figure may be bounded by two curved lines DG and EN, and the two straight lines DE, FG (Fig. 23). The ordinates would then correspond to mn, rq, etc. If the two curved boundaries are symmetrical about a line AB, it is only necessary to give the half-ordinates pm, rs, etc., and

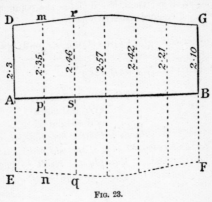

FIG. 23.

each of these ordinates may be doubled. Or, by substituting the values of the half-ordinates in Simpson's rule, half the area is obtained, and this, when doubled, is the area required.

So far in applying Simpson's rule it has been assumed that the ordinates divide the base into equal spaces. When this is not the case the figure may be drawn to scale, and ordinates at equal distances drawn; the lengths of these ordinates can be measured, and the area obtained by Simpson's rule.

Ex. 2. The half-ordinates of two curved lines GD, EF (Fig. 23), the common interval being 1·5 feet, are as follows: 2·3, 2·35, 2·46, 2·57, 2·42, 2·21, 2·10. Find the area.

Extreme ordinates $2·3 + 2·10 = 4·4$.
Remaining odd ordinates, $2·46 + 2·42 = 4·88$.
Even ordinates $2·35 + 2·57 + 2·21 = 7·13$.

$$\text{Area} = \frac{1·5}{3}(4·4 + 4 \times 7·13 + 2 \times 4·88) = 21·34 \text{ square feet.}$$

Hence, area of $DEFG = 2 \times 21·34 = 42·68$ square feet.

When the area is *not* symmetrical about a line; parallel lines
such as FG and ED (Fig. 24)
are drawn touching the curve,
and GD, FE are also drawn
perpendicular to the former
and touching the curve.

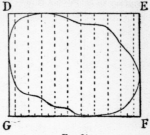

As before, the base GF is
divided into a number of equal
parts and the ordinates of the
curve measured; from these
values, proceeding as before,
the area can be obtained.

FIG. 24.

Ex. 3. The ordinates of a curve (Fig. 24) are in feet, 4·8, 6·5,
7·0, 7·7, 7·5, 7·8, 7·6, 7·2, 5·5, 3·0, respectively and the common
interval is 2 feet. Find the area (*a*) by common rule, (*b*) by
trapezoidal rule.

(*a*) The sum of the ordinates = 64·6, as there are 10 ordinates, and
base GF = 20 ft.

$$\therefore \; \text{Area} = \frac{64 \cdot 6}{10} \times 20 = 129 \cdot 2 \text{ sq. ft.}$$

(*b*) If ordinates dividing the base into equal parts are drawn,
their sum is found to be 64·8; ∴ the area = 64·8 × 2 = 129·6 sq. ft.

Ex. 4. A force P acts along a line AE; the values of the force at
A and at points 3, 6, 9, and 12 from A are respectively 50, 35, 28, 25,
and 24 lbs. Draw a diagram of the work done by the force and
calculate its amount in foot-pounds.

In Fig. 25 at the points along AE ordinates (equal to the respective values of P at those points) are drawn as shown. If a fairly
even curve FG be drawn through the points so obtained, the area
$AFGE$ represents work done.

If we add all the ordinates together the sum is 162; dividing this
by 5, the number of ordinates, we obtain very roughly the mean
ordinate to be $\frac{162}{5}$ lbs. This, multiplied by the length AE = 12 ft.,
gives the work done by the force in foot-pounds;

$$\therefore \; \tfrac{162}{5} \times 12 = 388\tfrac{4}{5}.$$

A much better result is obtained by Simpson's Rule, thus:

$$\text{Area of curve} = \tfrac{3}{3}\{50 + 24 + 4(35 + 25) + 2(28)\}$$
$$= 74 + 240 + 56 = 370 \text{ foot-pounds.}$$

This example also furnishes a good instance of the superior accuracy of Simpson's Rule. If we assume that no more than the

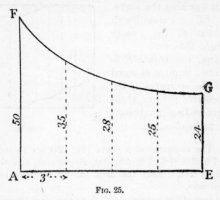

FIG. 25.

three values at **50, 28,** and **24** are given, as the common interval will now be 6 ft.

$$\text{Area} = \tfrac{6}{3}(50 + 24 + 4(28) + 2 \times 0)\}$$
$$= 2(74 + 112) = 372 \text{ foot-pounds.}$$

Although, as shown in the preceding examples, the most accurate results are obtained by Simpson's Rule; in all cases the area obtained may if necessary be checked by the rough method.

Ex. 5. The length of the base is 16 inches, and the lengths of nine equidistant ordinates are as follows: 0, 1·5, 2·5, 3, 4 5, 5·5, 6·5, 7, 0; the common interval is 2 inches; find the area.

$$\text{Area} = \tfrac{2}{3}\{(0 + 0) + 4(1·5 + 3 + 5·5 + 7) + 2(2·5 + 4·5 + 6·5)\}$$
$$= \tfrac{2}{3}(68 + 27) = \tfrac{2}{3} \times 95 = 63\tfrac{1}{3} \text{ sq. inches.}$$

As the area of an irregular figure is the product of the length of the base GF and the mean ordinate, it follows that when the area is obtained the mean ordinate may be found by dividing the area by the length of the base. Thus in Fig. 20, p. 47, where GF denotes 6 inches, the division into 10 equal parts will give the common distance between each ordinate to be ·6 inch. On p. 48 a rough result for the mean ordinate has been obtained. A more accurate result can be found by Simpson's Rule, as follows :

$$\text{Extreme ordinates} = 55 \cdot 8 + 13 \cdot 6 = 69 \cdot 4,$$
$$\text{Even ordinates} = 71 \cdot 2 + 70 + 48 \cdot 2 + 36 \cdot 2 + 28 \cdot 4 = 254,$$
$$\text{Odd ordinates} = 72 \cdot 8 + 58 \cdot 4 + 40 \cdot 8 + 33 = 205.$$

$$\therefore \text{ Area of figure} = \frac{\cdot 6}{3}(69 \cdot 4 + 4 \times 254 + 2 \times 205)$$
$$= 299 \cdot 08 \text{ sq. in.}$$

$$\therefore \text{ Mean ordinate} = \frac{299 \cdot 08}{6} = 49 \cdot 85 \text{ in.}$$

By using 10 instead of 11 ordinates, and adopting the rough method, an approximate result 50·2 has been already obtained, (see p. 47.)

Average Cross-Section.—The volume of a solid is obtained by multiplying together its average cross-section and its length. Simpson's rule may be applied with advantage to obtain the average cross-section, when the cross-sections of an irregular body at given intervals are known. In the rule it is only necessary to substitute the words 'area' for 'ordinate' and 'volume' for 'area.' If h denote the mean height or average cross-section, then as the area is given by

$$A = \frac{s}{3}(A + 4B + 2C),$$

and the length AB is known, the value of h can be obtained.

An important practical case occurs when only three ordinates (Fig. 26) are given.

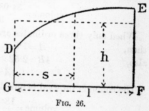

FIG. 26.

In this case C is 0 ; $\therefore$ area of $GFED = \frac{s}{3}(A + 4B)$;

but $2s \times h = l \times h$ is also the area of $GFED$;

$$\therefore \quad 2s \times h = \frac{s}{3}(A + 4B) ;$$

$$\therefore \quad h = \frac{1}{6}(A + 4B),$$

or average section $= \frac{1}{6} \left\{ \begin{array}{l} \text{sum of first and last sections} \\ \quad + 4 \text{ times the middle section} \end{array} \right\}$.

This is known as the **Prismoidal Rule.**

In using Simpson's rule, to avoid, as far as possible, mistakes finding their way into the work, other methods consisting of the arrangement of the given numbers into vertical columns are used. This can be best shown by an example.

Ex. 7.   Find the cubical contents of a log of timber 30 feet long, the cross-sectional areas at intervals of 5 feet being respectively 7·5, 5·08, 3·54, 2·52, 1·86, 1·34, 0·92 square feet.   Find also what the volume would be if only the cross-sectional areas of the two ends and the middle were given.

(1) Ordinate,	7·5	5·08	3·54	2·52	1·86	1·34	0·92
(2) Simpson's Multiplier,	1	4	2	4	2	4	1
(3) Product,	7·5	20·32	7·08	10·08	3·72	5·36	·92

Adding the numbers in the last row (3) together, the sum is found to be 54·98.

As the common interval is 5 feet,

$$\text{volume} = \frac{54 \cdot 98 \times 5}{3} = 91 \cdot 6 \text{ cub. ft.}$$

When only three ordinates are given,

then, $A = 7 \cdot 5 + \cdot 92 = 8 \cdot 42$;
also, $4B = 2 \cdot 52 \times 4 = 10 \cdot 08$;
             $\therefore A + 4B = 18 \cdot 5.$

The common interval is now 15 feet ;

$$\therefore \text{volume} = \frac{18 \cdot 5 \times 15}{3} = 92 \cdot 5 \text{ cub. ft.}$$

Or, by the **Prismoidal Rule**, we could find the mean or average cross-section, and multiplying by the length obtain the volume.

Thus,   average section $= \frac{1}{6}(8 \cdot 42 + 4 \times 2 \cdot 52) = \frac{18 \cdot 5}{6}$;

$$\therefore \text{volume} = \frac{18 \cdot 5}{6} \times 30 = 92 \cdot 5, \text{ as before.}$$

Other methods of finding the area of an irregular figure, instead of those which have now been studied, are by means of weighing, and by using a planimeter.

By Weighing.—Draw the figure to some convenient scale, or, if possible, full size, on thick paper or cardboard of uniform thickness. Cut it out carefully. Also cut out a rectangular piece from the same sheet ; find the weight of the rectangular piece and hence deduce the weight of a square inch. Then knowing the weight of the irregular figure and the weight of unit area, the area of the figure can be calculated.

Planimeters.—The planimeter is an instrument for estimating the areas of irregular figures. There are many forms of the instrument to which various names—Hatchet, Amsler, etc.—are applied. Of these the more expensive and accurate forms are mostly modifications of the *Amsler planimeter*.

Hatchet Planimeter.—A hatchet planimeter in its simplest form may consist of a ∩-shaped piece of metal wire (Fig. 27), one end terminating in a round point, the other in a knife edge.

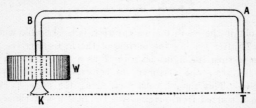

FIG. 27.—Hatchet planimeter.

This knife edge is rounded or hatchet-shaped, the distance between the centre of the edge K and the point T may be made 5, 10, or some such convenient number. This length may be denoted by TK.

To determine the area of a figure we proceed as follows :

(*a*) Estimate approximately the centre of gravity of the area (p. 58), and through this point draw a straight line across the figure.

(*b*) Set the instrument so that it is roughly at right angles to this line, with the point T at the centre of gravity. When in this position a mark is made on the paper by the knife edge K. Holding the instrument in a vertical position, the point T is made to pass from the centre to some point P in the periphery of the figure (Fig. 28), and then to trace once round the outline of the figure until point P is again reached, thence to the centre again. In this position a mark is again made with the edge K. The distance between the two marks is measured, the product of this length and the constant length TK gives the area of the figure approximately.

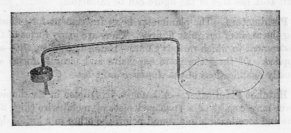

FIG. 28.—Hatchet planimeter.

To obtain the result more accurately, it is advisable when the point T (after tracing the outline of the figure) arrives at the centre to turn the figure on point T as a pivot through about 180°, and trace the periphery as before, but in the opposite direction. This should, with care, bring the edge K near to where it started from originally. The nearness of these marks depends to some extent on the accuracy with which the centre of area has been estimated.

The area of the figure is the product of TK, and the mean distance between the first and third marks.

To prevent the knife edge K from slipping, a small weight W (Fig. 27) is usually threaded on to the arm BH; the portion of the arm on which the weight is placed is flattened to receive it. The arm BA is usually adjustable, and this enables the instrument to be used, not only for small, but also for comparatively large diagrams.

Amsler Planimeter.—One form of the instrument is shown in Fig. 29, and consists of two arms A and C, pivoted together at a point B. The arm BA is fixed at some convenient point s. The other arm BC carries a tracing point T. This is passed

round the outline of the figure, the area of which is required.
The arm *BC* carries a wheel *D*, the rim of which is usually
divided into 100 equal parts.

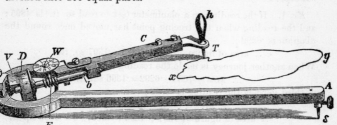

FIG. 29.—Amsler planimeter.

When the instrument is in use the rim of the wheel rests on
the paper, and as the point *T* is carried round the outline of the
figure, the wheel, by means of a spindle rotating on pivots at *a*
and *b*, gives motion to a small worm *F*, which in turn rotates
the dial *W*.

One rotation of the wheel corresponds to one-tenth of a
revolution of the dial. A vernier, *V*, is fixed to the frame of
the instrument, and a distance equal to 9 scale divisions on the
rim of the wheel is divided into ten on this vernier. The readings on the dial are indicated by means of a small finger or
pointer shown in Fig. 29. If the figures on the dial indicate
units, those on the wheel will be $\frac{1}{10}$ths ; as each of these is
subdivided into 10, the subdivisions indicate $\frac{1}{100}$ths. Finally,
the vernier, *V*, in which $\frac{9}{100}$ of the wheel is divided into 10
parts, enable a reading to be made to three places of decimals.

To obtain the area of a figure, the fixed point *s* is set at some
convenient point outside the area to be measured, and the point
T at some point in the periphery of the figure. Note the
reading of the dial and wheel. Carefully follow the outline of
the figure until the tracing point *T* again reaches the starting-
point, and again take the reading. The difference between the
two readings will give the area of the figure.

To obtain proficiency in the use of the instrument it is advisable to first use it to find the area of a square or other simple
figure.

To find the area of an irregular figure with accuracy, the mean of two or three readings may be taken, as in the following example :

Ex. 1.   If the reading on a planimeter (set to read sq. ft.) is ·4895 ; and the reading when the tracing point has moved once round the diagram is ·6292 ;

$$\therefore \text{ area of figure} = ·6292 - ·4895 = ·1397 \text{ sq. ft.}$$

When another journey is made the reading is ·7688 ;

$$\therefore \text{ area} = ·7688 - ·6292 = ·1396 \text{ sq. ft.}$$

A third journey the reading is ·8083 ;

$$\therefore \text{ area} = ·8083 - ·7688 = ·1395.$$

$$\therefore \text{ area of figure} = (·1397 + ·1396 + ·1395) \div 3 = ·1396 \text{ sq. ft.}$$

Centre of Gravity.—Every particle of a body is attracted by the earth, and the total force exerted constitutes the weight of the body.   The separate forces due to the weights of the constituent particles are directed towards the centre of the earth, and are therefore practically parallel forces.   The resultant of all these parallel forces, or the weight of the body, will act through a definite point.   This point is called the *centre of gravity* of the body.

Centre of gravity of symmetrical figures.   The centre of gravity of symmetrical bodies is also their geometrical centres.   Thus, the centre of gravity of a disc is the centre of its circular surface ; of a rectangle, parallelogram, or square, the intersection of their diagonals.

Centre of gravity of a triangle.   In a triangle any line drawn parallel to the base will have its centre of gravity at its middle point.   Hence the centre of gravity of the triangle is in a line

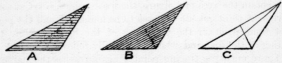

Fig. 30.—Centre of gravity of a triangle.

joining the vertex to the middle point *A* of the opposite side (Fig. 30.)

In a similar manner, as at *B*, taking another line as base, the centre of gravity is in the line joining the apex to the middle point of the opposite side. The point of intersection of the lines so obtained, as at C, Fig. 30, is the centre of gravity of the triangle; it is easy to verify by measurement or by a simple application of Euclid, Bk. I., that the point of intersection is at one-third the line measured from the base.

Centre of gravity of irregular figures. To find the centre of gravity of an irregular figure, the outline may be drawn on cardboard or sheet zinc, then carefully cut out and suspended, as shown in Fig. 31. The centre of gravity is in the vertical line passing through the point of suspension. Now suspend it from any other point, again the centre of gravity is similarly in the vertical line passing through the point of suspension. Hence the centre of gravity of the face is at G the intersection of the two lines found. If

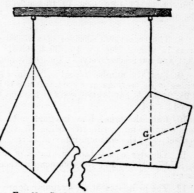

Fig. 31.—Centre of gravity of an irregular figure.

the body is of uniform thickness the centre of gravity of the body is at the middle point of a line passing through G at right angles to its plane surface.

EXERCISES. X.

1. Draw a semicircle of $1\frac{1}{2}$ inches radius; find its area by Simpson's Rule.

2. Draw an ellipse, major axis 12 in., minor axis 8 in., and find its area by Simpson's Rule.

3. The ordinates of a curve are 4, 5, 6, 7, 8, 12, and 14 ft. respectively; find the area, the common interval being 3 ft., (i) using the common rule, (ii) by Simpson's Rule.

4. The half ordinates of an irregular piece of steel plate of uniform thickness, and weighing 4 lbs. per sq. ft., are 0, 1·5, 2·5, 3

5, 6·75, 7·25, 9, 8·75, 7, 6, 5·25, 3·5, 2, and 0 ft. respectively; the common distance between the ordinates is 5 ft. Find its weight.

5. The ordinates of an irregular piece of land are 3·5, 4·75, 5·25, 7·5, 8·25, 14·75, 6, 9·5, and 4 yds. respectively; the common interval is 1¼ yds. Find its area.

6. The equidistant ordinates of an irregular piece of sheet lead, weighing 6 lbs. per sq. ft., are respectively 2, 4, 9, 5, and 3 ft.; the length of the base is 8 ft. Find its weight.

7. The half ordinates of the midship section of a vessel are 12·8, 12·9, 13, 13, 13, 12·9, 12·6, 12, 10·5, 6, and 1·5 feet respectively, and the distance between each of them is 18 inches; find the area of the section.

8. The transverse sections of a vessal are 15 ft. apart, and the areas in square feet are 4·8, 39·4, 105·4, 159·1, 183·5, 173·3, 127·4, 57·2, and 6·0 respectively. Find the volume of the vessel.

9. Find the number of cubic feet in a log of timber, 36 ft. long, whose cross sections every six feet are 16·4, 11·36, 8·08, 5·84, 4·32, 3·08, 2·04. What is its weight if the specific gravity of the timber is ·56?

10. Find the area of an irregular piece of land; the lengths of seven equidistant ordinates being 15, 19, 20, 23, 25, 30 and 33 ft. respectively, the common interval 12 ft.

11. The five equidistant ordinates of a curved space are in feet 8, 10, 12, 14, and 15; the common distance being 6 ft. What is the area?

12. The ordinates of an irregular figure are found to be 8·2, 7·4, 9·2, 10·2, and 8·6 ft. respectively; find the area by the three methods, the total length of the figure being 6 ft.

13. The length of a tree is 17¼ ft., its girth or circumference at five equidistant places being 9·43, 7·92, 6·15, 4·74, and 3·16 ft. respectively. Find the volume of the tree by three methods.

14. The length of an indicator diagram is 4 inches, the end ordinates are 1, ·22, and the other ordinates are 1, ·82, ·71, ·55, ·45, ·38, ·33, ·29, and ·26 inches; the scale of pressure is 60 lbs. per sq. in. to one inch. Find the mean pressure (i) by the common rule, (ii) by Simpson's Rule.

15. The transverse sections of a vessel are 18 ft. apart; the areas being 6·5, 55·8, 132·0, 210·9, 266·3, 289·5, 280·2, 235·7, 161·2, 77·8, and 10·9 sq. ft. respectively. Find the volume of the vessel.

16. The flagstaff at Kew is 215 ft. long; its diameter at the base is 3 ft. and at the top 1 ft. Find its weight, assuming a circular cross-section throughout, if its timber weighs 38·06 lb. per cub. ft.
[N.U.T.]

17. The depth of a railway cutting is 27 ft. Its breadth at the top is 74 ft., at the bottom 49 ft. Find the cost of excavating a length of 60 yards at 1s. 9½d. per cubic yard.
[L.C.U.]

18. A line of telephone wires is 1½ miles long. The poles on which the wires are hung are 30 ft. long, base diameter 10 in., top diameter 6 in., and are placed 60 ft. apart. Find cost of timber at 2s. 6d. per cub. ft.   [N.U.T.]

19. A bucket is 8 in. internal diameter at the bottom and 12 in. at the top. If the depth is 7½ in., find the volume and weight of water it will hold.   [L.C.U.]

20. The length of a trench is 30 ft., uniform depth 5 ft.; it is 12 ft. wide at the top and 10 ft. wide at the bottom. How many cubic yards of soil are removed in excavating the trench? How many gallons of water will it hold when full ?   [U.E.I.]

21. From equidistant points in a straight path 60 yards long, running along one side of a field, the perpendicular distances to the boundary are 0, 30·8, 50·6, 65, 66, 67·2, 64, 50, 34·2, 20·9, 15, 8, and 0 yds. respectively. Calculate the area of the field. [N.U.T.]

Summary.

The area of an irregular figure can be obtained thus :

Divide the figure into a number of equal spaces, and erect ordinates at the centre of each space :

(1) Add the lengths of all the ordinates together, and, to obtain the mean ordinate, divide the sum by the number of ordinates.

(2) Trapezoidal Rule.—Add half the sum of the end ordinates to the sum of all the others, and divide this by the number of ordinates to obtain the mean ordinate.

(3) Simpson's Rule.—Add together the extreme ordinates, four times the sum of the even ordinates, and twice the sum of the odd ordinates. Multiply the result by one-third the common interval.

In each of the above the area = length × mean ordinate.

Average Cross-Section = $\frac{1}{6}$ (sum of first and last sections + 4 times the middle section).

Area by use of Squared Paper.—Draw the figure on squared paper, estimate the number of whole squares within the boundary, and the fractional parts cut by it, and add the two together.

Area by Weighing.—Draw the figure on a sheet of uniform thickness, such as a sheet of cardboard : cut out the figure as carefully as possible : also cut out of the same piece of cardboard a rectangular piece, weigh the latter ; hence deduce the weight of a square inch, and from this, knowing the weight of the irregular figure, its area can be found.

A **Planimeter** is an instrument by means of which the area of an irregular plane figure can be mechanically determined.

CHAPTER VIII.

UNITS OF VOLUME. UNITS OF MASS. UNITS OF WEIGHT. DENSITY. SPECIFIC GRAVITY.

Measurement of Volume.—If you examine Fig. 32, which represents a cubic foot, and bear in mind what you have already learnt, you will easily understand that each edge of the solid there represented is measured as a length and is 1 foot, or 12 inches. Each of its faces has an area, which can be obtained by multiplying together the lengths of two of the edges which meet at a corner. But the size of the solid, or the amount of room it takes up, or the space it occupies is quite a different thing. This new measurement is what is called its **volume**.

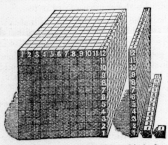

FIG. 32.—To explain why 1728 cubic inches make one cubic foot.

The volume of a solid body is obtained by measuring in three directions. Just as to find the area of a surface we measure its length and breadth, so to measure the volume of a solid we must find in addition to measurements of length and breadth, another distance called the thickness. If we multiply length, breadth, and thickness together we obtain a volume or cubical content.

Returning to our cubic foot for a moment, let us find how many cubic inches it contains. We know already that any one of its faces covers 144 square inches of surface. In the cube we can think of a layer of 144 cubic inches, or little cubes each edge of which is an inch, and each face of which is a square inch. How many such layers are there in the whole cubic foot? Evidently there are twelve layers.

Consequently, in the whole cube we have $144 \times 12 = 1728$ little cubes the edges of which are one inch long and the faces of which are each one square inch. Or, one cubic foot contains 1728 cubic inches.

We could reason in the same way to find out how many cubic feet are required to build up a cubic yard. We may write down, therefore,

$1728 (= 12 \times 12 \times 12)$ cubic inches make 1 cubic foot.

$27 (= 3 \times 3 \times 3)$ „ feet „ 1 „ yard.

Units of Capacity and Volume.—In the British system an arbitrary unit, the **gallon**, is the *standard unit of capacity and volume*, and is defined as the volume occupied by 10 lbs. of pure water at a temperature of 62° F.

With a few exceptions, all bodies expand by heat and contract when cooled; hence the temperature of the water must be given in thus defining the unit of volume.

The weight of a cubic foot of water depends upon its temperature. Thus at 32° F. the weight is 62·418 lbs., at 62° F. the weight is 62·355 lbs., and at 212° is 59·64 lbs. A good average value is 62·3 lbs. For convenience in calculations, a cubic foot is sometimes taken to be $6\frac{1}{4}$ gallons, and its weight 1000 oz., or 62·5 lbs. Hence the weight of a pint is about $1\frac{1}{4}$ lbs.

A larger unit is the volume of a cube on a base of which the length of each side is 1 foot and the height *BE* also 1 foot. The volume of such a cube is 1 cubic foot.

When the unit of length is *one inch*, the unit of volume is one *cubic inch*.

In Fig. 33 a cubic yard is represented. If *ABCD* represent a square having its edge 1 yard, the area of the square is 9 square feet. If the vertical sides, one of which is shown at *DE*, be divided into three equal parts, and the remaining lines be drawn parallel to *DE* and the base respectively. Then, as will be seen from the figure, there are nine perpendicular rows of small cubes, the sides being 1 foot in length, area of base 1 square foot, and volume 1 cubic foot. Also there are three of these

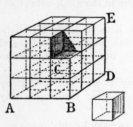

FIG. 33.—A cubic yard contains 27 cubic feet.

cubes in each row, making in all $3 \times 9 = 27$. Thus 1 cubic yard = 27 cubic feet, *i.e.* $3 \times 3 \times 3 = 27$, and the weight of a cubic yard of pure water would therefore be $27 \times 62\cdot3$ lbs. = $1682\cdot1$ lbs.

In this example, and also in considering the weight of a gallon, the student should notice that the specification "pure" water is necessary, for if the water contains matter either in solution or mixed with it, its weight would be altered. Thus, the weight of a cubic foot of salt water is 64 lbs., and the weight of a gallon of muddy water may be 11 or 12 lbs. instead of 10 lbs.

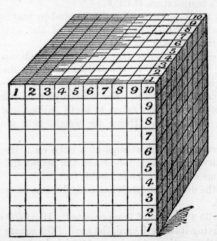

FIG. 34.—Cubic decimetre (1000 cubic centimetres) holds 1 kilogram or 1000 grams (1 litre) of water at 4° C.

Metric Measures of Volume.—We proceed in a similar way when we wish to measure volumes by the metric system.

A block built up with cubes representing cubic centimetres is shown in Fig. 34.

The cube measures 10 centimetres each way, and its volume is therefore a cubic decimetre. There are 10 centimetres in a decimetre, so the edge of the decimetre cube is 10 centimetres in length; the area of one of its faces is $10 \times 10 = 100$ square centimetres; and its volume is $10 \times 10 \times 10 = 100 \times 10 = 1000$ cubic centimetres.

In the Metric System the unit of volume is called a **Litre.** At ordinary temperature it is very nearly a cubic decimetre, or 1000 cubic centimetres (Fig. 34), and is equal to 1·76 English pints.

We have found that the unit of area is, for convenience, taken to be one square centimetre, the corresponding unit of volume is then the cubic centimetre (c.c.).

MEASURES OF VOLUME OR CAPACITY.

British.

Unit volume *is the volume occupied by a gallon, or 10 lbs. of water at a temperature of* 62° F.

One fourth part of a gallon is a quart, and an eighth part of a gallon is a pint.

1728 cubic inches = 1 cubic foot.   27 cubic feet = 1 cubic yard.

Metric.

Unit Volume.—*The litre is the volume occupied by 1 kilogram of water at* 4° C.   1000 cubic centimetres = 1 litre.

The standard temperature 4° C. is not very convenient, and the temperature 62° F., or $16\frac{2}{3}$° C., may be used instead; a suitable correction for the expansion of substances for an increase of temperature must be made if necessary.

Volume.
Conversion Table.

1 cub. in.	= 16·387 cub. cm.		1 c.cm.	= ·061	cub. in.
1 „ ft.	= 28316 „		1 litre	= 61·027	„
1 „ yard	= 764535 „			= 1·76	pint, or
1 pint	= 567·63 „			= ·22	gallon.
1 gallon	= 4541 „				

The **mass** of a body is the quantity of matter it contains.

The **British Unit of Mass** is the **Pound Avoirdupois.** The mass of a body is ascertained by comparing it with the Standard mass.

The British Pound is defined as the quantity of matter in a platinum cylinder deposited in the offices of the Board of Trade.

Accurate copies of the Standard, as well as multiples and sub-multiples of it, are to be found in various parts of the country. The sub-multiples of the unit are obtained by dividing the unit into sixteen equal parts, each called an **ounce.** A smaller measure of mass is obtained by dividing the pound avoir-dupois into 7000 equal parts, each of which is called a **grain.** Thus, one-sixteenth part of the unit is an ounce, and one seven-thousandth part a grain.

By the operation of weighing very accurate copies of the standard can be made. The choice of platinum as a suit-able material for the standard is made on account of its being a substance not liable to be affected by atmospheric influences.

The Metric Unit of Mass is the Kilogram.—The metric standard of mass is conveniently obtained from the correspond-ing unit of volume. The **kilogram,** for such the standard is called, was originally defined to be the quantity of matter in a cubic decimetre, or litre, of pure water, at its temperature of maximum density 4° C. It is now defined to be the mass of a platinum cylinder deposited in the French Archives. For all practical purposes a litre of pure water at 4° C. weighs 1 kilo-gram or 1000 grams. Hence, since, as has been seen, the litre contains 1000 cubic centimetres (c.c.) a *gram is the mass of a cubic centimetre of water at a temperature of* 4° C. The gram is the usual unit used, and hence when we know the volume in cubic centimetres of any quantity of water at 4° C., we know also its mass in grams.

It is advisable to remember that there are 453·593 grams in a pound ; that 1 gram = 15·432 grains ; and a kilogram = 2⅕ lbs.

British and Metric Measures of Mass.

1 grain = ·0648 gm.	1 gram = 15·432 grains.
1 ounce avoirdupois = 28·35 gm.	1 kilo. = 2·2 lbs.
7000 grains ⎫ = 453·593 gm 1 pound (lb.) ⎭	
1 ton = 1·01605 × 10⁶ gm.	

$$10 \text{ milligrams} = 1 \text{ centigram.}$$
$$10 \text{ centigrams} = 1 \text{ decigram.}$$
$$1000 \text{ grams} = 1 \text{ kilogram.}$$

Weight.—The *weight of a body* is the *attractive* force which the earth exerts on the body at or near its surface. It varies with the position of the body on the earth's surface, being greatest at the poles and least at the equator.

Hence the *weight of a pound* is a quantity of force, viz., the force equal to the tension of a string supporting a mass of 1 lb., or, as it is commonly called, a pound weight. The force of gravity varies with the distance from the earth's centre; thus, at a place where gravity is nil, such as at the centre of the earth, the weight would also be nil.

The weight of the body, equal to the tension of the string supporting it, could be ascertained by attaching the string to a spring balance. If the mass attached to the balance could be carried from the pole to the equator, although the mass remains constant, its weight, as indicated by the balance, would vary continuously.

By means of an ordinary balance or pair of scales the mass of a body in terms of the unit mass, or the weight of a body in terms of the weight of the unit mass, can be obtained at the particular place where the estimation is made.

The operation of finding the weight of a body is called *weighing*. The body whose weight is to be found is placed in one pan of a balance, and known weights are placed in the other pan until the two are balanced; the sum of the weights used is the *weight* of the body.

Density.—*The density of a substance is the mass of the unit volume of it.* Assuming the density to be uniform, the density of a substance (when the unit of mass is one pound and the unit of volume one cubic foot), is the number of pounds in a cubic foot of the substance.

When metric units are adopted, the density is the number of grams in a cubic centimetre of the substance.

Relative Density.—*The relative density of a substance is the ratio of its weight to the weight of an equal volume of a standard substance.* It is obvious that the standard substance should be at any place easily obtainable in a pure state ; pure distilled water fulfils these conditions. The only precaution necessary is with regard to temperature.

The *relative density* is usually called the **specific gravity** ; the specific gravities of various substances are tabulated in Table II. Thus, if the specific gravity of cast iron is 7·22, then the weight of a cubic foot is 7·22 times the weight of a cubic foot of water $= 7·22 \times 62·3 = 450$ lbs.

The specific gravity of mercury being 13·596, the weight of a cubic foot is $13·596 \times 62·3$ lbs.

The weight of a cubic centimetre of cast iron will evidently be 7·22 grams.

The weight of V cubic feet of water $= Vw$, where w is the weight of unit volume.

Hence, if V denote the volume of a body in cubic feet, and S its specific gravity, the weight of the body is

$$VS \times w \, (1).$$

If w be the weight of unit volume, then the weight of the body is $\qquad VSw = VS \times 62·3$ lbs. [Eq. (1)].

In this manner it is customary to define *specific gravity as the ratio of the weight of a given volume of a substance to the weight of the same volume of water.*[*]

If the volume of the body is obtained in cubic inches, then in Eq. (1) w will denote the weight of one cubic inch (the weight of one cubic inch of water $= 62·3 \div 1728 = ·036$ lb.).

EXERCISES. XI.

1. Find the number of litres in one cubic foot of water.

2. If a cup contains ·7735 litre, how often must it be filled to obtain 1575 pints ?

---

[*] The term specific gravity is usually shortened to sp. gr.

3. Five kilograms of gold are divided among 110 persons. Show that each person receives nearly 45 grams 4 decigrams 5 centigrams 5 milligrams.

4. Find the number of square metres in $7\frac{1}{2}$ acres.

$$[1 \text{ sq. yd.} = 8361 \text{ sq. cm.}]$$

5. Find the difference in cubic inches between the volume of a cubic yard and $\frac{4}{5}$ that of a cubic metre.

6. Find the number of kilograms in a ton, also the number of grains in a gram.

7. If the weight of a cubic foot of water be 62·3 lbs., find the error in calculating the weight of 1000 cub. ft., on the assumption that a cubic foot weighs 1000 oz.

8. Find the weight of a cubic metre of air if 100 cubic inches weigh 31 grains.

9. Find the number of gallons in 50 litres of water, also in a kilolitre.

10. What is the number of litres in 100 pints?

11. Find the number of litres in 10 gallons, 3 quarts, 2 pints.

12. In 120 lbs. how many grams?

13. Find the number of grains in 100 grams, and the number of pounds in 100 kilograms.

14. The specific gravity of mercury being 13·6, find the weight of 12 litres of mercury in kilograms.

15. The internal dimensions of a tank are: length 10·5 m., width 2·25 m., depth 2·75 m. Find the number of litres of water in it when the tank is full.

16. The diameter of a lead pencil of circular cross-section is 8 mm., and the length of one side of square graphite enclosed is 2 mm. If the specific gravity of the whole pencil is 0·63, and of graphite 2·25, what is the specific gravity of the wood? [N.U.T.]

17. The weights of equal volumes of two substances A and B are in the ratio 3·5. The weights of equal volumes of B and C are in the ratio 6:7. If 100 c.c. of C weigh 90 grams, what is the volume of 25 grams of A?

[N.U.T.]

18. Convert a pressure of 500 lbs. per sq. in. into kg. per sq. cm. 1 kg. = 2·2 lb., 1 m. = 39·37 in.

[N.U.T.]

19. Find the sp. gr. of an iron casting weighing 10 lb., and when immersed in water 8 lb. 10 oz.

20. The sp. gr. of cast iron is 7·2. If the volume of a cast-iron bracket is 100 cub. in. and sp. gr. 6·2, what volume is not occupied by metal?

21. If the sp. gr. of glycerine is 1·26, how much water has been added to 10 pints of glycerine of sp. gr. 1·2?

22. Find the amount of gold and silver in an alloy of sp. gr. 16, weighing 600 grams; sp. gr. of gold 19·3, of silver 10·5.

23. A gold ornament weighing 77·2 grams, sp. gr. 19·3, when immersed, displaces 5 grams of water. Is the gold hollow, and if so, what is the size of the cavity?

24. An iron shell, volume 18 cub. in., sp. gr. 7·2, loses half its weight when immersed in water. What part of its volume is hollow?

Summary.

Unit of volume in the British system is the **gallon**, defined as the volume occupied by 10 lbs. of pure water at a temperature 62° F. A larger unit is the **cubic foot**. A cubic foot of water is taken to weigh 62·3 lbs., or approximately 6¼ gallons, equal to 62½ lbs., or 1000 ounces.

A Pint of pure water weighs about 1¼ lbs. The sub-multiple (the cubic inch) is often used; a cubic inch of water weighs

$$\frac{62\cdot3 \times 7000}{1728} = 252\tfrac{1}{2} \text{ grains} = ·036 \text{ lbs. nearly.}$$

A cubic yard contains 27 cubic feet.

The metric unit of volume is the **litre**, or the space occupied by a kilogram of water at 4° C.; a more convenient unit for many purposes is the **cubic centimetre** (c.c.). The mass of a c.c. of pure water at 4° C. is **one gram.**

The **mass of a body** denotes the quantity of matter it contains.

Unit of mass is **one pound** (1 lb.) defined as the quantity of matter in a platinum cylinder deposited in the Standards Office.

Multiples of the unit are 1 cwt. = 112 lbs., and 1 ton = 20 cwts., or 2240 lbs.

Sub-multiples are obtained by dividing one pound into 16 equal parts, each an *ounce*, or into 7000 parts called *grains.*

The metric unit of mass is the **Kilogram**, which is defined as the mass of a certain platinum cylinder deposited in the French Archives.

The kilogram of water at ordinary temperatures has a volume of very nearly 1 litre, or 1000 c.c. A more convenient unit of mass is that of 1 c.c. of water, or 1 gram.

Weight.—The weight of a body is the attractive force which the earth exerts on it at or near its sea-level. The *weight* of a body denotes a *quantity of force.* The *mass* of a body denotes a *quantity of matter.*

The **density** of a body is the mass of unit volume. **Relative density** of a body is the ratio of its weight to that of an equal volume of a standard substance. The standard substance is pure water, and relative density is usually known as **specific gravity.**

Sp. gr. $= \dfrac{W}{W-w}$, where W = weight of body, w = apparent weight of body in water.

CHAPTER IX.

MENSURATION OF SOLIDS. VOLUME AND SURFACE
OF A RIGHT PRISM. VOLUME AND SURFACE OF A
CUBIC PRISM. VOLUME AND SURFACE OF AN
OBLIQUE PRISM. APPROXIMATIONS. ESTIMATING.
SIMILAR FIGURES.

A solid figure or **solid** is a figure having the three dimensions of length, breadth, and thickness. When the surfaces
bounding a solid are plane, they are called faces, and the edges
of the solid are the lines of intersection of the planes forming
its faces.

What are called the regular solids are five in number, viz.,
the *cube, tetrahedron, octahedron, dodecahedron,* and *icosahedron.*

The *cube* is a solid having six equal
square faces.

The *tetrahedron* has four equal faces,
all equilateral triangles.

The *octahedron* has eight faces, all equilateral triangles.

The *dodecahedron* has twelve faces, all
pentagons.

The *icosahedron* has twenty faces, all
equilateral triangles.

Cylinder.—If a rectangle *ABCD* (Fig.
35) be made to revolve about one side
AB, as an axis, it will trace out a
cylinder. Or, a cylinder is traced by a
straight line always moving parallel to itself round the boundary
of a curve, called the *guiding curve*.

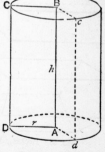

FIG. 35.—Cylinder.

Pyramid.—If one end of the line *AB* always passes through a fixed point, and the other end be made to move round the boundary of a curve, a *pyramid* is traced out.

Cone.—If the curve be a circle and the fixed point is in the line passing through the centre of the circle, and at right angles to its plane, a *right cone* is obtained; an *oblique cone* results when the fixed point is not in a line at right angles to the plane of the base.

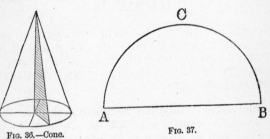

FIG. 36.—Cone.   FIG. 37.

Sphere.—If a semicircle *ACB* (Fig. 37) revolve about a diameter *AB*, the surface generated is a *sphere*.

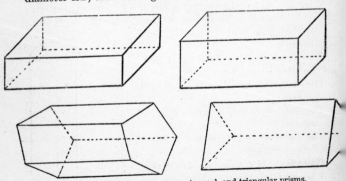

FIG. 38.—Rectangular, square, pentagonal, and triangular prisms.

Prism.—When the line remains parallel to itself and is made to pass round the boundary of any rectilinear polygon, the solid formed is called a *prism*.

The ends of a prism and the base of a pyramid may be polygons of any number of sides, *i.e.*, triangular, rectangular, pentagonal, etc.

A prism is called *rectangular, square, pentagonal, triangular, hexagonal*, etc. (Fig. 38), according as the end or base is one or other of these polygons.

A prism which has six faces all parallelograms is also called a *parallelopiped.*

A right or **rectangular prism** has its side faces perpendicular to its ends. Other prisms are called **oblique.**

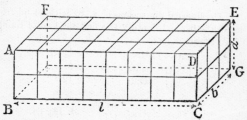

Fig. 39.—Volume of a right prism or parallelopiped.

In (Fig. 39) a right prism, the ends of which are rectangles, is shown ; to find its volume, sometimes called the *content*, or *solidity*, it is necessary to find the area of one end *DCGE*, and multiply by the length *BC*. Let *l*, *b*, and *d* denote the length, breadth, and depth or altitude of the right prism respectively.

Then area of one end $= b \times d$.

And *volume of prism* $= b \times d \times l$.

As $b \times l =$ area of base ; volume $=$ *area of base × altitude.*

When the volume of any solid is obtained, the weight can be determined by multiplying the volume by the weight of unit volume. The weight of unit volume of various materials in common use may be obtained from Table II., p. 163.

Ex. 1. If the length of a wrought iron slab be 8 ft., the depth 2 ft., and breadth 3 ft.,

Area of one end $= 3 \times 2 = 6$ sq. ft.

$\therefore$ volume $= 6 \times 8 = 48$ cub. ft.

Weight $= 48 \times 480 = 23040$ lbs.

A similar case is illustrated in Fig. 39, in which the length BC is divided into 8 equal parts, the breadth into 3, and the depth into 2. Then it is seen that there are 6 square units in the end $DCGE$ of the slab, and these are faces of a row of six unit cubes. There are 8 such rows; hence the volume is $8 \times 6 = 48$ cub. ft.

Total Surface of a Right Prism.—The total surface is, from Fig. 39, seen to be twice the area of the face $ABCD$, and twice the area of $ADEF$, together with the area of the two ends;

$$\therefore \text{ surface} = 2(ld + bl + bd);$$

or, *perimeter of base multiplied by altitude together with areas of the two ends.*

Ex. 2. The internal dimensions of a box without lid are: length 8 ft., breadth 3 ft., and depth 2 ft.; find the cost of lining it with zinc at 7d. per square foot.

$$\text{Area of base} = 8 \times 3 \quad = 24 \text{ sq. ft.}$$
$$\text{,,} \quad \text{sides} = 2\,(8 \times 2) = 32 \quad \text{,,}$$
$$\text{,,} \quad \text{ends} = 2\,(3 \times 2) = 12 \quad \text{,,}$$
$$\therefore \qquad \text{Total area} = 68 \text{ sq. ft.}$$
$$\therefore \text{ Cost} = \frac{68 \times 7}{12} = \pounds 1. \text{ 19s. 8d.}$$

Volume of a Cube.—When the length, breadth, and depth are equal, the solid is called a *cube*; if a denote the length of an edge of the solid, the area of the base is a^2 and the volume is $\mathbf{a}^3$.

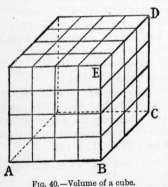

FIG. 40.—Volume of a cube.

Ex. 3. Let the length of the edge of the cube be 4 inches (Fig. 40). It is seen by dividing two adjacent sides (or edges), as EB and BC, each into 4 equal parts, and drawing through the points of division lines parallel to EB and BC, that one end $EBCD$ contains 16 squares, each of which is a face of a unit cube; and as there are four slabs of 16 cubes each, the volume is $4 \times 16 = 64$ cubic inches.

Thus, when the number denoting the length of the edge of a cube is known, the volume is obtained by cubing the given number. The converse operation, *i.e.*, given the volume to find the length of an edge, requires the extraction of the cube root, but this and the operations of division and multiplication can be readily effected by using logarithms.

Ex. 4. Find the edge of a cubical block of cast-iron, whose weight is equal to that of a rectangular bar of steel measuring 10 ft. 6 in. long, 4 in. wide, and 2 in. thick.

If a denote the length of the edge of the cube, its volume will be a^3. The volume of the steel bar is $126 \times 4 \times 2 = 1008$ cub. in. From Table II. the weights of a cubic inch of cast-iron and steel are ·26 and ·29 lb. respectively.

Hence
$$a^3 \times \cdot 26 = 1008 \times \cdot 29$$
$$\therefore a^3 = \frac{1008 \times \cdot 29}{\cdot 26}.$$
$$\log 1008 = 3 \cdot 0033$$
$$\log \cdot 29 = \overline{1} \cdot 4624$$
$$\overline{2 \cdot 4657}$$
$$\log \cdot 26 = \overline{1} \cdot 4150$$
$$3\,)\,3 \cdot 0507$$
$$1 \cdot 0169.$$

antilog ·0169 = 1040.

$\therefore$ length of edge = 10·4 in.

Volume of an Oblique Prism.—The volumes of all parallelopipeds, having the same or equal bases and the same or equal altitudes, are equal.

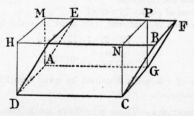

FIG. 41.—Volume of an oblique prism.

In Fig. 41 an oblique prism $ADCGFBAE$ is shown. By drawing CN and DH perpendicular to DC and NP parallel to BF, wedge-shaped pieces are obtained. Assuming the wedge-shaped piece *CNPFB* transferred to the left, as indicated, the oblique prism becomes a right prism on a rectangular base.

Thus *the volume of an oblique prism or parallelopiped is equal to the area of the base multiplied by its altitude.*

Perhaps the best and the easiest method is to build up a rectangular prism from a number of thin rectangles (of millboard, cardboard, or thin wood). By shearing the solid so constructed, as in Fig. 42, any degree of obliquity can be obtained, and the height, which is obviously the sum of the thicknesses of the rectangles, remains the same. Hence the volume of the solid is unaltered.

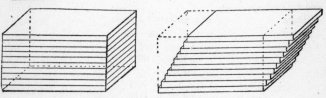

FIG. 42.—Model to illustrate a right and an oblique prism.

Assuming the volume of a solid to be unaltered when its shape is altered, then, given two of the new dimensions, the remaining one can be found.

Ex. 5. A bar of copper 1 ft. long, 9 in. wide, and $\frac{5}{8}$-in. thick is rolled into a plate 6 ft. long and 4 ft. wide. What will be the thickness of the plate?

Let t denote the thickness.

Then volume of plate $= 72 \times 48 \times t$.

As the volume is unaltered, this must be equal to the original volume. $\qquad \therefore\ 72 \times 48 \times t = 12 \times 9 \times \frac{5}{8}$

$$t = \frac{12 \times 9 \times 5}{72 \times 48 \times 8} = \cdot 01953 \text{ in.}$$

The value of t is easily obtained by using logarithms as in the preceding example.

Approximations.—Those who have made measurements of the internal dimensions of any forms of hollow vessels, such as tanks, cylinders, etc., used for commercial purposes, and from such observations calculated the volume and weight of water filling the vessel to any measured height, are quite aware that the results obtained are at best only a good approximation. This is shown at once when the calculation can be checked by actually weighing the enclosed volume of water. When this is done, it is at once seen that to express an answer to a practical question concerning the weight of water in such a vessel in tons, pounds, ounces and decimals of an ounce is to give an appearance of accuracy impossible actually to attain.

Another case of close approximation may be shown by weighing a block of any ordinary material, and then comparing the result with the product of the calculated volume and the weight of unit volume which only gives the weight of the block approximately.

These inaccurate results may be due to many causes, such as, the difficulty of obtaining sufficiently accurate measurements ; the edges or lines which are measured and are assumed to be mutually perpendicular may not be strictly so ; the material may vary in density, or the tabulated value of unit volume may only roughly represent the weight of unit volume of the given material.

In multiplying simple numbers together the result may as an exercise in arithmetical methods be obtained to any degree of accuracy, but when applied to practical questions it is not advisable to give results which imply a degree of accuracy not obtainable from the observed data.

Estimating.—In previous pages reference has already been made to some methods in use by practical men for estimating in any given case the amount of material required, the cost of labour, etc. Methods in use where volume is concerned are very numerous, and it is only possible to refer here to a few of the more important.

Unit of Cost.—In the case of buildings an approximate computation of the expense necessary to carry out a given design is effected by calculating the cubic content as though the building were a solid instead of a hollow structure. *The volume* so obtained *multiplied by the unit of cost* gives the total cost. In such a computation the dimensions, length and width, are the outside dimensions of the walls ; the third dimension is the distance from the top of the concrete, or from the upper side of the top course of the footings, to half the height of the roof.

The *unit of cost*, also called the *cost per foot cube*, may vary from 4d. to 6d. for cottage property, to 1s. or 1s. 6d. for more important structures.

Brickwork.—In large engineering works brickwork is usually measured by the cubic yard, and in a few cases by the **rod** or square perch, *at a standard thickness of* $1\frac{1}{2}$ *bricks*. As a rod is $5\frac{1}{2}$ yds. or $16\frac{1}{2}$ ft., a square rod (abbreviated into rod) contains $16\frac{1}{2} \times 16\frac{1}{2} = 272\frac{1}{4}$ sq. ft. It is usual to use 272 instead of the more accurate number $272\frac{1}{4}$. Hence, as the thickness is $1\frac{1}{2}$ bricks or $13\frac{1}{2}$ inches it follows that a rod of brickwork contains

$$272 \times \frac{13\frac{1}{2}}{12} \text{ cub. ft.} = 306 \text{ cub. ft.} = 11\frac{1}{3} \text{ cub. yds.}$$

To estimate the number of standard rods of brickwork in a wall we may use the rule :

Multiply the area of the wall in square feet by the number of half bricks in the thickness, and divide by 272×3.

Ex. 1. Find the number of standard rods of brickwork in a wall $52\frac{1}{2}$ feet long, 8 feet high, and $2\frac{1}{2}$ bricks thick.

The area is $52\frac{1}{2} \times 8$ square feet.

The number of half bricks in the thickness is 5.

$$\therefore \text{ number of rods} = \frac{52 \cdot 5 \times 8 \times 5}{272 \times 3} = 2 \cdot 574 = 2 \cdot 6 \text{ approx.}$$

Similar Solids.—Solids which have the same shape, but the dimensions not necessarily the same, are called *similar solids*.

Right prisms. Two right prisms, the bases of which are similar, and their heights proportional to corresponding edges of the bases, are similar solids. The same test also applying to right pyramids, right cylinders, and right cones.

All *spheres* and all *cubes*, are similar solids.

Ex. 1. The lengths of the edges of two cubes are 2 in. and 4 in. respectively. Compare the surfaces and volumes of the two solids. If the first cube weighs 2 lbs. what is the weight of the second?

The area of each face of a cube of 2 in. edge is 2^2. As there are 6 similar faces the surface is $6 \times 2^2 = 24$ square inches.

In a similar manner the surface of the second cube is $6 \times 4^2 = 96$ sq. in.

Thus the surface of the second is 4 times that of the first.

The volume of the first cube is $2^3=8$.

The volume of the second cube is $4^3=64$.

Hence the volume of the second is 8 times that of the first.

As the weight of the first is 2 lbs., the weight of the second is $8 \times 2 = 16$ lbs.

EXERCISES. XII.

1. Find the volume of a piece of timber 10 ft. 6 in. long, 4 in. wide, and 2 in. thick.

2. If the inside edge of a cubical tank is 4 ft., find its volume; also find the number of gallons it will hold when full.

3. The internal dimensions of a rectangular tank are 4 ft. 4 in., 2 ft. 8 in., and 1 ft. $1\frac{1}{2}$ in. Find its volume in cubic feet, the number of gallons in, and the weight of the water it will hold when full.

4. A cistern measures 7 ft. in length, 3 ft. 4 in. in width. What is the depth of the water when the tank contains 900 gallons?

5. A tank is 4 metres long, ·75 metres wide, and 1 metre deep; find the weight of water it will hold.

6. A metal cistern is 12 ft. long, 8 ft. wide, and 4 ft. deep, external measurements. If the average thickness of the metal is $\frac{1}{4}$ in., find the number of gallons of water it will hold when full.

7. Three edges of a rectangular prism are 3, 2·52, and 1·523 ft. respectively. Find the volume in cubic feet. Find also the cubic space inside a box of the same external dimensions made of wood one-tenth of a foot in thickness.

8. The content of a solid block of stone, 12 ft. 6 in. broad, and 3 ft. 9 in. thick, is 27 cub. yds. 1 cub. ft. 810 cub. in. What is its length, and its price at 6d. per cubic foot?

9. How much would it cost to have a cellar dug 18 ft. 4 in. long, 12 ft. broad, and 13 ft. 6 in. deep, at 6d. per cubic yard?

10. It is required to cut a piece equal to 1 cubic foot from a plank $2\frac{1}{2}$ in. thick and 8 in. wide; find the length of the piece to be cut off.

11. A rectangular tank is 13 ft. 6 in. long by 9 ft. 9 in. wide; how many cubic yards of water must be drawn off to make the surface of the water sink a foot?

12. A cubical cistern, open at the top, costs £16. 6s. 8d. to line with lead at 1s. 4d. per square foot. How many cubic feet does it contain?

13. A cistern is 5 ft. long, 2 ft. wide, and 8 feet deep; find the weight of water it will contain when full.

14. If the length of the edge of a cubical box be 2 ft., find the cost of painting the outside at 6d. per square yard.

15. The length of the edge of a cube is 7·5 ft. ; find its volume.

16. How many square feet of metal are there in a rectangular tank (open at the top), 12 ft. long, 10 ft. broad, and 8 ft. deep ?

17. An open square box, 9 in. side and $1\frac{1}{2}$ in. deep, is made out of a square piece of cardboard 1 ft. side ; how much of the cardboard will be wasted ?

18. A bar of metal, 9 in. wide, 2 in. thick, and 8 ft. long, weighs 1 lb. to the cubic inch. Find the length and thickness of another bar of the same metal, width, and solid content, if 2 in. cut off from its end weigh 27 lbs.

19. A box without a lid, made of wood an inch thick, measures on the outside 30 in. long, 21 in. wide, and 16 in. deep ; find the cubic contents of the interior, and the cost of painting the outside at 7d. per square foot.

20. How many cubic feet of lead, $\frac{1}{16}$ inch thick, will be required to cover the sides and bottom of a cistern 10 ft. long, 6 ft. 6 in. wide, and 7 ft. deep ? What weight of water will the cistern hold when full ?

21. A reservoir is 24 ft. 8 in. long, 12 ft. 9 in. wide, and 9 ft. deep ; how far will the surface rise when a cube of stone, edge 7 ft., is placed in the reservoir ?

22. Find the expense of lining with tin the whole of the interior of a cubical box, one end of which is 4 ft. 6 in., at 1s. 8d. a square yard.

23. A cubical cistern, open at the top, costs 15 guineas to line with lead at 1s. 9d. per square foot ; find its volume.

24. The external dimensions of a deal box are $4\frac{1}{2}$ ft., 3 ft., and 2 ft. If the thickness is 2 in. find the weight of the box, specific gravity of deal being ·53.

25. Find the weight of a box, with a lid, made of wood $\frac{3}{4}$ of an inch thick, and measuring externally 4 ft. by 3 ft. by 3 ft., the weight of a cubic foot being 38·4 lbs.

26. Find the cost of making a road 200 yds. long and 24 ft. wide. The soil to be excavated to a depth of 1 ft. at a cost of 1s. per cubic yard ; rubble laid in 9 in. deep at 1s. 4d. per cubic yard ; and gravel 3 in. deep at 3s. 6d. per cubic yard laid on top. Afterwards a steam-roller is used at a cost of 2d. per square yard.

27. Outside a lawn, 100 yds long and 96 yds. wide, a ditch is dug. If the width of the ditch is 6 ft. find its depth, when the earth obtained from it is sufficient to raise the surface of the lawn a distance of 4 inches.

28. A Dantzic oak plank is 24 ft. long and $3\frac{3}{4}$ in. thick. It is 7 in. wide at one end and tapers gradually to $5\frac{3}{4}$ in. at the other. Find its volume and weight, the specific gravity being ·93.

29. A Riga fir deck plank is 22 ft. long and 4 in. thick, and tapers in width from 9 in. at one end to 6 in. at the other. If the specific gravity of the timber be ·53, find the volume and weight of the plank.

30. Find what weight of lead will be required to cover a roof 48 ft. long, 32 ft. wide, with lead $\frac{1}{12}$ in. thick, allowing 5 per cent. of weight for roll joints, etc.

31. A reservoir is 25 ft. 4 in. long, 6 ft. 4 in. wide; how many tons of water must be drawn off for the surface of the liquid to fall 7 ft. 6 in.?

32. If the weight of a cube of 2 in. edge is 2·08 lbs., what will be the weight of a cube of the same material 5 in. edge?

33. The length of a wall is 57 ft. 3 in., height 24 ft. 6 in., the thickness $2\frac{1}{2}$ bricks. Find the number of standard rods of brickwork in the wall.

34. The base of a right prism is a square of 2 ft. side, the height of the solid is 4 ft. The base of another prism is a square of 4 ft. side, and its height is 8 ft. Compare the surfaces and the volumes of the two prisms.

If the weight of the first is 4·25 lbs., what is the weight of the second if it is of the same material?

35. The dimensions of a rolled iron girder are length 15 ft., flanges 8 in. by $1\frac{1}{2}$ in., depth 24 in. (Fig. 43); find its weight.

36. In Fig. 44 the cross-section of a wrought-iron joist is given, flanges 6 in. by 1 in., depth 12 in., length 18 ft.; find its weight.

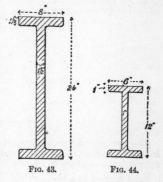

FIG. 43.   FIG. 44.

37. A cast-iron plate, $1\frac{1}{4}$ in. thick, is of the form and dimensions shown in Fig. 45, its height at the centre being 3 ft.; find its volume and weight.

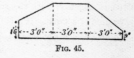

FIG. 45.

38. A cast-iron plate, mean thickness $1\frac{7}{8}$ in., is of the form and dimensions shown in Fig. 46; find its volume and weight.

FIG. 46.

39. A rectangular cast-iron trough one inch thick ; internal dimensions, length 30 in., breadth 16 in., depth 11 in. Find (*a*) volume and weight of water it will hold, (*b*) volume and weight of iron.

[U.E.I.]

40. The depth of water in a rectangular swimming bath is 2·5 metres at one end and 1·5 m. at the other, the bottom having a uniform slope. If the bath is 25 m. long and 10 m. wide, how many litres of water are there in it ?   [N.U.T.]

41. A rectangular plate, breadth 7 ft. 6 in., thickness ¼ in., weight 656¼ lbs., is made of brass, specific gravity 8·4. Find its length.

[L.C.U.]

42. (*a*) How many bricks, 9 in. by 4½ in. by 3 in., are needed to build a wall *x* yd. long. *y* ft. high, and *z* in. thick ?

(*b*) The length, breadth, and height of a room are *x*, *y*, and *z* ft. respectively. Find (i) the surface area of the walls, (ii) the length of the diagonal of the floor, (iii) the length of the diagonal of the room.   [N.U.T.]

43. A swimming bath is 35 yd. long and 12 yd. wide. The depth of water varies uniformly from 3 ft. at one end to 6 feet at the other. Find the number of cubic feet of water the bath contains.

[L.C.U.]

44. A metal sash weight for a window is to be 2½ in. square in section and it must weigh 30 lb. Find its length if 1 cu. in. of the metal weighs 0·48 lb.   [L.C.U.]

45. Steel bars of octagonal section have a width across the flat sides of ⅞ in. Estimate the weight of one foot-length of this material, which weighs 489·3 lb. per cub. ft.   [L.C.U.]

Summary.

The portion of space included under the three dimensions of length, breadth, and thickness is called the *cubical content*, the *volume*, or the *solidity* of a figure.

Total Surface of a Right Prism.—Perimeter of base multiplied by altitude, together with the areas of the two ends.

Volume of a Cube.—If *a* is the length of one side, the volume is a^3.

Volume of a Right Prism = *length* × *breadth* × *depth*

= *area of base* × *altitude.*

Volume of an Oblique Prism = *area of base* × *altitude.*

CHAPTER X.

VOLUME AND SURFACE OF A CYLINDER. VOLUME AND SURFACE OF A FRUSTUM OF A CYLINDER. VOLUME AND SURFACE OF A HOLLOW CYLINDER.

Cylinder.—It has been seen that the volume of a prism is equal to the area of the base multiplied by the altitude (or perpendicular height).

In the case of a cylinder the base is a circle.

If r denote the radius of the base and h the altitude or height of the cylinder (Fig. 47).

$$Area\ of\ base = \pi r^2;\quad \therefore\quad volume = \pi r^2 \times h.$$

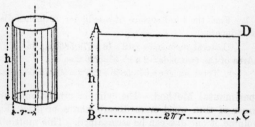

Fig. 47.—Surface of a cylinder.

Ex. 1. Find the volume and weight of a cast-iron cylinder, 18·5 inches diameter, height 20 inches.

$$Area\ of\ base = \pi \times (9\cdot25)^2 = 268\cdot8 \text{ sq. in.}$$
$$Volume = 268\cdot8 \times 20 = 5376 \text{ cub. in.}$$
$$Weight = 5376 \times \cdot26 = 1397\cdot76 \text{ lbs.}$$

Ex. 2.   A piece of round steel wire 12 inches long weighs 0·65 lbs., and its specific gravity is 7·8 ; find the area, also the diameter of the wire.

If A denote the area of a cross-section of the wire in square inches,

Volume in cubic inches $= 12 \times A$.

Also from Table II. weight of a cubic inch of water $= ·036$ lb.

Weight $= 12A \times 7·8 \times ·036$, but this is equal to ·65 lb. ;

$$\therefore \quad 12A \times 7·8 \times ·036 = ·65 ;$$

$$\therefore \quad A = \frac{·65}{12 \times 7·8 \times ·036} = ·193 \text{ sq. in.}$$

From this (p. 36) the diameter is found to be $\frac{1}{2}$ inch.

Lateral Surface.—The surface of a cylinder consists of two parts, the curved surface of the solid, called the *lateral surface*, and that of the two ends which are plane circles.

If the cylinder were covered by a piece of thin paper this when unrolled would form a rectangle of height h and base $2\pi r$. Thus, if the lateral surface of a cylinder be conceived as unrolled and laid flat, it will form a rectangle of area $2\pi r \times h$ (Fig. 47) ;

$$\therefore \quad \text{lateral surface of cylinder} = 2\pi rh.$$

To obtain the whole surface the areas of the two ends must be added to this ;

$$\therefore \quad \text{total surface of cylinder} = 2\pi rh + 2\pi r^2$$
$$= 2\pi r(h+r).$$

Ex. 1.   Find the total surface of a cylinder 12 inches diameter, height 18 inches.

Lateral surface $= \pi \times 12 \times 18 = 678·5856$ sq. in.

Area of the two ends $= 2 \times \pi \times 6^2 = 226·2$ sq. in.

$$\therefore \quad \text{Total surface} = 678·5856 + 226·2 = 904·7856 \text{ sq. in.}$$

Experimental Method.—The cylinder can be built up from a number of thin wood or cardboard plates, or discs (Fig. 48). The volume of one disc can be ascertained. This multiplied by the number of discs will give the volume of the cylinder.

Ex. 2.   If 20 discs are used, each 3 inches diameter and $\frac{1}{4}$ inch in thickness,

the area of base of one disc $= \pi \times \left(\frac{3}{2}\right)^2 = 7$ sq. in.,

and volume $= 7 \times \frac{1}{4} = \frac{7}{4}$ cub in. ;

$$\therefore \quad \text{volume of cylinder} = 20 \times \frac{7}{4} = 35 \text{ cub. in.}$$

Oblique Cylinder.—By using a simple arrangement of the kind suggested in the case of an oblique prism, then by shearing the solid (Fig. 48) any degree of obliquity can be obtained, the volume remaining unaltered.

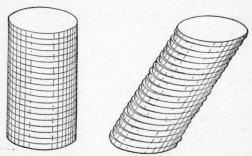

FIG. 48.—Model to illustrate a right and an oblique cylinder.

Hence

volume of oblique cylinder = area of base × altitude = $\pi r^2 \times h$.

Section of a Cylinder.—When a cylinder (Fig. 49) is cut by a plane neither perpendicular nor parallel to the axis, the section is an ellipse.

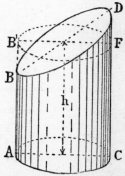

The volume of the solid is the product of the area of base and altitude.

The altitude h is the perpendicular distance from the centre of the base AC to the centre of the ellipse BD.

If points B and D are the lowest and highest points respectively; then the height h is half the sum of AB and CD.

For if we assume the cylinder to be cut by a plane parallel to the base and passing through the centre

FIG. 49.—Frustum of a cylinder

of the ellipse, a wedge-shaped portion is obtained which may be transferred as shown.

Frustum of a Cylinder.—The part of a cylinder cut off by a *plane not parallel* to the base is called the *frustum of a cylinder*.

In Fig. 49 the frustum of a cylinder is shown by the figure *BACD*.

Volume of Frustum of Cylinder.—This, as will be seen from Fig. 49, is the area of the base multiplied by the altitude h ;

$$\therefore \text{ volume} = \pi r^2 \times h = \pi r^2 \times \left(\frac{h_1 + h_2}{2} \right).$$

Where $\qquad\qquad BA = h_1,$

and $\qquad\qquad CD = h_2.$

Cross-Section.—The term cross-section should be clearly understood ; a section of a cylinder by any plane perpendicular to the axis of the cylinder is a circle ; any oblique section gives an ellipse. Hence, the term *area of cross-section* is used to indicate the area of a section (a circle) at right angles to the axis.

It is advisable, in working out any numerical example, to express as clearly as possible the given quantities in the form of an equation. When this is done much unnecessary labour may be avoided by cancelling common terms.

Ex. 1.   A piece of copper 4 inches long, 2 inches wide, and $\frac{1}{2}$ inch thick is drawn out into a wire of uniform thickness and 100 yards long ; find the diameter of the wire.

Volume of copper = $4 \times 2 \times \frac{1}{2} = 4$ cubic inches.

Length of wire $= 100 \times 3 \times 12 = 3600$ inches.

Let d denote the diameter of the wire.

Then $\qquad\qquad$ volume of wire $= \dfrac{\pi}{4} d^2 \times 3600.$

Hence $\qquad\qquad \dfrac{\pi}{4} d^2 \times 3600 = 4$;

$$\therefore \ d^2 = \frac{4 \times 4}{\pi \times 3600} = \frac{1}{225 \times \pi} \ ;$$

$$\therefore \ d = \cdot 0376 \text{ inches.}$$

Hollow Cylinder.—The volume is as before, area of base multiplied by the altitude.

If R and r denote the radii of the outer and inner circles respectively, D and d the corresponding diameters (Fig. 50),

area of base $= \pi R^2 - \pi r^2 = \pi (R^2 - r^2)$,

and volume $= \pi (R^2 - r^2)h$

$= \cdot 7854 (D^2 - d^2)h$.

To use logarithms, it is better to write this as

$\cdot 7854 (D - d)(D + d)h$.

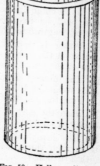

FIG. 50.—Hollow cylinder.

Ex. 1. The external diameter of a hollow steel shaft is 18 inches, its internal diameter 10 inches. Calculate the weight of the shaft if the length is 30 feet.

Area of cross section $= \cdot 7854 (18^2 - 10^2)$

$= \cdot 7854 (18 + 10)(18 - 10)$

$= \cdot 7854 \times 28 \times 8$,

volume $= \cdot 7854 \times 28 \times 8 \times 30 \times 12$ cubic inches,

weight $= \dfrac{\cdot 7854 \times 28 \times 8 \times 360 \times \cdot 29}{2240}$ tons

$= 8 \cdot 2$ tons.

EXERCISES. XIII.

1. Find the curved surface and solid content of a cylinder 8 feet long, the radius of the base being 8 feet.

2. A cylindrical column is 5 feet high, and the diameter of its base is 4·25 feet. Find the total surface and the volume of the column.

3. Find the radius of a cylinder whose volume is 10,000 cubic inches and height 50 inches.

4. Find the external surface, including that of the two ends of a cylinder, whose diameter is 40 inches and height 14 inches.

5. Find the number of square feet of felt required to cover the external surface of a cylinder, diameter 33 inches, height 2 ft. 7½ in.; find also the internal or rubbing-surface, the thickness of the cylinder being ⅞ inch.

6. Find the volume and weight of a brass cylinder, diameter 12 inches, height 20 inches.

7. The diameter of a cylinder is 12 inches, length of stroke 2 feet, find the volume.

8. The height of the discharge orifice in a lifting pump is 28 feet above the level of the water in the well; if the diameter of the pump bucket is 5 inches, find the weight of water lifted per stroke.

9. Find the volume and weight of the water in a shaft 560 feet deep, mean diameter 5 feet, when the shaft is half full.

10. If 30 cubic inches of powder weigh 1 lb., what weight of powder will be required to fill a cylinder of 8 inches internal diameter, length 5 feet?

11. Water is poured into a cylindrical reservoir, 20 feet in diameter, at the rate of 400 gallons a minute; find the rate at which the water rises in the reservoir.

12. The internal diameter of a cylinder open at the top is 2 feet, and its weight is $167\frac{1}{2}$ lbs. When filled with water it weighs 2131 lbs. Find the height of the cylinder.

13. Find the cost of sinking a well 80 feet deep and 4 ft. 6 in. diameter at an average cost of 14s. per cubic yard.

14. How many cubic inches are there in a garden roller which is half an inch thick, with an internal diameter of 20 inches, and length 3 ft. 6 in.?

15. A pond of water is 25 feet diameter, what weight of water is removed when the surface of the water is lowered 12 inches?

16. A cylinder, 2 inches diameter and 8 inches in height, contains equal volumes of mercury, water, and oil. If the specific gravity of mercury be 13·59, that of oil ·915, find the total weight of mercury, water, and oil.

17. A rectangular "steel" deck plate is 14′ 3″ long, 3′ 3½″ wide, and $\frac{1}{2}''$ thick. A circular piece 13″ in diameter is cut out of the centre of the plate. What is the weight of the plate?

18. A $\frac{5}{8}$-inch steel plate (Fig. 51) is 16 feet long, 4′ 6″ wide, at one end, tapering to 3′ 6″ at the other end, and has two circular holes

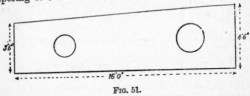

FIG. 51.

cut in it, 2 feet and 1′ 6″ in diameter respectively. What is its weight?

19. A portion of a cylindrical steel stern shaft casing is $12\frac{3}{4}$ ft. long, $1\frac{1}{4}$ in. thick, and its external diameter is 14 inches; find its weight.

20. What is the external surface and weight of a cast-iron pipe $1\frac{1}{2}$ ft. internal diameter, 48 ft. long, and $\frac{1}{2}$ in. thick?

21. The outer circumference of a cast-iron cylinder is 127·235 in., the thickness ½ in., and length 3 ft. 6 in.; show that its weight is 686 lbs., and find its internal diameter.

22. A well 5 ft. in diameter and 30 ft. deep is to have a lining of bricks (fitted close together without mortar) 9 in. thick; required approximately in tons the weight of the bricks, supposing a brick 9 × 4½ × 3 in. to weigh 7·8 lbs.

23. Find the weight of a copper tube $\frac{5}{8}$-in. outside diameter, ·05 in. thick, and 5 ft. 10 in. long.

24. What length of a gun of 6 in. bore will be filled with 20 lb. of powder, of which 30 cubic inches weigh 1 lb.?

25. Find the surface, volume, and weight of a cast-iron cylinder, radius of base 1 ft. 9 in., height 4 ft. 6 in.

26. How many cubic inches of iron are there in a cast-iron garden roller which is half an inch thick, with an outer circumference of 5½ ft. and a length of 5¼ ft.? Find its weight.

27. A cylindrical pipe 14 ft. long contains 396 cub. ft.; find its diameter and the cost of gilding its surface at 9¾d. per square foot.

28. The greater diameter of a hollow cast-iron roller is 1 ft. 9 in., the thickness of the metal 1½ in., and the length 5 ft.; find its weight, also the cost of the roller at 16s. per cwt.

29. The specific gravity of petroleum is ·87; find the weight of petroleum which can be put into a cylinder 4 ft. 6 in. diameter and 8 ft. long.

30. The piston of a steam engine is 18 inches diameter, and the effective pressure of the steam beneath it is 150 lbs. per square inch; find in tons weight the thrust of the piston rod.

31. In a rectangular plot of land, length 80 ft., width 70 ft., a round hole is dug to receive a tank, the mean dimensions being, diameter 14 ft., depth 10 ft. If the earth so taken out be spread evenly over the plot, find by how much the surface of the plot is raised.

32. If a cube of stone whose edge is 9 in. is immersed in a cylinder of 12 in. diameter half full of water, how far will it raise the surface of the water in the cylinder?

33. The pull on the wire in a testing machine is obtained by raising a cast-iron disc, 16 inches diameter, thickness 7¾ inches. Find the magnitude of the pull when it is equal to the weight of the disc.

34. Find the weight of a lead pipe 6 feet long, external and internal diameters 7 inches and 6 inches respectively, assuming that the weight of the two flanges are equivalent to one foot length of pipe.

35. A circular pond 95·9 feet diameter is surrounded by a fence 8 feet high. Find the surface of the fence and the cost of tarring it on both sides at 8d. per 10 sq. yds. of surface.

36. The length of a coil of steel wire is 9778·48 yards, and it weighs 49 lbs. Find the diameter of the cross-section.

37. A cylindrical gas holder, closed by a flat top and open at the bottom, has both its internal diameter and height equal to 233·5 feet ; find its volume. Determine its weight approximately, assuming the average weight of the iron plate to be $2\frac{1}{2}$ lbs. per sq. ft.

38. Find the weight of a cast-iron roller, internal diameter $22\frac{1}{2}$ inches, thickness of metal $\frac{3}{4}$ inch, and length 3 feet.

39. What weight of water can be held in a hose pipe 2 inches bore and 30 feet long ?

40. The dimensions of two lengths of 3 inch wrought-iron shafting connected together by a cast-iron muff coupling are given in Fig. 52,

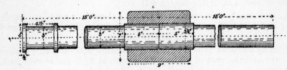

FIG. 52.—Shafts and coupling.

the length of each shaft is 15 feet ; find the weight of the coupling and the weight of the shaft.

41. The 10-lb. weights for a small testing machine require to be flat discs of cast-iron 6 inches diameter, with a rectangular slot 3 inches long and $\frac{11}{16}$ inch wide. Find the thickness of the discs.

42. How many cubic feet of water will be discharged from a pipe in 24 hours ; diameter of pipe $3\frac{3}{20}$ inches, mean velocity of water 2 feet per second ?

43. The amount of water discharged at each stroke by a pump equals the area of the plunger multiplied by the length of stroke. If the diameter of the plunger is 4·3 in., stroke 16 in., and 20 strokes are made per minute, how long will it take to empty a full cistern 6 ft. wide, 4 ft. deep, and 14 feet extreme length, the ends being semi-circular in plan ? [N.U.T.]

Summary.

Volume of a Cylinder = area of base × height = $\pi r^2 \times h$.

Lateral Surface of a Cylinder = circumference of base × height
$$= 2\pi r \times h.$$

Volume of an Oblique Cylinder = *area of base × altitude*.

Volume of a Hollow Cylinder = area of base × altitude = $\pi(R^2 - r^2)h$.

CHAPTER XI.

VOLUME AND SURFACE OF A PYRAMID. VOLUME AND SURFACE OF A FRUSTUM OF A PYRAMID. VOLUME AND SURFACE OF A CONE. VOLUME AND SURFACE OF FRUSTUM OF A CONE.

Pyramid.—Let $ABCD$ be one of the six faces of a cube. Join each of these points to the middle point or centre of the cube (Fig. 52). It is evident that a square pyramid is formed, and also that the cube consists of six such pyramids, the base of each pyramid being one of the faces of the cube. Hence the volume of the pyramid = $\frac{1}{6}$ that of the cube.

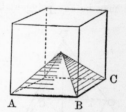

FIG. 53.—Volume of a pyramid.

If h denote the height of the pyramid, then $h = \frac{a}{2}$ where a is length of side, BC, of the cube;

$$\therefore \text{ volume of pyramid} = \frac{1}{6}a^3, \text{ or } \frac{1}{3}a^2 \times \frac{a}{2} = \frac{1}{3}a^2h.$$

Hence, *volume of pyramid* $= \frac{1}{3}(area\ of\ base \times height)$.

or, the volume of a pyramid is one-third that of a prism on the same base and the same altitude.

Experimental Verification.—A model showing how to obtain the volume of a pyramid may be made as follows :

In Fig. 54, the four corners of the base $EFGH$ are joined to A, a pyramid is formed with A as apex and base that of the cube. It will be seen that three such pyramids can be **formed**

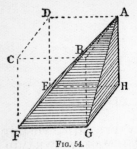

FIG. 54.

from a cube, by means of three
saw-cuts which are made to meet
in one diagonal *FA*.

In this manner the cube is
divided into three equal square
pyramids. The height of each
pyramid will be equal to the
height of the cube, and the base
of each, one of the faces of the
cube.

Hence *volume of each pyramid*
$=\frac{1}{3}$ *(area of base × height).*

Ex. 1.   Find the volume of a square pyramid, side of base 2 feet,
height 3 feet.   Area of base $= 2^2 = 4$;

∴ volume $= \frac{1}{3}(4 \times 3) = 4$ cub. ft.

The **surface area** of a pyramid is the area of the base (which
may be any polygon), together with the area of a number of

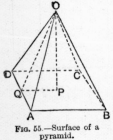

FIG. 55.—Surface of a
pyramid.

triangles which form the faces or sides
of the figure.

If the polygon forming the base be
a regular polygon, the faces *ABO*,
BCO, etc., of the solid (Fig. 55) consist
of equal isosceles triangles.

The perpendiculars let fall from the
vertex *O* to each side *AB*, *BC*, etc., will
all be equal in length ; the length may
be found either graphically or by calculation. Let the length *OQ* be denoted
by *l*, then

Area of each triangle $= \dfrac{a \times l}{2}$,

where *a* denotes the length of the equal sides *AB*, or *BC*, etc.

∴ lateral surface $= \left(\dfrac{a + a + \ldots}{2}\right) l = \dfrac{l}{2}\Sigma a.$

And, if *n* denote the number of sides in the base,

lateral surface $= \dfrac{n \times a \times l}{2}$,

or *the lateral surface equals half the perimeter of the base multiplied by the slant height ;*

∴ total area = lateral surface together with the area of the base.

To obtain the lateral surface when the height h and side of base a are given, it is necessary to find the slant height, or length of OQ.

From the right-angled triangle OPQ (Fig. 55). we have

$$OQ^2 = OP^2 + PQ^2 ;$$

but $OP = h$ and $PQ = \dfrac{a}{2}$;

$$\therefore \ OQ^2 = h^2 + \left(\dfrac{a}{2}\right)^2 ;$$

$$\therefore \ l = \sqrt{h^2 + \left(\dfrac{a}{2}\right)^2}.$$

Ex. 1.   Find the volume and total surface of a square pyramid, side of base 4 feet, height 5 feet.

$$\text{Area of base} = 4^2 = 16 \text{ sq. ft.}$$
$$\text{Volume of pyramid} = \tfrac{1}{3} \times 16 \times 5 = \tfrac{80}{3}$$
$$= 26\tfrac{2}{3} \text{ cub. ft.}$$

$$\text{The slant height} = \sqrt{5^2 + \left(\tfrac{4}{2}\right)^2} = \sqrt{25 + 4} = \sqrt{29}$$
$$= 5 \cdot 385 ;$$

The perimeter of the base is 4×4 ;

$$\therefore \ \text{lateral surface} = \dfrac{4 \times 4 \times 5 \cdot 385}{2} = 43 \cdot 08 \text{ sq. ft.}$$

$$\text{Area of base} = 16 \text{ sq. ft. ;}$$
$$\therefore \ \text{total surface} = 43 \cdot 08 + 16 = 59 \cdot 08 \text{ sq. ft.}$$

Frustum of a Pyramid.—When a pyramid is cut by a plane parallel to its base, the sloping faces are found to consist of a number of trapeziums.

As shown on p. 134, Part I., the area of a trapezium is the product of half the sum of the parallel sides and the distance between them.

Hence if in Fig. 56, l denote the sloping height of the frustum or

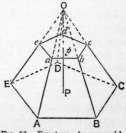

Fig. 56.—Frustum of a pyramid.

trapezium $ABab$, *i.e.* the perpendicular distance between the parallel lines ab and AB.

$$\text{Area of trapezium} = \tfrac{1}{2}(ab + AB)l.$$

If n denote the number of sides in the regular polygon forming the base,

$$\text{Lateral surface} = \frac{n}{2}(ab + AB)l.$$

∴ *Lateral surface = sum of perimeter of the end polygons multiplied by half the distance between them.*

Ex. 1. Find the lateral surface of the frustum of a square pyramid ; the side of the base 18 ft., the top surface 11 ft.; and the slant height 12 ft.

Here, perimeter of the ends $= 4(18 + 11) = 116$.

∴ Lateral surface $= 116 \times \tfrac{12}{2} = 696$ sq. ft.

Cone.—As we have already seen, when the base of a pyramid

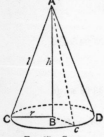

FIG. 57.—Cone.

is a circle, the solid is called a cone (Fig. 57), and is therefore a pyramid on a circular base, and as before :

Volume of pyramid
$$= \tfrac{1}{3}(\textit{area of base} \times \textit{altitude})$$
$$= \tfrac{1}{3}\pi r^2 \times h.$$

Where $r =$ radius of base,
and $h =$ altitude of cone.

Thus, the volume of a cone is one-third that of a cylinder on the same base and the same altitude.

This result may be checked in a laboratory in many different ways. Thus, if a cone of brass and a cylinder of the same material, of equal heights, and with equal bases, be weighed, the weight of the cylinder will be found to be three times that of the cone. Or, the cone and cylinder may both be immersed in a graduated glass vessel, and the height to which the water rises measured. Or, if a cylindrical vessel of the same diameter and height as the cone, is filled with water, it will be found, by inserting the cone point downwards, that one-third the water will be displaced by the cone, and will overflow.

Lateral Surface of a Cone.—If the base of the cone be divided into a number of equal parts AB, BC, etc. (Fig. 58), then by joining A, B, C, etc., to the vertex V, the lateral surface of the solid is divided into a number of triangles, VAB, VBC, etc.

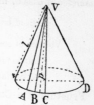

If a line be drawn perpendicular to BC, and passing through V; and its length be p,

Then,

area of triangle $VBC = \frac{1}{2}(BC \times p)$.

Fig. 58.—Lateral surface of a cone.

If n denote the number of triangles into which the base is divided, and a the length of BC,

Then,   lateral surface $= \dfrac{n}{2} \times ap$ approximately.

As the number of parts into which the base is divided is increased, the product na becomes more nearly equal to the circumference of the base ; and becomes equal to the circumference when the number of parts is indefinitely increased, also p becomes at the same time equal to l, the slant height.

$$\therefore \text{ Lateral surface} = \tfrac{1}{2} 2\pi rl = \pi rl.$$

Or, we may proceed as follows : Cut out a piece of thin paper to exactly cover the lateral surface of a cone.   When opened out it will form a sector of a circle of radius l (Fig. 59).

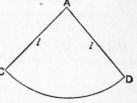

The length of arc CD
= circumference of base of cone
$= 2\pi r$.

But as we have seen on p. 39, the area of a sector is equal to half the arc multiplied by the radius,

Fig. 59.—Development of a cone.

$$\therefore \text{ Lateral surface} = \tfrac{1}{2}(CD \times l) = \tfrac{1}{2}(2\pi r \times l) = \pi rl,$$

the lateral surface of a cone equals half perimeter of base multiplied by the slant height.

If h denote the height of the cone, then

$$l = \sqrt{(h^2 + r^2)}.$$

Ex. 1.   Find the volume and lateral surface of a right cone, diameter of base 67 in., height 30 in.

$$\text{Area of base} = 67^2 \times \frac{\pi}{4} = 3525 \cdot 66 \text{ sq. in.}$$

$$\text{Volume of cone} = \tfrac{1}{3}(3525 \cdot 66 \times 30) = 35256 \cdot 6 \text{ cub. in.}$$

$$\text{Slant height} = \sqrt{33 \cdot 5^2 + 30^2} = 44 \cdot 98.$$

$$\therefore \text{ Surface} = \tfrac{1}{2}(\pi \times 67 \times 44 \cdot 98) = 4733 \cdot 85 \text{ sq. in.}$$

Frustum of a Cone.—The area of the surface of the frustum of a pyramid consists of a number of trapeziums.

Similarly the curved surface of a cone may be assumed to consist of an indefinite number of trapeziums, the parallel sides forming parts of the circular ends, and the distance between them the length of the slant side.

$$\therefore \textit{ Lateral surface} = \tfrac{1}{2}(\text{sum of circumferences of ends} \times \text{slant side})$$
$$= \tfrac{1}{2}(2\pi R + 2\pi r)l = \pi(R + r)l.$$

Where R is the radius of the base, and r the radius of the smaller end.   To obtain the total area the areas of the two ends must be added,

$$\therefore \text{ Total area} = \pi(R + r)l + \pi(R^2 + r^2).$$

Ex. 2.   Find the lateral surface and total area of the frustum of a cone ; the radii of the ends are 11 ft. and 3 ft., and the slant side 14 ft.

$$\text{Lateral surface} = \pi(11 + 3)14 = 196\pi = 615 \cdot 75 \text{ sq. in.}$$

$$\text{Area of the two ends} = \pi(11^2 + 3^2) = 408 \cdot 4.$$

$$\therefore \text{ Total area} = 615 \cdot 75 + 408 \cdot 4 = 1024 \cdot 15 \text{ sq. in.}$$

Volume.—The volume of the frustum of a pyramid, or cone, is most easily obtained by the **Prismoidal Rule,** pp. 53, 54.

EXERCISES.   XIV.

1. Find the whole surface and the content of a square pyramid ; side of base 10 feet, height 19·36 feet.

2. Find the weight of a solid right circular cone of cast-iron ; height 6 inches, diameter of base 4 inches.

3. Find the total area and volume of a square pyramid ; side of base 4 feet, height 6 feet.

4. Find the volume and lateral surface of a cone ; radius of base 3 inches, height 5 inches.

5. Find the weight of a cast-iron cone; diameter of base 7 inches, height 10 inches. What would be the weight of a lead cone of the same dimensions?

6. Find the weight of petroleum in a conical vessel; diameter of base 7 inches, height 8 inches. Specific gravity of petroleum ·87.

7. The altitude of a hexagonal pyramid is 8 feet. Each side of the base is 6 feet, find the volume.

8. A regular pyramid has a square base each side of which is 12·97 inches long. Its volume being 1322 cubic inches, find its height.

9. Find the content of a circular right cone, when the diameter of the base is 174 inches, and the length of the slope from the vertex to the base is 145 inches.

10. What length of canvas ¾ yard wide will be required to make a conical tent 10 feet high and base 12 feet diameter?

11. The base of a square pyramid covers an area of 13·4 acres, the height is 480 feet. Find the side of the square and the volume of the pyramid.

12. A right pyramid (base a square of 7 inches, side and height 8 inches) is cut into two parts by a plane parallel to the base and 6 inches from it. Find the volumes of the two parts and their total surface.

13. The great pyramid of Egypt is 481 feet in height and its base 764 feet in length. Find the volume in cubic yards.

14. What length of canvas, which is 1 yard wide, will be required to make a conical tent 8 feet in perpendicular height, with a radius of 6½ feet?

15. Find what length of canvas ⅔ yard wide is required to make a conical tent 7 yards in diameter and 12 feet high.

16. A piece of paper in the form of a circular sector, of which the radius is 7 inches and the length of the arc 11 inches, is formed into a conical cap. Find the area of the conical surface and the base of the cone.

17. Find the number of cubic feet in a hexagonal room, each side of which is 20 feet and its height 30 feet, which is finished above with a roof in the form of a hexagonal pyramid 15 feet high.

18. A pyramid has a square base, the area of which is 20·25 sq. feet; each of the edges of the pyramid passing through the vertex is 30¾ feet in length. Find the volume of the pyramid.

19. The interior of a building is in the form of a cylinder of 40 feet radius and 20 feet in height. A cone surmounts it; radius of base 40 feet and height 10 feet. How many cubic feet of air will the building contain?

20. Find the area of each of the sloping surfaces of a frustum of a pyramid, perpendicular height 6 inches, and a square base, side 6 inches, the side of the upper square being 1 inch.

21. If 30 cubic inches of powder weigh 1 lb., what is the radius of the base of a cone whose altitude is 6 feet, and which contains 350 lbs. of powder?

22. The base of a cone is an ellipse ; major axis 4 inches, minor axis 2 inches, height 6 inches. Find the volume of the cone.

23. The base of a cone is 10 in. diameter, slant height 13 in. Calculate (a) area of curved surface, (b) the volume. [U.E.I.]

24. The base of a cone is 4·8 in. diameter, height 6·2 in. Find (a) slant height, (b) volume, (c) area of curved surface. [U.E.I.]

25. A tent in the form of a cone has a base 9·6 ft. diameter, height 10 ft. Find :
(a) Volume of air the tent will hold, (b) slant height, (c) area of canvas necessary to make the tent. [U.E.I.]

26. Compare the weights of a silver cone and a cast-iron square pyramid, each of the same height, the diameter of cone equal to side of square. Specific gravity of silver is 10·5, of cast iron 8·3. [N.U.T.]

27. Find the area of leather needed to cover a cone, base 12 in. diameter, height 18 in. The leather in one piece is a sector of a circle ; find the angle between the straight lines. [N.U.T.]

28. An iron nut is in shape a regular hexagon of 2·07 cm. side, and is 1·69 cm. thick. In plan, the distance from a corner of the hexagon to the nearest point on the boundary of the hole is 1·38 cm. Neglecting the internal screw, find the weight per gross of these nuts, the specific gravity of iron being 7·62. [N.U.T.]

29. Eight tons of earth are tipped into a conical heap of base-diameter 12 ft., with sides at an angle of 35° with the horizontal. Estimate from these data the density of the earth. [N.U.T.]

Summary.

Volume of a Pyramid $=\frac{1}{3}$(area of base) × height.

Lateral Surface of a Right Pyramid = *half the perimeter of the base multiplied by the slant height.*

Frustum of a Pyramid : lateral surface $=\frac{1}{2}$(sum of perimeters of the ends multiplied by the perpendicular distance between them).

Volume of a Cone $=\frac{1}{3}$(area of base) × height $=\frac{1}{3}\pi r^2 \times h$.

Lateral Surface of a Cone $=\frac{1}{2}$ (*circumference of base × slant height*).

Lateral Surface of Frustum of a Cone $=\frac{1}{2}$(sum of circumferences of ends × slant side) $=\pi(R+r)S$.

CHAPTER XII.

VOLUME AND SURFACE OF A SOLID RING. VOLUME
AND SURFACE OF A SOLID SPHERE. VOLUME
AND SURFACE OF A HOLLOW SPHERE.

Solid Ring.—If a circle, with centre C, rotate about an axis such as AB (Fig. 60), the solid described is called a *solid circular ring*, or simply a solid ring. By bending a length of

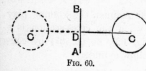

FIG. 60.

round solid indiarubber, a ring such as that shown in Fig. 61 may be obtained. The length of such a piece of rubber is the distance DC from the axis multiplied by 2π.

Examples of solid rings are found in curtain rings, in anchor rings, etc. It will be obvious that any cross-section of such a ring will be a circle, also that it may be considered as a cylinder, bent round in a circular arc until the ends meet. *The mean length of the cylinder will be equal to $2\pi CD$, or, the circumference of a circle which passes through the centres of area of all the cross-sections.*

Instead of considering the case of a cylinder bent to form a ring, we may imagine a bar having a rectangular cross-section to be bent in the same way to form a ring as in Fig. 62.

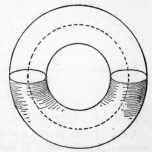

FIG. 61.—Solid ring.

Area of a Ring.—*The surface area of the ring or curved surface will be equal to the circumference or perimeter of a cross-section multiplied by the mean length of the ring.*

If r denote the radius of the cylinder from which the ring may be imagined to be formed, and R the mean radius of the ring, then

Perimeter or circumference of cross-section $= 2\pi r$.

Mean length $= 2\pi R$.

$$\therefore \text{ Area of ring} = 2\pi r \times 2\pi R \dotfill (1)$$
$$= 4\pi^2 Rr. \dotfill (2)$$

Eq. (1) will probably be easier to remember than Eq. (2).

Volume of a Ring.—*The volume of a ring is the area of a cross-section multiplied by the mean length.*

Area of cross-section $= \pi r^2$.

Mean length $= 2\pi R$.

$$\therefore \text{ Volume} = \pi r^2 \times 2\pi R$$
$$= 2\pi^2 Rr^2. \dotfill (3)$$

In a similar manner the volume may be obtained when the cross-section is a

FIG. 62.   rectangle (Fig. 62), or (p. 87) by considering the ring to form a short hollow cylinder.

Ex. 1.   The cross-section of a solid wrought-iron ring, such as an anchor ring, is a circle of 5 inches radius, the inner radius of the ring is 3 ft.; find (*a*) the area of the curved surface, (*b*) the volume of the ring, (*c*) its weight.

(*a*) Here $r = 5$; $R = 36 + 5 = 41$.
Area of curved surface $= 4\pi^2 \times 41 \times 5$ sq. in.
$$= \frac{\pi^2 \times 20 \times 41}{144} \text{ sq. ft.} = 56 \cdot 2 \text{ sq. ft.}$$

(*b*) *Volume.*—Area of cross-section $= \pi \times 5^2$.
Mean length $= 2\pi \times 41$.
$$\therefore \text{ volume} = \frac{2\pi^2 \times 5^2 \times 41}{1728} \text{ cub. ft.} = 11 \cdot 71 \text{ cub. ft.}$$

(*c*) Weight $= 11 \cdot 71 \times 480$ lbs. $= 5620 \cdot 8$ lbs.

Ex. 2.   The cross-section of the rim of a cast-iron fly-wheel is a square of 5 inches side.   If the inner diameter of the ring is 5 ft., find (*a*) the area, (*b*) the volume, (*c*) the weight of the rim.

As the inner diameter is 60 inches, the outer diameter will be 70.
$$\therefore \text{ Mean diameter} = \tfrac{1}{2}(60 + 70) = 65 \text{ inches.}$$

The rim may be considered as a square prism, side of base 5 inches, length $\pi \times 65$.

(a) Perimeter of square $= 4 \times 5 = 20$ inches.

$\therefore$ Total surface, or area $= 20 \times \pi \times 65$ sq. in.

$= 1300\pi$ sq. in.

(b) Volume $= $ (area of base) $\times$ (length) $= 5^2 \times \pi \times 65 = 1625\pi$ cub. in.

(c) Weight $= 1625\pi \times \cdot 26$ lb.

EXERCISES. XV.

1. The section of the rim of a fly-wheel is a rectangle 6 inches wide and 4 inches deep, the inner radius of the rim is 3 ft. 6 in. ; find the volume and weight of the rim, the material being cast iron.

2. In a cast-iron wheel the inner diameter of the rim is 2 feet and the cross-section of the rim is a circle of 6 inches radius, find the weight of the rim.

3. The inner diameter of a wrought-iron anchor ring is 12 inches, the cross-section is a circle 4 inches diameter ; find the surface, volume, and weight of the ring.

4. The cross-section of the rim of a cast-iron fly-wheel is a rectangle 8 inches by 10 inches. If the mean diameter is 10 feet, find the weight of the rim.

5. The volume of a solid ring is $741 \cdot 125$ cubic inches, and the inner diameter 21 inches ; find the diameter of the cross-section.

6. The outer diameter of a solid ring is $12 \cdot 6$ inches ; if the volume is $54 \cdot 2$ cubic inches, find the inner diameter of the ring.

7. Find the volume of a cylindrical ring whose thickness is 27 inches and inner diameter 96 inches.

The Sphere.—A semicircle of radius r if made to rotate about its diameter as an axis, will trace out a sphere.

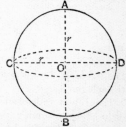

Any line such as AB or CD (Fig. 63) passing through the centre and terminated both ways by the surface, is a **diameter**, and any line such as OA or OC passing from the centre to the circumference is a **radius**.

By cutting an orange or a ball of soap it is easy to verify that *any section of a sphere by a plane is a circle*.

FIG. 63.—Sphere.

The section by any plane which passes through the centre of the sphere is called a **great circle**.

Surface and Volume of a Sphere.—The following formulae for the surface and volume of a sphere of radius r should be carefully remembered :

$$\text{Surface of a sphere} = 4\pi r^2. \quad \dots\dots\dots\dots\dots(1)$$
$$\text{Volume of a sphere} = \tfrac{4}{3}\pi r^3. \quad \dots\dots\dots\dots\dots(2)$$

The formula for the area of the curved surface may be easily remembered as follows :

The area of a great circle CD (Fig. 63) is πr^2, where r is the radius of the sphere.

The area of the curved surface DAC or hemisphere is twice that of the plane surface, and is therefore $2\pi r^2$.

Hence, the area of the surface of the sphere is $2 \times 2\pi r^2 = 4\pi r^2$.

To obtain the volume it is only necessary to multiply this by $\tfrac{1}{3}r$.

The area of the surface of a sphere is equal to that of the circumscribing cylinder.

FIG. 64.—Sphere and its circumscribing cylinder.

Thus, in Fig. 64, the circumscribing cylinder, or the cylinder which just encloses a sphere of radius r is shown. The curved surface of the cylinder will be the circumference of the base $2\pi r$ multiplied by the height $2r$;

$\therefore$ curved surface of cylinder
$$= 2\pi r \times 2r = 4\pi r^2.$$

The volume of the sphere is two-thirds that of the circumscribing cylinder.

Thus,   area of base of cylinder $= \pi r^2$,
and   height of cylinder $= 2r$;
$\therefore$ volume of cylinder $= 2\pi r^3$;

two-thirds of $2\pi r^3$ is $\tfrac{4}{3}\pi r^3$, and this is equal to the volume of the sphere.

The rule for determining the volume of a sphere may be deduced by assuming the sphere to be divided into a large number of pyramids by means of planes passing through the centre of the sphere. The bases of the pyramids, if small enough, may be considered to be plane surfaces. The height of each pyramid is equal to the radius of the sphere. The sum of the bases of all the pyramids is equal to the area of the surface of the sphere, and the total volumes of the pyramids are equal to the volume of the sphere. But the volume of a pyramid is one-third the area of the base multiplied by the height ; therefore the volume of the sphere considered as made up of pyramids is equal to the surface of the sphere multiplied by one-third the radius. The surface of a sphere has already been shown to be four times the area of the hemispherical section, that is $4\pi r^2$. It will therefore be seen that *the volume of the sphere may be found by multiplying four times the area of a great circle of the sphere by the radius, and taking one-third the product.*

The formulae for the surface and volume of a sphere assumes a much more convenient form when expressed in terms of the diameter of the sphere.

Let d denote the diameter, then $r = \dfrac{d}{2}$.

$$Surface \ of \ a \ sphere = 4\pi \left(\frac{d}{2}\right)^2 = \pi d^2.$$

$$Volume \ of \ a \ sphere = \frac{4}{3}\pi \left(\frac{d}{2}\right)^3 = \frac{\pi}{6}d^3$$

$$= \cdot 5236 d^3. \quad \dots\dots\dots\dots\dots(3)$$

From Eq. (3) (as $\cdot 5$ is one-half), the *approximate* method of quickly obtaining the volume of a sphere is readily obtained, *i.e.* To find *the volume of a sphere take half the volume of the cube on the diameter and add 5 per cent. to it.*

Ex. 1. Find the surface, volume, and weight of a cast-iron ball ; radius 6·25 in.

$$Surface = \pi \times 12 \cdot 5^2 \text{ sq. in.}$$

$$2 \log 12 \cdot 5 = 2 \cdot 1938$$
$$\log \pi = \underline{\cdot 4972} \qquad \text{antilog } 6910 = 4909$$
$$2 \cdot 6910 \qquad \therefore \text{ Surface} = 490 \cdot 9 \text{ sq. in.}$$

$$Volume = \cdot 5236 d^3 \text{ cub. in.}$$

$$3 \log 12 \cdot 5 = 3 \cdot 2907$$
$$\log \cdot 5236 = \overline{1} \cdot 7190 \qquad \text{antilog } \cdot 0097 = 1023.$$
$$3 \cdot 0097 \qquad \therefore \text{ Volume} = 1023 \text{ cub. in.}$$

Weight of ball = (volume) × (weight of unit volume)
$$= 1023 \times \cdot 26 \text{ lbs.} = 266 \text{ lbs.}$$

Hollow Sphere.—If the external and internal diameters of a hollow sphere be denoted by r_2 and r_1 respectively, then the volume of the material forming the sphere would be

$$\tfrac{4}{3}\pi r_2{}^3 - \tfrac{4}{3}\pi r_1{}^3, \quad \text{or} \quad \tfrac{4}{3}\pi (r_1{}^3 - r_2{}^3).$$

This may be replaced by its equivalent

$$\cdot 5236 (d_1{}^3 - d_2{}^3).$$

Ex. 1. Find the weight of a cast-iron ball, external diameter 9 inches, internal diameter 4 inches.

$$\text{Volume} = \cdot 5236 (9^3 - 4^3) = \cdot 5236 (729 - 64) = \cdot 5236 \times 665.$$

Weight of ball $= \cdot 5236 \times 665 \times \cdot 26 = 90 \cdot 53$ lbs.

EXERCISES. XVI.

1. Find the surface and weight of a cast-iron ball 7 inches diameter.

2. A hemispherical basin (Fig. 65) holds 1 gallon of water ; find its internal diameter.

3. If 30 cubic inches of powder weigh 1 lb., show that it will require nearly 9 lbs. to fill a shell whose internal diameter is 8 inches. What must be the diameter to contain (i) 10 lbs., (ii) 37·699 lbs. of powder ?

FIG. 65.

4. A spherical cast-iron ball 15 inches diameter, is melted down and cast into a conical mould, the base of which is 20 inches diameter ; find the height of the cone.

5. A sphere has a radius of $25\tfrac{1}{4}$ feet ; find its surface, and determine the radius of a sphere whose surface is $\tfrac{1}{4}$ of that of the former.

6. Find the diameter of a hemispherical cup which holds half a pint.

7. How long will it take to fill a hemispherical tank of 10 feet diameter by a pipe supplying 6 gallons per minute ?

8. What is the volume of a sphere when its surface is equal to that of a circle 4 feet in diameter ?

9. Determine (i) the radius of a sphere whose volume is 1 cubic foot, (ii) of a sphere whose surface is 1 square foot.

10. A sphere, whose diameter is 1 foot, is cut out of a cubic foot of lead, and the remainder is melted down into the form of another sphere. Find the diameter of the second sphere.

11. Determine the number of yards of material, 3·239 feet wide, necessary to make a spherical balloon containing 1000 cubic feet of gas.

12. What is the weight of a hollow sphere of cast-iron, inside diameter $1\frac{1}{2}$ feet, and thickness 2 inches?

13. Find the weight of a ball composed of a cast-iron sphere 8 inches in diameter, coated with a layer of lead 7 inches thick.

14. Find the weight of a metal shell, the exterior and interior diameters being 10 inches and 8 inches respectively; specific gravity of the metal 7·21.

15. The weights of two spheres, which are solid and made of the same material, are 512 lbs. and 729 lbs., respectively. If the radius of the first sphere is 16 inches, what will it cost to gild the surface of the second sphere at $1\frac{3}{4}$d. per square inch.

16. If 30 cubic inches of powder weigh 1 lb., find the internal diameter of a spherical shell that is just filled by 37·699 lbs. of powder.

MISCELLANEOUS EXERCISES. XVII.

1. A wrought-iron hollow pontoon, thickness $\frac{1}{8}$th inch, has a cylindrical body 20 feet long and hemispherical ends. If the outside diameter is 3 ft. 4 in., find its weight.

2. The area of the sector of a circle is 2240·567 square feet and the radius 33·5 feet, find the length of the arc.

3. A wrought-iron boiler is made in the form of a cylinder 1 foot radius. The ends of the boiler are hemispherical, the length of the cylindrical part of the boiler is 4 feet; find the weight of water the boiler can hold.

4. Find the surface and volume of a regular pyramid on a square base, side of base 6 inches, altitude 8 inches.

5. An area of 200 square yards has to be covered by a conical tent having a height of $7\frac{1}{2}$ feet; find the amount of canvas required.

6. Find the radius of a cylindrical vessel 11 inches in height, which will contain as much water as two cylindrical vessels, radius of the first 6 inches, height 1 foot; radius of the second 8 inches, height $1\frac{1}{2}$ feet.

7. A cylindrical boiler with plane ends is internally 15 feet long and 4 feet diameter, and is traversed lengthwise by 50 tubes, each 3 inches external diameter; determine the volume of water the boiler will contain.

8. A leaden sphere 1 inch diameter is beaten out into a circular sheet of uniform thickness of $\frac{1}{100}$ inch. Find the radius of the sheet.

9. Find the weight of a hollow cast-iron sphere internal diameter 2 inches, thickness one-fifth of an inch.

10. Prove that the area of a triangle is half the product of the base and height, and that the volume of a right-circular cone is one-third the product of the area of the base, and the height.

11. The radius of a sphere is equal to the radius of the base of a cone; find the height of the cone when its volume is equal to that of the sphere.

12. The slant side of a cone is 25 feet, and the area of its curved surface is 550 square feet; find its volume.

13. If the surface of a cube be 491·306 square inches, what is the length of its edge?

14. A cistern is 9 ft. 4 in. long, and 7 ft. 6 in. wide, and contains 6 tons 5 cwts. of water; find the depth of the water in the cistern.

15. If a reservoir of water be 6 ft. 4 in. wide and 25 ft. 4 in long, how many tons of water must be drawn off in order that the surface may sink 7 ft. 6 in?

16. The base of a cone is an ellipse, major axis 8 inches, minor axis 6 inches, the height of the cone is 15 inches; find the volume.

17. Find the number of gallons of water which pass in ten seconds under a bridge, the stream being 10 ft. 11 in. deep, 17 ft. 8 in. wide, and its velocity 8 miles per hour.

18. A plate of metal is 106·58 inches long, 14·6 inches wide, and 2 inches thick. Supposing it to be melted and cast into an exact cube, what would be the edge of the cube?

19. What weight of lead will be required to cover a roof 48 feet long and 32 feet wide with a sheet of lead $\frac{1}{12}$ inch thick?

20. The length of a field of 50 acres is to its breadth as 4 : 3; find the length and breadth.

21. In a schoolroom 77 feet long and 32 feet wide there is a raised platform with straight sides and back and a semicircular front; the length of each straight portion of the platform is 10 feet. Find the area of the floor not occupied by the platform.

22. If a cubical cistern open at the top costs 15 guineas to line with lead at 1s. 9d. per square foot, how many cubic feet will it contain?

23. Two thin vessels, without lids, each contain a cubic foot. The one is a rectangular parallelopiped on a square base, whose height is half its length; the other a right-circular cylinder whose height is equal to the radius of its base. Compare the amounts of material which it would require to make them, the thickness being the same for each.

24. Water is flowing at the rate of 10 miles an hour, through a pipe 15 inches in diameter, into a rectangular reservoir 187 yards long and 84 yards wide; calculate the time in which the surface will be raised 1 inch.

25. A gravel walk 6 feet wide runs round a grass plot 60 feet long and 40 feet wide. If gravel is 3s. per cubic yard, find the cost of a coat of gravel on the path 3 inches deep.

26. Find the radius of a spherical balloon which contains 17974·21 cubic feet.

27. A solid metal sphere 6 inches diameter is formed into a tube 1 inch internal diameter and 4 feet long; find the thickness of the tube.

28. Find the lateral surface of the frustum of a cone, the slant height of the frustum being 25 feet and the diameters of the two ends 5 feet and 27 feet respectively.

29. Water is flowing at the rate of 10 miles an hour through a pipe 16 inches diameter into a rectangular reservoir 197 yards long and 87 yards wide; calculate the time in which the surface will be raised 3 inches.

30. A rectangular reservoir whose length and breadth are 135 feet and 67 feet respectively is supplied by a cylindrical pipe, diameter $3\frac{3}{4}$ inches, through which the water runs at the rate of 9 miles per hour; find how much the surface will be raised in 11 hours and also what number of gallons will be poured in during that time.

31. If a 14-lb. shot be of 2·34 inches radius find the weight of a square plate of the same material, each side of square being 3 ft. 5 in., and its thickness $1\frac{1}{8}$ inch.

32. Find the cost of building a wall 100 yards long, 6 feet high, and 18 inches thick, at £16 per rod. (A rod of brickwork is $16\frac{1}{2}$ feet square and 14 inches thick.)

33. Find the weight of an open slate cistern 4 feet deep, 6 ft. 4 in. long, and 2 ft. 9 in. wide, the mean thickness of the slate being 1 inch and specific gravity of slate 2·8.

Summary.

Surface of a solid ring.—The area of the curved surface of a solid ring is $4\pi^2 Rr$, where r is radius of cross-section, and R is mean radius of ring.

Volume of a solid ring.—The volume is the area of cross-section multiplied by mean length of ring $= 2\pi^2 r^2 R$.

Surface of a sphere is four times the area of a great circle $= 4\pi r^2$, where r denotes the radius of the sphere.

Volume of a sphere.—Volume of a sphere is $\frac{4}{3}\pi r^3$, where r is the radius.

Circumscribing cylinder.—The area of the surface of a sphere is equal to the area of the circumscribing cylinder; the volume of the sphere is two-thirds that of the circumscribing cylinder.

Hollow sphere.—Volume of a hollow sphere is $\frac{4}{3}\pi(r_2^3 - r_1^3)$, where r_2 and r_1 denote the external and internal radii respectively.

SECTION III.—ALGEBRA.

CHAPTER XIII.

FACTORS. INDICES.

The elements of Algebra have been already explained in Part I. of this work. In addition to what is there presented, some knowledge of factors must be obtained before the student can hope to deal successfully with algebraic expressions and their simplification.

Factors.—When an algebraic expression is the product of two or more quantities, each of these quantities is called a **factor** of it.

Thus, if $x+5$ be multiplied by $x+6$, the product is

$$x^2 + 11x + 30,$$

and the two quantities $x+5$ and $x+6$ are said to be the factors of

$$x^2 + 11x + 30.$$

The determination of the factors of a given expression, or, as it is called, the **resolution** of the expression into its factors, may be regarded as the inverse process of multiplication.

The following results, easily obtained by multiplication, occur so frequently and are of such great importance that they should be carefully remembered :

$$(a+b)(a+b) \text{ or } (a+b)^2 = a^2 + 2ab + b^2 \ldots\ldots\ldots\ldots(1)$$
$$(a-b)^2 = a^2 - 2ab + b^2 \ldots\ldots\ldots\ldots\ldots(2)$$

The results are true when any other letters are used instead of a and b. We can write with equal correctness

$$(x+y)^2 = x^2 + 2xy + y^2.$$

Or, *The square of the sum of two quantities is equal to the sum of the squares of the quantities increased by twice their product.*

Similarly, *The square of the difference of two quantities is equal to the sum of the squares of the quantities diminished by twice their product.*

By multiplying $(x+y)(x-y)$ we obtain x^2-y^2. Conversely given x^2-y^2 we can at once write down the factors as $x+y$ and $x-y$. The first of these relations may be expressed as : *The product of the sum and the difference of two numbers is equal to the difference of their squares.*

Ex. 1. $40^2 - 39^2 = (40+39)(40-39) = 79 \times 1 = 79$.

Ex. 2. $1000^2 - 998^2 = (1000+998)(1000-998) = 1998 \times 2 = 3996$.

Ex. 3. To obtain the factors of $x^4 - y^4$.

First $\qquad (x^4 - y^4) = (x^2 + y^2)(x^2 - y^2)$.

Also as $\qquad x^2 - y^2 = (x+y)(x-y)$,

we can write $\qquad x^4 - y^4 = (x^2 + y^2)(x+y)(x-y)$.

Ex. 4. Multiplying $a^2 - ab + b^2$ by $a+b$, the product is found to be
$$a^3 + b^3.$$
$$\therefore \ a^3 + b^3 = (a+b)(a^2 - ab + b^2).$$

Similarly $\qquad a^3 - b^3 = (a-b)(a^2 + ab + b^2)$.

The quantities $(a+b)(a^2 - ab + b^2)$ are the factors of $a^3 + b^3$, and $(a-b)(a^2 + ab + b^2)$ are the factors of $a^3 - b^3$.

Generally $a^n + b^n$ is divisible by $a+b$ when n is an odd number, 1, 3, 5, etc. Thus, in Ex. 4, n is 3.

Also $a^n - b^n$ is divisible by $a-b$ when n as before is an odd number. The case of $n=3$ is shown, and by actual division, assuming n to be any odd number, the rule can be further verified.

When n is an even number, 2, 4, etc., it will be found that $a^n - b^n$ is divisible by both $(a+b)$ and $(a-b)$.

Ex. 5. Let $n=6$; $\therefore \ a^n - b^n$ becomes $a^6 - b^6$.

We know that $a^6 - b^6 = (a^3 + b^3)(a^3 - b^3)$, and in Ex. 4 the factors of $(a^3 + b^3)$ and $(a^3 - b^3)$ have been obtained.

Hence the factors of $a^6 - b^6$ are
$$(a+b)(a^2 - ab + b^2)(a-b)(a^2 + ab + b^2).$$

Thus $a^6 - b^6$ is divisible by both $a+b$ and $a-b$.

When the preceding simple examples are clearly made out it is advisable to consider the more general expression $a^n \pm b^n$, and to find that :

$a^n + b^n$ is divisible by $a + b$ when n is odd.

$a^n - b^n$,,   ,, $a - b$,,   ,,

$a^n - b^n$,,   ,,   both $a + b$ and $a - b$ when n is even.

The cases where $n = 2$, 3, 4, 6 have already been taken. Other values of n should be used and more complete verifications be obtained of the rules given.

By multiplying $x + 2$ by $x + 3$ we obtain $x^2 + 5x + 6$;

$$\therefore \ (x + 2)(x + 3) = x^2 + 5x + 6.$$

Hence given the expression $x^2 + 5x + 6$ to find the quantities $x + 2$, and $x + 3$, or the factors of the given expression, we find that

The first term is the product of x and x, or x^2.

  ,, last   ,,   ,,   ,,   2 and 3, or 6.

  ,, middle ,,   ,,   ,,   the first term, and the sum of 2 and 3, or $5x$.

Proceeding in this manner the factors of a given expression are readily obtained.

Ex. 6.   Resolve into factors $x^2 + 8x + 12$.

Here the two numbers required must have a sum of 8 and a product equal to 12. Of such pairs of numbers, the sum of which is 8, are 4 and 4, 7 and 1, and 6 and 2, but only the last pair have a product 12. Hence the factors required are

$$(x + 2)(x + 6).$$

Or, we could write the given expression

$$x^2 + 8x + 12 \text{ as } x^2 + 2x + 6x + 12.$$

Taking out the quantity common to two terms we obtain

$$x(x + 2) + 6(x + 2).$$

This shows that $x + 2$ is common to both terms, hence we may write

$$x^2 + 8x + 12 = (x + 2)(x + 6).$$

Ex. 7.   In a similar manner,

$$x^2 - 9x + 20 = x^2 - 5x - 4x + 20$$
$$= x(x - 5) - 4(x - 5) = (x - 4)(x - 5).$$

Ex. 8. $x^2 + 11x + 30 = x^2 + 5x + 6x + 30 = (x + 5)(x + 6)$.

Factors obtained by Substitution.—The factors in the preceding and in other examples may also be found by substituting for x some quantity which will reduce the given expression to zero. Such a quantity is a factor. Thus in $x^2 - 9x + 20$ the last term suggests that two of the following, 4 and 5, 10 and 2, or 20 and 1, are the factors, but the middle term denoting the sum of the numbers gives -4 and -5. To ascertain if 4 and 5 are the factors, put $x = 4$;

$$\therefore \ 16 - 36 + 20 = 0.$$

Hence $x = 4$, or $x - 4 = 0$ is a factor.

Similarly putting $x = 5$ we obtain $25 - 45 + 20 = 0$;

$$\therefore \ x - 5 \text{ is a factor.}$$

Hence $\qquad x^2 - 9x + 20 = (x - 4)(x - 5).$

Ex. 9. $\quad x^2 + 6x - 55.$

Put $x = -11$; this reduces the given expression to zero;

$$\therefore \ x + 11 \text{ is a factor.}$$

Next put $x = +5$, and it is found to be a factor ;

$$\therefore \ x^2 + 6x - 55 = (x + 11)(x - 5).$$

The preceding examples involving x^2 and x are known as quadratic equations, the factors are called in each case the roots of the equation. Thus in Ex. 9 the two values, $x = -11$, $x = 5$ are the roots of the given **quadratic equation** ; in a similar manner the two roots of the quadratic

$$x^2 - 9x + 20 \text{ are } x = 4, \ x = 5.$$

EXERCISES. XVIII.

What are the factors of the following expressions :

1. $x^2 - 16x - 57.$
2. $10x^2 + 79x - 8.$
3. $x^2 - 12x - 85.$
4. $11x^2 + 75x - 14.$
5. $10x^2 + x - 2.$
6. $x^2 + 4x - 4y^2 + 4.$
7. $a^3 - 3a^2b + 3ab^2 - b^3 + c^3.$

8. Add to $a^2 - 2ab$ a quantity of one term so that it is exactly divisible by $a - b$.

Find the factors of

9. (1) $x^2 - 7x - 44$; (ii) $x^2 - 11x - 102.$
10. $14x^2 - 25xy + 6y^2.$
11. $x^2 - 5x - 14.$

Find the factors of

12. $x^2y - 15xy^2 + 36y^3$.   **13.** $(a + 3b + 2c)^2 - 9(2a + b - c)^2$.

14. (i) $6x^2 + 5xy - 6y^2$;   (ii) $x^3 - 13x^2y + 42xy^2$;

(iii) $(a + 2b + 3c)^2 - 4(a + b - c)^2$;   (iv) $81x^4 - 625y^4$.

15. $21x^2 - 13xy - 20y^2$.   **16.** $(x - 2y)^3 + y^3$.

Deduce without division the quotient of

17. $x^8 + 16x^4y^4 + 256y^8$ by $x^2 - 2xy + 4y^2$.   **18.** $11x^2 + 75x - 14$.

Indices.—The number which expresses the power of a quantity is called the **index**. Thus in a^5, a^7, a^9 the numbers 5, 7, and 9 are called the **indices** of a, and are read "a to the power five," "a to the power seven," etc.

Since $a^3 \times a^2 = (a \times a \times a)(a \times a) = a^{3+2} = a^5$, we may say that in the case of positive whole numbers, *to multiply together different powers of the same quantity, it is only necessary to add the index of one to that of the other. When one power is divided by another, the index of the divisor is subtracted from the index of the dividend.*

This may be written in a more general manner as follows :

$$a^m = (a \times a \times a \dots \text{ to } m \text{ factors}),$$

when m is a positive integer. Similarly,

$$a^n = (a \times a \times a \dots \text{ to } n \text{ factors}) ;$$

$$\therefore \ a^m \times a^n = (a \times a \times a \dots \text{ to } m \text{ factors})(a \times a \times a \dots \text{ to } n \text{ factors})$$
$$= (a \times a \times a \dots \text{ to } m + n \text{ factors})$$
$$= a^{m+n}.$$

Ex. 1. $(a^2)^3 = (a \times a)^3$
$$= (a \times a)(a \times a)(a \times a) = a^6,$$

or in words, the cube of a^2 is equal to a^6.

This most important rule has been shown to be true when $m = 3$ and $n = 2$. Other values of m and n should be assumed, and a further verification obtained.

Also $\dfrac{a^5}{a^3} = \dfrac{a \times a \times a \times a \times a}{a \times a \times a} = a^{5-3} = a^2$.

Similarly $\dfrac{a^m}{a^n} = \dfrac{a \times a \times a \text{ to } m \text{ factors}}{a \times a \times a \text{ to } n \text{ factors}} = a^{m-n}$.

It is found convenient to use both fractional and negative indices.

Thus
$$\sqrt{a} \text{ is written as } a^{\frac{1}{2}},$$
$$\sqrt[3]{a} \text{ is written as } a^{\frac{1}{3}}.$$

Also
$$\frac{1}{\sqrt{a}} = a^{-\frac{1}{2}},$$

and
$$\frac{1}{\sqrt[3]{a}} = a^{-\frac{1}{3}}.$$

The meaning attached to fractional and negative indices is such that the previous rule holds for them also. When one fractional power of a quantity is multiplied by another fractional power the indices are added, and when one fractional power is divided by another the indices are subtracted.

$$a^{\frac{1}{2}} \times a^{\frac{1}{2}} = a^{\frac{1}{2}+\frac{1}{2}} = a^1 = a$$
$$a^{\frac{1}{3}} \times a^{\frac{1}{3}} = a^{\frac{2}{3}}, \ a^{\frac{1}{3}} \times a^{\frac{1}{3}} \times a^{\frac{1}{3}} = a^{\frac{1}{3}+\frac{1}{3}+\frac{1}{3}} = a^1 = a.$$

Thus, the meaning to attach to $a^{\frac{1}{2}}$ is the square root of a; to $a^{\frac{2}{3}}$ is the cube root of a squared, and to $a^{\frac{1}{3}}$ the cube root of a.

Again
$$\frac{a^{\frac{1}{3}}}{a^{\frac{1}{2}}} = a^{\frac{1}{3}} \times a^{-\frac{1}{2}} = a^{\frac{1}{3}-\frac{1}{2}} = a^{-\frac{1}{6}}.$$

Also
$$\frac{a^{\frac{1}{3}}}{a^{\frac{1}{3}}} = a^{\frac{1}{3}-\frac{1}{3}} = a^0 = 1.$$

Since $a^m \times a^n = a^{m+n}$ is true for all values of m and n. If n be 0, then
$$a^m \times a^0 = a^{m+0} = a^m;$$
$$\therefore \ a^0 = \frac{a^m}{a^m} = 1.$$

The general form is $(a^n)^m = a^{mn}$.

Hence
$$a^{\frac{m}{n}} = \sqrt[n]{a^m},$$
which is read as the nth root of a to the power m.

Ex. 1. Explain why the product is a^{12} when a^5 is multiplied by a^7, and why the quotient is a^5 when a^8 is divided by a^3.

a^5 is a short way of writing $a \times a \times a \times a \times a$, and a similar meaning is attached to a^7;
$$\therefore \ a^5 \times a^7 = a^{7+5} = a^{12}.$$

Also
$$\frac{a^8}{a^3} = \frac{a \times a \times \dots \text{ to 8 factors}}{a \times a \times a};$$
$$\therefore \ \frac{a^8}{a^3} = a^{8-3} = a^5.$$

Ex. 2. Simplify $\left(\dfrac{bc}{a}\right)^{m+n}\left(\dfrac{a}{c}\right)^m\left(\dfrac{a}{b}\right)^n$.

Also find its value when $a=7$, $b=3$, $c=2$, $m=2$, $n=1$.

$$\left(\frac{bc}{a}\right)^{m+n}\left(\frac{a}{c}\right)^m\left(\frac{a}{b}\right)^n=\left(\frac{bc}{a}\right)^m\left(\frac{bc}{a}\right)^n\left(\frac{a}{c}\right)^m\left(\frac{a}{b}\right)^n$$

$$=\frac{a^m b^m c^m a^n b^n c^n}{a^m c^m a^n b^n}=b^m c^n.$$

Numerical value $=3^2\times 2=18$.

Ex. 3. Explain why $(a^2)^3=(a^3)^2=a^6$.

$$(a^2)^3=(a\times a)(a\times a)(a\times a)=(a\times a\times a)(a\times a\times a)$$
$$=(a^3)^2=a^6.$$

Ex. 4. Simplify $(a^2b)^2\times(ab^2)^3\div(a^2b^2)^4$.

$$(a^2b)^2\times(ab^2)^3\div(a^2b^2)^4=\frac{a^4b^2\times a^3b^6}{a^8b^8}=\frac{1}{a}.$$

EXERCISES. XIX.

1. How are the squares and cubes of numbers represented in Algebra? Show that $a^3\times a^2=a^5$; and prove that $a^7\div a^5=a^2$.

2. Explain the meaning of a^2, a, a^m, a^n, a^{-n}.

3. Prove that $a^m\div a^n=a^{m-n}$ and $a^m\times a^n=a^{m+n}$; also that $(a^m)^n=a^{mn}$.

Simplify

4. $\dfrac{(a^{p-q})^{p+q}\times(a^q)^{q+r}}{(a^p)^{p-q}}$.

5. $\dfrac{(a^{p-q}\times a^{q-r})^2}{(a^2)^p\times(a^{-q})^2}$.

6. $b^{2p+q}\times b^{p+4q}\div b^{q-p}$.

7. $x^{a+3b}\times x^{a+b}\div x^{b-a}$.

8. Find the product of
$$ax^{\frac{1}{4}}+2a^{\frac{1}{2}}x^{\frac{1}{2}}+4x^{\frac{3}{4}}\text{ and } a-2a^{\frac{1}{2}}x^{\frac{1}{4}}+4x^{\frac{1}{2}}.$$

9. Multiply $9a^{\frac{5}{6}}x^{\frac{1}{3}}+6a^{\frac{5}{12}}x^{\frac{5}{6}}+4x^{\frac{4}{3}}$ by $9a-6a^{\frac{7}{12}}x^{\frac{1}{2}}+4a^{\frac{1}{6}}x$.

Simplify

10. (i) $\sqrt{75a^5b^3}$; (ii) $\sqrt[3]{135}$; (iii) $(a^{\frac{q}{p-q}}\times a^{\frac{p}{q-p}})^{\frac{1}{p^2-q^2}}$.

11. $[a^{\frac{1}{3}}b^{\frac{1}{2}}(a^{-\frac{1}{6}}b^{-\frac{1}{4}})^{-\frac{1}{2}}]^{-\frac{4}{5}}$.

12. $\dfrac{\left(\frac{1}{2}\right)^4+\left(\frac{1}{3}\right)^4+\left(\frac{1}{6}\right)^2}{\left(\frac{1}{2}\right)^2+\left(\frac{1}{3}\right)^2+\frac{1}{6}}-\dfrac{1}{36}$.

13. $a^9b^{10}c^{11}\div a^4b^5c^8$.

14. $x^{m-n}y^{n-p}\times x^{2n-m}y^{n+p}$.

15. $\sqrt[3]{(4a^{-1}b^2c^{\frac{1}{2}})}\times\sqrt[4]{(12a^3b^{-\frac{2}{3}}c^2)}\div\sqrt[12]{(108a^{-3}b^2c^{-4})}$.

MISCELLANEOUS EXERCISES. XX.

1. Add together $x+y$, $3x-y-3z$, $2y-2x+z$, and multiply the result by $x-y-z$.

2. (i) Multiply x^3-2x^2+x-1 by x^3+2x^2-x-1, and (ii) divide $(x^2-5x+6)(x^2-5x-14)$ by $(x+2)(x^2-10x+21)$.

3. Determine the highest factor which will divide each of the expressions:

$$x^4-10x^2+9, \quad x^4+7x^3+11x^2-7x-12, \quad \text{and} \quad x^4+2x^3-16x^2-2x+15.$$

4. Simplify $\dfrac{2(x^2-1)^2}{(x^2+2)(x^2-16)}-\dfrac{(x-4)(x-1)^2+(x+4)(x+1)^2}{2x(x^2-16)}$.

5. Multiply $2x^5+4x^4+6x^3+8x^2+10x+5$ by x^2-2x+1.

6. Find an algebraic expression such that when it is divided by a^2-ab+b^2 the quotient is $a^2-2ab+b^2$ and the remainder is $2a^2b^2$.

7. Show that x^n-a^n is divisible by $x-a$; find the quotient when $n=3$.

8. Find the value of $x^2-5x^{\frac{1}{2}}+x^{-2}$ when $x=5$.

9. Find the value of $x^2-\frac{3}{4}x^{\frac{3}{2}}+x^{-1}$ when $x=3$.

10. Simplify $(a+b+c)^2-(a-b+c)^2+(a+b-c)^2-(-a+b+c)^2$.

11. (i) Divide $x^4-2ax^3-a^3x+2a^4$ by $x^2-3ax+2a^2$, and
(ii) multiply the quotient by x^2-ax+a^2.

12. If $x+y=2z$, show that $\dfrac{x}{x-z}+\dfrac{y}{y-z}=2$.

13. Obtain an expression which will divide both $4x^2+3x-10$ and $4x^3+7x^2-3x-15$ without remainder.

14. Divide $729x^6-y^6$ by $(3x-y)(9x^2+3xy+y^2)$.

15. (i) Multiply $ax^2+ax+\dfrac{1}{a}$ by $\dfrac{x^2}{a}-ax+a$;

(ii) divide
$$x^4+5ax^3-(n^2+n-7)a^2x^2-5na^3x-6a^4 \text{ by } x^2-(n-2)ax-2a^2.$$

16. Show that $(x-2)^2$ is a common factor of
$$x^7-6x^6+13x^5-12x^4+4x^3 \text{ and } x^7-5x^6+8x^5-4x^4.$$

17. From $3(a-2b)-2(2c-d)$ take $2(a-2b)-3(2c-d)$, and find the value of the difference when $a+c=b+d$ and $c=b+1$.

18. Prove that $\dfrac{(x+y)^4-(x-y)^4}{8x^2y^2}=\dfrac{x}{y}+\dfrac{y}{x}$.

19. What values of x and y will make $ax-by$ and $bx-ay=a^2+b^2$?

20. For what value of x will the two following fractions become equal:
$$\frac{2x-a}{3x-2a}; \; \frac{2x+3a}{3x+2a}?$$

21. Simplify $\dfrac{[(a^m)^{\frac{1}{r}}(a^q)^{\frac{1}{n}}]^{nr}}{[\sqrt[q]{b^n} \cdot (\sqrt[n]{b})^r]^{mq}} \div \left[\left(\dfrac{a}{b}\right)^q\right]^r$.

22. Prove that if $y-z=ax$, $z-x=by$, $x-y=cz$, then
$$abc+a+b+c=0.$$

23. Express in factors the three quantities
$$4a^2-9b^2, \quad 4a^2-12ab+9b^2, \quad 4a^2-9ab+2b^2.$$

24. Find the factors of
(a) $8a^3+27b^3$, (b) $2x^3+11x^2+14x$. [U.E.I.]

25. Write down the following products :
(a) $(2p+3q)(3p-2q)$, (b) $(2p-3q)^2$, (c) $(2p+3q)(3q-2p)$, and factorize x^2+5x+6, x^2+5x-6. [U.E.I.]

26. Resolve into factors: (a) 871^2-801^2; (b) $ac+bd+bc+ad$; (c) $x^2-y^2+xy^2-x^2y$. [L.C.U.]

27. $(a+b)x-(a+b)y$ and x^2-3x+2. [L.C.U.]

28. $x^2+0{\cdot}7x-144$; $x^2+14x+32$, x^3+27. [L.C.U.]

29. If $a:b=3:7$, find the value of $\dfrac{ab+b^2}{a^2-b^2}$. [N.U.T.]

30. Find a number whose 8th power is 40 times the number. [N.U.T.]

Summary.

Factors.—When an algebraic expression consists of the product of two or more quantities, each of those quantities is called a factor of the expression.

Index.—The number placed near the top and to the right of a quantity, and which expresses the *power* of a quantity, is called the *index*.

Multiplication.—To multiply together different powers of the same quantity, it is only necessary to add the index of one to the index of the other.

Division of different powers of the same quantity is performed by subtracting the index of one from the index of the other.

a^n+b^n is divisible by $a+b$ when n is an odd number.

a^n-b^n „ „ $a-b$ „ is odd.

a^n-b^n „ „ both $a+b$ and $a-b$ when n is even.

The product of the sum and difference of two numbers is equal to the difference of their squares.

CHAPTER XIV.

APPROXIMATIONS. FRACTIONS.

WE have already found that

$$(a+b)^2 = a^2 + 2ab + b^2,$$

and by multiplying again by $a+b$ we obtain

$$(a+b)^3 = a^3 + 3a^2b + 3ab^2 + b^3.$$

It is seen at once that some definite arrangement of the coefficients and indices can be made so that another power, say $(a+b)^4$, can be written down : the method used, and called the *Binomial Theorem*, is very important. The rule should be applied to the operation of expanding several simple expressions, such as $(a+b)^3$, $(a+b)^4$, etc., and afterwards committed to memory.

$$(a+b)^n = a^n + \frac{na^{n-1}b}{1} + \frac{n(n-1)}{1 \cdot 2} a^{n-2}b^2 + \dots.$$

Take $n=2$, then

$$a^n = a^2, \text{ and } \frac{na^{n-1}b}{1} = 2ab.$$

Hence $\quad (a+b)^2 = a^2 + \dfrac{2ab}{1} + \dfrac{b^2 \cdot (2 \cdot 1)}{1 \cdot 2} = a^2 + 2ab + b^2.$

Take $n=3$; here $a^n = a^3$; $\dfrac{na^{n-1}b}{1} = 3a^2b$, etc. ;

$$\therefore \ (a+b)^3 = a^3 + \frac{3a^2b}{1} + \frac{3 \cdot 2ab^2}{1 \cdot 2} + \frac{3 \cdot 2 \cdot 1}{1 \cdot 2 \cdot 3} a^0b^3$$
$$= a^3 + 3a^2b + 3ab^2 + b^3.$$

As a handy check, the reader should notice, that in each term the sum of the powers of a and b are equal to n. Thus, when $=3$, in the second term a is raised to the power 2, and b to the power 1. Therefore sum of powers = 3. Also, the coefficient has for denominator a series of factors $1 . 2 . 3 \ldots r$, where r has the same numerical value as the power of b in the term. Thus, in the term containing b^3, a must be raised to the power $n - 3$, and the coefficient must be

$$\frac{n(n-1)(n-2)}{1 . 2 . 3}.$$

Writing down terms in the numerator to be afterwards cancelled by corresponding numbers in the denominator, would appear to the beginner to be a tedious and unnecessary process, but to avoid mistakes it is better to write out in full, as above, and afterwards to cancel any common factors in the numerator and denominator.

The expansion of

$$(1+a)^n \text{ is } 1 + \frac{na}{1} + \frac{n(n-1)a^2}{1 . 2} + \cdots$$

when a is a very small quantity, the two first terms are for all practical purposes sufficient; thus, when a is small,

$$(1+a)^n = 1 + na \text{ approximately.}$$

Thus if $a = \cdot 01$ and $n = 2$, then

$$(1 + \cdot 01)^2 = 1 + 2 \times \cdot 01 = 1 \cdot 02.$$

Ex. 1. $(1 + \cdot 05)^2 = 1 + 2 \times \cdot 05 = 1 \cdot 1$;
more accurately $(1 \cdot 05)^2 = 1 \cdot 1025.$

Ex. 2. $(1 + \cdot 05)^3 = 1 + 3 \times \cdot 05 = 1 \cdot 15.$

Ex. 3. $\sqrt[3]{(1 \cdot 05)} = (1 + \cdot 05)^{\frac{1}{3}} = 1 + \frac{1}{3} \times \cdot 05 = 1 \cdot 0167.$

Ex. 4. $\dfrac{1}{\sqrt[3]{1 \cdot 05}} = (1 + \cdot 05)^{-\frac{1}{3}} = 1 - \frac{1}{3} \times \cdot 05 = 1 - \cdot 0167 = \cdot 9833.$

Fractions.—The rules and methods adopted in dealing with fractions in Algebra are almost identical with those already considered in Arithmetic. In both cases fractions are of frequent occurrence and their consideration is of the utmost importance. Some little practice is necessary before even a simple fraction can be reduced to its lowest terms. Perhaps the best method in the simplification of fractions is, as already shown, to write out the given expressions in factors wherever possible. To do this easily the factors already referred to on page 109 should be carefully learnt by heart.

When required to add, subtract, or compare fractional expressions, it is necessary that they shall all have a common denominator, and to lessen the work it is desirable that this denominator shall be as small as possible.

Ex. 1.   Add $\dfrac{1}{2} + \dfrac{1}{3x}$.

First reduce to a common denominator $6x$; mentally multiply both numerator and denominator of the first fraction by $3x$, and obtain $\dfrac{3x}{6x}$; and similarly, by multiplying $\dfrac{1}{3x}$ by 2, get $\dfrac{2}{6x}$.

$$\therefore \; \frac{1}{2} + \frac{1}{3x} = \frac{3x+2}{6x}.$$

Ex. 2.   Simplify $\left(\dfrac{1}{2} + \dfrac{1}{3x}\right) \div \left(9x - \dfrac{4}{x}\right)$.

$$\frac{\dfrac{1}{2} + \dfrac{1}{3x}}{9x - \dfrac{4}{x}} = \frac{\dfrac{3x+2}{6x}}{\dfrac{9x^2-4}{x}} = \frac{x(3x+2)}{6x(3x+2)(3x-2)} = \frac{1}{6(3x-2)}.$$

The factors $x(3x+2)$, which are common to both numerator and denominator, are cancelled.

Ex. 3.   Simplify $\dfrac{x-a}{\dfrac{1}{a} - \dfrac{1}{b}} \times \dfrac{a-b}{1 - \dfrac{a}{x}}$.

$$\frac{x-a}{\dfrac{1}{a} - \dfrac{1}{b}} \times \frac{a-b}{1 - \dfrac{a}{x}} = \frac{x-a}{\dfrac{b-a}{ab}} \times \frac{a-b}{\dfrac{x-a}{x}}$$

$$= \frac{(x-a)ab}{b-a} \times \frac{(a-b)x}{x-a} = -abx.$$

The terms common to numerator and denominator are cancelled; the term $b - a$ is for this purpose written in the form $-(a-b)$.

When the denominators of two or more fractions can be written in the form of factors, the reduction of the fractions to their simplest form can be readily effected.   But the process of factorisation cannot in all cases be easily carried out, and in such cases we may proceed to find the *Highest Common Factor* (H.C.F.).   The process is analogous to that of finding the G.C.M. in arithmetic.   The H.C.F. of two or more given expressions may be defined as *the expression of highest dimensions which can be divided into each of the given expressions without a remainder.*

Ex. 4. Simplify the fraction $\dfrac{x^4+x^3+2x-4}{x^3+3x^2-4}$.

To find the H.C.F. we proceed as follows :

$$x^3+3x^2-4 \,\Big)\, x^4+\ x^3+2x\ -4 \,\Big(\, x-2$$
$$\underline{x^4+3x^3-4x}$$
$$\quad\ -2x^3\qquad\ +6x-\ 4$$
$$\quad\ \underline{-2x^3-6x^2\qquad\ +\ 8}$$
$$\qquad\qquad 6x^2+6x-12$$
$$=6\,(x^2+x-2)\,;$$
$$x^2+x-2 \,\Big)\, x^3+3x^2-4 \,\Big(\, x+2$$
$$\underline{x^3+\ \ x^2-2x}$$
$$\qquad 2x^2+2x-4$$
$$\qquad \underline{2x^2+2x-4}$$

Therefore the H.C.F. $=x^2+x-2$.

Hence $\qquad \dfrac{x^4+x^3+2x-4}{x^3+3x^2-4}=\dfrac{(x^2+x-2)(x^2+2)}{(x^2+x-2)(x+2)}=\dfrac{x^2+2}{x+2}.$

Lowest Common Multiple.—When required to add, subtract, or compare two fractions, it is often necessary to obtain the *Lowest Common Multiple* (L.C.M.) of the denominators, i.e., *the expression of lowest dimensions into which each of the given expressions can be divided without a remainder.*

To find the L.C.M. we may find the H.C.F. of two given expressions, *divide one expression by it and multiply the quotient by the other.* Thus the H.C.F. of the two expressions

$$x^3-3x^2-15x+25 \quad \text{and} \quad x^3+7x^2+5x-25$$
is $\qquad\qquad x^2+2x-5\,;$

dividing the first expression by this H.C.F. the quotient is $x-5$.

Hence the L.C.M. is

$$(x-5)(x^3+7x^2+5x-25) \quad \text{or} \quad (x-5)(x+5)(x^2+2x-5).$$

Ex. 5. Simplify the following :
$$\frac{1}{x^3-3x^2-15x+25}-\frac{1}{x^3+7x^2+5x-25}.$$

The common denominator will be the L.C.M. of the two denominators, and the fractions become

$$\frac{x+5}{(x^2+2x-5)(x-5)(x+5)}-\frac{x-5}{(x^2+2x-5)(x-5)(x+5)}$$
$$=\frac{10}{(x-5)(x+5)(x^2+2x-5)}.$$

Ex. 6. Simplify $\dfrac{x-2y}{x+2y}+\dfrac{x+2y}{x-2y}+\dfrac{8xy}{x^2-4y^2}$.

As, $\qquad x^2-4y^2=(x+2y)(x-2y)$,
the common denominator is $\ x^2-4y^2$.

Hence we multiply the numerator of the first fraction by $x-2y$, the numerator of the second by $x+2y$, and to the sum add the numerator of the third fraction; thus

$$\frac{(x-2y)^2+(x+2y)^2+8xy}{x^2-4y^2}=\frac{2x^2+8xy+8y^2}{x^2-4y^2}=\frac{2(x+2y)(x+2y)}{(x+2y)(x-2y)}$$

$$=\frac{2(x+2y)}{x-2y}.$$

EXERCISES. XXI.

Simplify the following expressions:

1. $\dfrac{x^2-14x+13}{x^2-8x-65}$.

2. $\dfrac{x^2+2x-15}{x^2+8x-33}\div\dfrac{x^2+9x+20}{x^2+7x-44}$.

3. $\dfrac{x-2a}{x+a}+\dfrac{2(a^2-4ax)}{a^2-x^2}-\dfrac{3a}{x-a}$.

4. $\dfrac{x^2-7xy+12y^2}{x^2+5xy+6y^2}\div\dfrac{x^2-5xy+4y^2}{x^2+xy-2y^2}$.

5. $\dfrac{x-a}{x+a}+\dfrac{a^2+3ax}{a^2-x^2}+\dfrac{x+a}{x-a}$.

6. $\dfrac{x^2-16x-17}{x^2-22x+85}$.

7. $\dfrac{1}{x-2}+\dfrac{1}{x^2-3x+2}-\dfrac{2}{x^2-4x+3}$.

8. $\dfrac{a-3b}{a+2b}-\dfrac{a+3b}{a-2b}-\dfrac{5ab}{a^2+4b^2}$.

9. $\dfrac{x^6+y^6}{x^6-y^6}\times\dfrac{x-y}{x+y}\div\dfrac{x^4-x^2y^2+y^4}{x^4+x^2y^2+y^4}$.

10. $\dfrac{x^2-7xy+12y^2}{4x^2-11xy-3y^2}-\dfrac{2x^2+7xy-4y^2}{8x^2-6xy+y^2}$.

11. $\dfrac{x^3-6x^2+11x-6}{x^3-9x^2+26x-24}$.

12. $\left(x-\dfrac{x^3-2x^2y}{x^2-y^2}\right)\left(y+\dfrac{xy-y^2}{x+3y}\right)\div\dfrac{2x-y}{x-y}$.

13. $\dfrac{\dfrac{x^2}{y^2}+\dfrac{x}{y}+1}{\dfrac{x^2}{y^2}-\dfrac{x}{y}+1}\times\dfrac{\dfrac{x^3}{y}+y^2}{x^2-\dfrac{y^3}{x}}\times\dfrac{x^2-xy}{y^2+xy}$.

14. $\dfrac{f}{g-\dfrac{g^2}{f}}+\dfrac{g}{f-\dfrac{f^2}{g}}$.

15. Find the sum of

$$\frac{1}{3x^2-14xy+15y^2} \quad\text{and}\quad \frac{2}{3x^2-2xy-5y^2}.$$

Simplify

16. $\dfrac{9}{x^2 - x - 20} - \dfrac{7}{x^2 + x - 12} - \dfrac{2}{x^2 - 8x + 15}.$

17. $\dfrac{1}{x^2 - 4x + 3} - \dfrac{4}{x^2 + 2x - 15} + \dfrac{3}{x^2 + 4x - 5}.$

18. $\dfrac{\dfrac{1}{x} + \dfrac{1}{y-z}}{\dfrac{1}{x} - \dfrac{1}{y-z}} \left\{ 1 - \dfrac{y^2 + z^2 - x^2}{2yz} \right\}.$

19. $\dfrac{x^3}{(x-y)(x-z)} + \dfrac{y^3}{(y-z)(y-x)} + \dfrac{z^3}{(z-x)(z-y)}.$

20. $\dfrac{a^3 - y^3}{a^4 - y^4} \cdot \dfrac{a - y}{a^2 - y^2} - \dfrac{1}{2} \left\{ \dfrac{a+y}{a^2 + y^2} - \dfrac{1}{a+y} \right\}.$

21. $\dfrac{2(x^2 - 1)^2}{(x^2 + 2)(x^2 - 16)} - \dfrac{(x-4)(x-1)^2 + (x+4)(x+1)^2}{2x(x^2 - 16)}.$

22. $\dfrac{2b}{a+b} - \dfrac{3a}{a-b} + \dfrac{a^2 + b^2}{a^2 - b^2}.$

23. $\left(\dfrac{x^2 + y^2}{x^2 - xy} \right) \left(\dfrac{xy - y^2}{x^4 - y^4} \right) \dfrac{x}{y}.$

24. $\left(\dfrac{x}{x-a} - \dfrac{a}{x+a} \right) \div \dfrac{x^2 + a^2}{x^2 - ax}.$

25. $\dfrac{1}{x(x-1)(x+1)(x-2)} + \dfrac{1}{x(x-1)(x+1)(x+2)}.$

26. $\left(x - \dfrac{xy - y^2}{x+y} \right) \left(x - \dfrac{xy^2 - y^3}{x^2 + y^2} \right) \div \left(1 - \dfrac{xy - y^2}{x^2} \right).$

27. Simplify $\dfrac{x - 4y^2}{xy(x + 2y)^2} \div \dfrac{2x - 4y}{x^3 y^3}.$ [L.C.U.]

28. When x and y are very small $(1+x)(1+y) = 1 + x + y$ approximately. What is the approximate value of $1\cdot006 \times 1\cdot002$, and what is the error?   [N.U.T.]

29. Simplify

    (a) $225\tfrac{1}{2} \times 1\tfrac{1}{7} \times 10$;   (b) $\dfrac{4a^2}{5b} \times \dfrac{15b}{2ab}$;   (c) $\dfrac{4y^2}{3x^2} \times \dfrac{6xy}{5}.$ [L.C.U.]

30. Simplify

    (a) $3x + (2y - z) + (x - 4z$;   (b) $15 - (2z - 4y + x) - (5 - x)$;

    (c) $4z - (3x + y) - (5z - 2y)$;   (d) $3(x - y) + 2(3z + x).$

Find the numerical values if $x = 4\cdot5$, $y = 5\tfrac{1}{4}$, and $z = 2$.   [L.C.U.]

CHAPTER XV.

SIMPLE EQUATIONS AND PROBLEMS INVOLVING THEM.

In Part I. of this course of work, in the chapters on Algebra, an attempt was made to give sufficient elementary information to enable a reader to solve a simple equation. In addition to this it is necessary that a practical man should be able to solve what are called simultaneous equations.

Before indicating the methods by which the solution of a given simultaneous equation may be obtained, it may be advantageous to briefly consider how the solutions of simple equations, rather more difficult than those already studied, may be effected.

Simple Equations.—Some methods which may often be used in solving equations have been already explained, but no general rules can be given which will apply to every case. It is only by practice that the student can hope to deal successfully with any ordinary example. Again, it will be found that if the attempt is made to solve all equations by fixed methods or rules, much unnecessary labour will often be entailed. Thus, in fractional equations the rule usually given would be to first clear of fractions by using the L.C.M. of the denominators; but, if this is done in all cases the multiplier may be a large number, troublesome to use. In such cases it is better, where possible, to simplify two or more terms before proceeding to deal with the remaining part of the equation.

Ex. 1. Solve $\dfrac{11x-13}{25}+\dfrac{17x+4}{21}+\dfrac{19x+3}{7}=28\tfrac{1}{7}+\dfrac{5x-25\tfrac{1}{3}}{4}.$

We may with advantage simplify three of the given terms, using 21 as a multiplier, thus :

$$\therefore\ \frac{21(11x-13)}{25}+17x+4+57x+9=591+\frac{21\left(5x-25\tfrac{1}{3}\right)}{4},$$

or $\qquad \dfrac{21(11x-13)}{25}+74x-\dfrac{21\left(5x-\tfrac{76}{3}\right)}{4}=578.$

Multiplying by 100 we obtain

$$84(11x-13)+7400x-525\left(5x-\tfrac{76}{3}\right)=57800,$$

or $\qquad 924x-1092+7400x-2625x+13300=57800.$

$$\therefore\ 5699x=45592.$$

$$\therefore\ x=\tfrac{45592}{5699}=8.$$

When decimal fractions occur in an equation it is often desirable to clear fractions by multiplying both sides of the equation by a suitable power of ten.

Ex. 2. Solve $\cdot015x+\cdot1575-\cdot0875x=\cdot00625x.$

We can clear of fractions by multiplying every term by 100000.

$$\therefore\ 1500x+15750-8750x=625x,$$

or $\qquad 15750=7875x.$

$$\therefore\ x=2.$$

Ex. 3. Solve $\qquad \dfrac{x-a}{x+a}+\dfrac{3b-x}{2b+x}=0.$

Multiplying all through by $(x+a)(2b+x)$, we get

$$\frac{(x-a)(2b+x)+(3b-x)(x+a)}{(x+a)(2b+x)}=0.$$

$$\therefore\ (x-a)(2b+x)+(x+a)(3b-x)=0.$$

Multiplying out and collecting terms,

$$x(5b-2a)=-ab\ ;\ \therefore\ x=\frac{-ab}{5b-2a}.$$

Ex. 4. Solve $\dfrac{3x-7}{5}-\dfrac{3x+7}{4}=\dfrac{5x-9}{8}-\dfrac{3x+9}{6}.$

Here the L.C.M. of the denominators is 120.

$$\therefore\ 24(3x-7)-30(3x+7)=15(5x-9)-20(3x+9).$$

Multiplying out and collecting terms, we get

$$33x=-63\ ;\ \therefore\ x=-\tfrac{21}{11}.$$

Ex. 5. Solve $\dfrac{a}{bx} - a^2 = b^2 - \dfrac{b}{ax}$.

First remove the fractions by multiplying all through by abx;

$$\therefore\ a^2 - a^3bx = ab^3x - b^2,$$

transposing, $\quad -a^3bx - ab^3x = -a^2 - b^2,$

changing sign or multiplying by -1,

$$x(a^2+b^2)ab = a^2 + b^2;$$

$$\therefore\ x = \dfrac{a^2+b^2}{ab(a^2+b^2)} = \dfrac{1}{ab}.$$

EXERCISES. XXII.

Solve the equations :

1. $(x-3)(x-5) - (x-4)(x-6) = 3.$ **2.** $\dfrac{3x-4}{2x+3} - \dfrac{2x-3}{4x+6} = \dfrac{5}{6}.$

3. $\dfrac{3}{5}(x-1) + \dfrac{2x}{7} - \dfrac{x-7}{14} = \dfrac{x-1}{5} + 13.$ **4.** $\dfrac{x}{6} + \dfrac{x}{8} = \dfrac{x+1}{7} + \dfrac{x}{12} + 3.$

5. $\dfrac{2x-7}{2x-3} = \dfrac{x+7}{x+11}.$ **6.** $\dfrac{x-a}{a-b} - \dfrac{x+a}{a+b} = \dfrac{2ax}{a^2-b^2}.$

7. $\dfrac{a-b}{x-c} = \dfrac{a+b}{x+2c}.$ **8.** $\dfrac{2x+1}{23} + \dfrac{4x-5}{13} = 2 - \dfrac{3x-47}{7}.$

9. $\dfrac{5}{7}\left(\dfrac{3x}{5} - 1\right) = \dfrac{2}{3}\left(\dfrac{x}{8} - 6\right) + 3\tfrac{4}{4}\tfrac{1}{2}.$ **10.** $\dfrac{x+a}{x-c} + \dfrac{x+c}{x-a} = 2.$

11. $\cdot006x - \cdot491 + \cdot723x = -\cdot005.$ **12.** $\cdot8x - \cdot067 = \cdot473 + \cdot071x.$

13. $\dfrac{1}{2(x-3)} = \dfrac{1}{3(x-2)} + \dfrac{1}{6(x-1)}.$ **14.** $4\left(x - \dfrac{3}{8}\right) - 3\tfrac{1}{5}\left(\dfrac{x}{2} - 1\right) = 5\tfrac{9}{10}.$

15. $\dfrac{x}{x+1} - \dfrac{3x}{x+2} = -2.$ **16.** $\dfrac{x}{12} - \dfrac{1}{8}(8-x) - \dfrac{1}{4}(1+x) + \dfrac{7}{4} = 0.$

17. $7(1-x) - \tfrac{1}{2}(21x-1) = 10\cdot5x + 6\tfrac{1}{6}.$

18. $\dfrac{ax}{b} + b = \dfrac{bx}{a} + a.$

19. $\tfrac{1}{3}(\cdot75 - x) + \tfrac{1}{5}(\cdot47 + 2x) = (3 - 1\tfrac{1}{5})x.$

20. $x - \dfrac{2x - \cdot3}{\cdot7} = \dfrac{5-x}{\cdot35}.$ **21.** $\dfrac{ax}{a+c} + 2ac - a^2 = \dfrac{cx}{a-c} - c^2.$

22. $\tfrac{1}{4}(x-3) + \tfrac{1}{5}(x-2) = 1 + \tfrac{1}{40}(x-1).$

23. $\dfrac{x}{2} - \dfrac{\cdot05x - 7\cdot5}{\cdot6} = \dfrac{\cdot25x + 3\cdot8}{\cdot3}.$

Solve the equations :

24. $\frac{5}{7}(x-9) + \frac{7}{9}(x-5) = \frac{9}{5}(x-7) + 1\frac{2}{3}$.

25. $5 - 3(4-x) + 4(3-2x) = 0$.   **26.** $\frac{9x-8}{7} + \frac{x + \cdot2}{\cdot4} + \frac{2}{9} = 0$.

27. $3x - 4\{9 - (2x+7) + 3x\} = 13$.   **28.** $\frac{(x-1)(x-2)(x-6)}{(x-3)^3} = 1$.

29. $\frac{x}{ab} + \frac{x}{bc} + \frac{x}{ac} = a + b + c$.   **30.** $\frac{1}{x-a} + \frac{1}{x-b} = \frac{2}{x}$.

31. $\frac{1}{4}(2x-5) - \frac{1}{6}(x-2) = \frac{1}{7}x - \frac{1}{4}$.   **32.** $a\frac{x-b}{a-b} + b\frac{x-a}{b-a} = 1$.

Problems involving simple equations with one unknown quantity.

—When a question or problem is to be solved, its true meaning ought in the first place to be perfectly understood, and its conditions exhibited by algebraical symbols in the clearest manner possible. When this has been done the equation can be written down and the solution obtained.

Ex. 1. The sum of two numbers is 100; 8 times the greater exceeds 11 times the smaller part by 2; find the numbers.

Let x denote the smaller part.

Then $\qquad\qquad 100 - x = $ greater part,

and $\qquad$ 8 times the greater $= 8(100-x)$.

Hence $\qquad\qquad 8(100-x) = 11x + 2$,

or $\qquad\qquad 800 - 8x = 11x + 2$;

$\qquad\qquad \therefore\ 798 = 19x$,

$\qquad\qquad\qquad x = 42$.

Also $\qquad\qquad (100 - x) = 58$.

Hence the two numbers are 58 and 42.

Ex. 2. A post which projects 7 feet above the surface of water is found to have $\frac{1}{3}$ its length in the water and $\frac{1}{4}$ its length in the mud at the bottom ; find its total length.

Let x denote its length in feet.

Then $\frac{x}{3}$ is the length in the water.

And $\frac{x}{4}$ is the length in the mud.

But the length in the mud, the length in the water, together with 7, is equal to the total length.

Hence
$$\frac{x}{3} + \frac{x}{4} + 7 = x,$$

or
$$4x + 3x + 84 = 12x ;$$
$$\therefore \; 5x = 84, \; \text{or} \; x = 16\tfrac{4}{5} \text{ feet.}$$

Ex. 3. Two rectangular boards are equal in area. The breadth of one is 18 inches, and that of the other 16 inches ; the difference of their lengths is 4 inches. Find the length of each board and their common area.

Let x denote the length of one board.

Then $x + 4$ will denote the length of the other.

The areas of the two boards are respectively $18x$ and $16(x+4)$. But these areas are equal ;

$$\therefore \; 18x = 16(x+4),$$

or
$$18x = 16x + 64.$$

Transposing,
$$2x = 64,$$
$$\therefore \; x = 32, \; \text{and} \; x + 4 = 36.$$

Hence length of one board is 32 inches.

And   ,,   other   ,,   36   ,,

$\therefore$ Common area $= 18 \times 32 = 16 \times 36 = 576$ square inches.

Ex. 4. A rectangle is 6 feet long ; if it were 1 foot wider its area would be 30 square feet. Find the width.

Let x denote the width in feet.

Then $x + 1$ is the width when one foot wider.

The area is $6(x+1)$, but the area is 30 square feet ;

$$\therefore \; 6(x+1) = 30,$$
$$6x + 6 = 30.$$

Transposing,
$$6x = 24 ; \; \therefore \; x = 4.$$

In electrical work equations are of the utmost importance. As a simple case we may consider what is known as **Ohm's Law.** This may be expressed by the equation

$$R = \frac{E}{C}, \dots\dots\dots\dots\dots\dots\dots\dots\dots\dots(1)$$

where R denotes the resistance of a circuit in ohms, E the electromotive force, and C the current in amperes. An explanation of the law may be obtained from any book on electricity. In (1) and in all such equations involving three terms, when two of the terms are given, the remaining one (or unknown quantity) may be found.

Ex. 5.   A battery contains 30 Grove's cells united in series; a wire is used to complete the circuit. Find the strength of the current, assuming the E.M.F. of a Grove's cell to be 1·8 volts, the resistance of each cell ·3 ohm, and the resistance of the wire 16 ohms.

Here   E.M.F. $= 30 \times 1·8$ $= 54$ volts.

Resistance $= 30 \times ·3 + 16 = 25$ ohms.

$$\therefore \; C = \tfrac{5\,4}{2\,5} = 2·16 \text{ amperes.}$$

EXERCISES.   XXIII.

1. An uncle is older than his nephew by 10 years; 15 years ago the uncle was twice as old as his nephew. What are their respective ages?

2. The difference of the ages of two brothers three years ago was $\frac{1}{6}$ the age of the elder, whereas it is now $\frac{1}{7}$. What are their ages?

3. A rectangular court is 20 yards longer than it is broad, and its area is 4524 square yards. Find its length and breadth.

4. If 3 yards be taken from one side of a rectangle whose perimeter is 14 yards, and added to the other side, its area will be doubled. Find the lengths of the sides.

5. A house and a garden were bought for £1000; the cost of the house was 5 times that of the garden, find the price given for each.

6. A bath can be filled by means of a tap in 3 minutes, and by a second in 5 minutes, and emptied by a third in $7\frac{1}{2}$ minutes. If when the bath is empty all three taps are opened, how long will it take to fill?

7. Divide £90 6s. 0d. among A, B and C, so that A may receive $\frac{3}{4}$ as much as B receives, and C $\frac{1}{5}$ as much as A and B together.

8. Divide £1000 between two persons so that one may have £10 more than half of what the other has.

9. The difference of two numbers is 20 and their sum 122; find the numbers.

10. Find two numbers such that their difference is 162, and $\frac{5}{1}$ of their sum is 162.

11. The sum of two numbers is 143, if the quotient of the greater number divided by the difference of the numbers is 7, find the two numbers.

12. At what time between three and four o'clock do the hands a watch point exactly in opposite directions?

13. Divide the number 42 into two parts, such that $\frac{2}{3}$ of one part may be the same as $\frac{8}{9}$ of the other.

14. If B gives to A 10s., A will have twice as much as B. If A gives B 10s., B will have three times as much as A. What money has each?

15. Find the two times between 6 and 7 o'clock when the hands of a watch are separated by 15 minutes.

16. A certain number is less than the number obtained by reversing the digits by 9; also the sum of the two numbers is 77. Find the number.

17. Each of two vessels A and B contains a mixture of wine and water, A in the ratio of 7 to 3, and B in the ratio of 3 to 1. Find how many gallons from B must be put with 5 gallons from A in order to give a mixture of wine and water in the ratio of 11 to 4.

18. Two farmers have each a flock of sheep containing the same number; when one farmer loses 390, and the other 930, it is found that one farmer has just twice as many sheep as the other : how many sheep had each at first?

19. A father's age is four times that of his elder son and five times that of his younger son. When the elder son has lived to three times his present age, the father's age will exceed twice that of his younger son by 3 years. What is the age of each?

20. Find a number which, after being multiplied by 4, will exceed 50 as much as it is now short of 50.

21. A can do a piece of work in 9 days, B in twice that time, C can only do $\frac{3}{4}$ as much work as A in one day; how long will A B and C, working together, require to do the same piece of work?

22. If 4 be added to the numerator of a fraction its value is $\frac{1}{2}$, but if 7 be added to the denominator the value is $\frac{1}{5}$. Find the fraction.

23. A Daniell's cell has an E.M.F. of 1·03 volts, and the circuit is completed by a wire whose resistance is 16 ohms. What will be the current sent through the wire assuming the internal resistance of the cell to be 3 ohms?

24. A man's wages are half-a-crown less than five times a boy's wages. If together they earn £2. 2s. 6d., what is the wage of each?

[N.U.T.]

25. When a man's weekly wage was £2. 15s. he saved 10s. per week. His wages were increased by 30 per cent., but owing to the increased cost of living he had to spend 40 per cent. more than before. By what percentage were his savings increased or decreased?

[N.U.T.]

26. Divide £46. 18s. between three persons, A, B, and C, so that C gets 20 per cent. more than B and 25 per cent. more than A.

[L.C.U.]

CHAPTER XVI.

SIMULTANEOUS EQUATIONS AND PROBLEMS INVOLVING THEM.

Simultaneous Equations.—If an equation contains two unknown quantities, denoted by x and y, then by giving definite values to one of the unknown quantities, a corresponding series of values can be obtained for the other.

Ex. 1.   Solve $3x - 5y = 6$.

This means that we require to find two numbers such that five times the second subtracted from three times the first will give 6.

By transposition, $3x = 5y + 6$; giving values 1, 2, 3, etc. to y, we obtain a corresponding series of values of x.

If $y = 1$, then $3x = 11$; $\therefore$ $x = \frac{11}{3}$.

$y = 2$, then $3x = 16$; $\therefore$ $x = \frac{16}{3}$.

Proceeding in this manner, a table of values can be arranged as follows :

x	$\frac{11}{3}$	$\frac{16}{3}$	7	$\frac{26}{3}$	....
y	1	2	3	4	....

Thus, for any assigned value of y a corresponding value of x can be obtained.

In a similar manner, if values are assigned to x, corresponding values of y can be found.

If, now, we have a second equation $4x + 3y = 37$, as before, by giving any assigned value to either x or y, a corresponding value of the other unknown is obtained, and a table of corresponding values of x and y can be tabulated as in the preceding case ; comparing the two sets of values so obtained, it will be found that only one pair of values of x and y will satisfy both equations at once, the two values being $x = 7$, $y = 3$.

Equations such as
$$3x - 5y = 6,$$
$$4x + 3y = 37,$$
which are satisfied by the same values of the unknown quantities, are called *simultaneous equations*.

To find two unknown quantities, we must have two distinct and possible equations.

Ex. 2. $4x + 3y = 37$, and $12x + 9y = 111$.

These form two equations, but they are not distinct, as the second can be obtained from the first by multiplying by 3.

Again, $3x - 5y = 6$ and $6x - 10y = 13$ are apparently impossible simultaneous equations, because, by multiplying the former by 2, the equation becomes $6x - 10y = 12$, but from the second equation, $6x - 10y = 13$. Hence simultaneous values of x and y satisfying the two equations and corresponding to the intersection of two plotted lines cannot be found. On plotting the lines as on p. 151 the lines are found to be parallel to each other.

To solve simultaneous equations, we require as many distinct and independent equations as there are unknowns to be found, *i.e.* if two unknowns have to be determined, two distinct equations are required ; if three unknowns, three equations, and so on.

If only one equation connecting two unknown quantities is given, although the value of each of the unknowns cannot be determined, it is possible to obtain the ratio of the quantities.

Ex. 3. If $\dfrac{5x - 4y}{3x - 2y} = 4$, find the ratio of x to y.

$$\therefore\ 5x - 4y = 4(3x - 2y) = 12x - 8y.$$
$$\therefore\ 4y = 7x,$$
or
$$\frac{x}{y} = \frac{4}{7}.$$

Elimination.—When in the data of a problem the given equations are not only distinct, but are sufficient in number, it is possible from these to obtain others, in which one or more of the unknown quantities do not occur. The process by which this is effected is called *elimination*. At the outset it is convenient in a few simple cases, to show some of the methods which may be adopted in dealing with simultaneous equations containing two or more unknown quantities.

Solution of Simultaneous Equations.—In the solution of a simultaneous equation containing two unknown quantities, there are two general methods by which their values may be obtained. The first, is by multiplication or division, to make the co-efficients of one of the unknowns the same in the two equations; then by addition, or subtraction, we can *eliminate* one unknown quantity. This leaves an equation containing only one unknown, the value of which can be found in the usual manner.

The other method is to find the value of one unknown in terms of the other unknown in one of the equations, and then to substitute the value so found in the other equation.

Ex. 4.

$$3x - 5y = 6, \quad \dots\dots\dots\dots\dots\dots\dots\dots \text{(i)}$$
$$4x + 3y = 37. \quad \dots\dots\dots\dots\dots\dots\dots\text{(ii)}$$

To apply the *first method*, multiply (i) by 3 and (ii) by 5. This will make the terms in y the same in both equations, and as these have opposite signs their sum is zero.

$$\therefore \quad 9x - 15y = 18$$
$$\underline{20x + 15y = 185}$$

By addition,
$$29x \qquad = 203$$

$$\therefore \quad x = \frac{203}{29} = 7.$$

Substitute this value in (i);

$$\therefore \quad 21 - 5y = 6;$$
or
$$5y = 21 - 6 = 15; \quad \therefore \quad y = 3.$$

On substituting these values of x and y in the given equations the equations are satisfied, thus substituting the values in (i), we get $3 \times 7 - 15 = 6$; the values obtained should always be substituted to ensure accuracy.

By the second method :
From (i)
$$3x = 6 + 5y;$$
or
$$x = \frac{6 + 5y}{3};$$

$$\therefore \quad 4x = \frac{24 + 20y}{3}.$$

Substitute this value in (ii);

$$\therefore \quad \frac{24+20y}{3}+3y=37.$$

Multiply both sides of the equation by 3;

or $\qquad\qquad 24+20y+9y=111.$

Hence $\qquad\qquad 29y=111-24=\ 87\ ;$

$$\therefore \quad y=\frac{87}{29}=\ \ 3.$$

Having found the value of y, then by substitution in (i) or (ii), the value of x is readily obtained.

Miscellaneous Examples.—As the solution of simultaneous equations is of the utmost importance, a few miscellaneous examples are worked here.

Ex. 5. $\qquad\qquad 6x+3y=33, \dots\dots\dots\dots\dots\dots\dots$ (i)

$\qquad\qquad\qquad 13x-4y=19. \dots\dots\dots\dots\dots\dots\dots$(ii)

Multiplying (i) by 4, we get $24x+12y=132$

$\quad$,, $\quad$ (ii) by 3, we get $\dfrac{39x-12y=\ 57}{}$

By addition $\qquad\qquad \overline{63x\qquad\ =189}$

$$\therefore \quad x=\tfrac{189}{63}=3,$$

and by substitution in (i), $\qquad y=5.$

If the known quantities are represented by the letters a, b, c, d, the solution is effected in the same manner.

Ex. 6. Solve $\qquad ax+by=c, \dots\dots\dots\dots\dots\dots\dots\dots$ (i)

$\qquad\qquad\qquad bx+ay=d, \dots\dots\dots\dots\dots\dots\dots\dots$(ii)

Multiplying (i) by b, we get $\quad abx+b^2y=bc$

$\quad$,, $\quad$ (ii) by a, we get $\quad \dfrac{abx+a^2y=ad}{}$

By subtraction, $\qquad\qquad \overline{b^2y-a^2y=bc-ad}$

or $\qquad\qquad y(b^2-a^2)=bc-ad\ ;$

$$\therefore \quad y=\frac{bc-ad}{b^2-a^2}.$$

To obtain x we may either substitute for y, or proceed to eliminate y from (i) and (ii).

Thus multiplying (i) by a, $\qquad a^2x+aby=ac$

$\quad$,, $\quad$ (ii) by b, $\qquad\qquad \dfrac{b^2x+aby=bd}{}$

Subtracting the upper line from lower, $\ \overline{(b^2-a^2)x=bd-ac}$

$$\therefore \quad x=\frac{bd-ac}{b^2-a^2}.$$

From the preceding examples the student will have seen that, in solving two simultaneous equations, the object is to determine from the two given equations a value of one of the unknowns. Using the value so obtained we proceed to find the other. The methods which may with advantage be employed in solving equations can only be quickly seen by practice.

The general methods previously explained may usually be employed. The following methods are also made use of when more than two unknowns have to be found.

Ex. 7.　Solve

$$x + y + z = 53 \dots\dots\dots\dots\dots \text{(i)}$$
$$x + 2y + 3z = 105 \dots\dots\dots\dots \text{(ii)}$$
$$x + 3y + 4z = 134 \dots\dots\dots\dots \text{(iii)}$$

Subtract (i) from (ii),　$\therefore\; y + 2z = 52 \dots\dots\dots\dots \text{(iv)}$

,,　　(ii) from (iii),　$\underline{\quad y + z = 29} \dots\dots\dots\dots \textbf{(v)}$

By subtracting (v) from (iv),　$z = 23$

Substitute this value for z in (v),

$$\therefore\; y + 23 = 29;$$
or　　　　　　　　$y = 29 - 23 = 6.$

Again substituting for y and z in (i),

$$x + 6 + 23 = 53;$$
$$\therefore\; x = 53 - 29 = 24.$$

Hence the values are
$$\left. \begin{array}{l} x = 24, \\ y = 6, \\ z = 23. \end{array} \right\}$$

EXERCISES.　XXIV.

Solve the equations :

1. $2x + 5y = 23,$
$4x - 3y = 7.$

2. $3x - 2y = 7,$
$7x - 3y = 18.$

3. $77x - 15y = 8,$
$14x + 21y = 6 \cdot 2.$

4. $14x - 9y = 5,$
$35x + 6y = 3.$

5. $\dfrac{3}{5}x + \dfrac{y}{4} = 13,$

$\dfrac{x}{3} - \dfrac{y}{8} = 3.$

6. $\dfrac{4x}{5} + \dfrac{5y}{6} = 18,$

$\dfrac{x}{2} - \dfrac{y}{3} = 1.$

7. $33x + 35y = 4$; $55x - 55y = -16$.

8. $\frac{1}{3}(x + y) = \frac{1}{5}(x - y)$; $3x + 11y = 4$.

9. $\frac{1}{5}(x + y) = \frac{1}{7}(x - y)$; $3x + 17y = 2$.

10. $\frac{x}{6} + \frac{y}{5} = 14$; $\frac{x}{9} + \frac{y}{2} = 24$.   11. $\frac{x}{8} + \frac{y}{3} = 15$; $\frac{x}{4} - \frac{y}{5} = 4$.

12. $x + \frac{y - 11}{3} = 15$; $\frac{x - 5}{4} + 2y = 36$.

13. $91x + 8y = 15$,
    $21x - 35y = -5 \cdot 75$.

14. $x + 2y + 3z = 4$,
    $x + 3y + 2 = 4z$,
    $x + 2z + 3 = 4y$.

15. $(a - b)x + (a + b)y = a^2 - b^2$,
    $(a + b)x - (a - b)y = 2ab$.

16. $(b - a)x - (c - b)y = c - a$,
    $(a - c)x - (b - a)y = b - c$.

17. $ax - by = a^2$,
    $bx - ay = b^2$.

18. $11x - 13y = 40$,
    $10x - 12y = 35 + \frac{9}{11}$.

19. $3x + 5y = \frac{155}{14}$,
    $9x - 10y = -\frac{30}{7}$.

20. $x + y = a + b$,
    $\frac{x + a}{y + b} = \frac{b}{a}$.

21. $5abx + 2y = 16b$; $3abx + 4y = 18b$.

22. $(b - a)x - (c - b)y = c - a$; $(a - c)x - (b - a)y = b - c$.

23. $\frac{2}{x} + y = 1$; $\frac{1}{x} + 2y = 1\frac{1}{4}$.

24. $2x + \frac{y - 2}{5} = 21$; $4y + \frac{x - 4}{6} = 29$.

25. $\frac{1}{2}(4x + 5y) = 20(x - y)$; $\frac{1}{6}(4x - 2y) + 2y = \frac{1}{2}$.

26. $3x - \frac{4y}{3} = 1$; $\frac{5x}{3} - 2y = -7$.   27. $ax + by = c$; $cx - ay = b$.

28. $3x + 2\frac{2}{3} = 4(y - 1) = 2(x + y - 1)$.

Problems involving Simultaneous Equations.—We have
already found that to solve a simultaneous equation it is essential to have as many independent equations as there are unknown quantities to determine.

Therefore, in the solution of any problem which produces a simultaneous equation, it is necessary in the statement of the question that there should be as many equations involved as there are unknowns to be determined.

Ex. 1. If 3 be added to the numerator of a certain fraction, its value will be $\frac{1}{3}$, and if 1 be subtracted from the denominator, its value will be $\frac{1}{5}$. What is the fraction?

Let x be the numerator and y the denominator of the fraction.

Add 3 to the numerator, then $\dfrac{x+3}{y} = \dfrac{1}{3}$.

Subtract 1 from the denominator, and $\dfrac{x}{y-1} = \dfrac{1}{5}$;

$$\therefore \frac{x+3}{y} = \frac{1}{3}, \text{ and } \frac{x}{y-1} = \frac{1}{5};$$

$$\therefore 3x + 9 = y, \dotfill \text{(i)}$$

and

$$5x = y - 1. \dotfill \text{(ii)}$$

Transposing we get

$$y - 3x = 9, \dotfill \text{(iii)}$$

$$y - 5x = 1. \dotfill \text{(iv)}$$

Subtracting (iv) from (iii), $\quad 2x = 8; \therefore x = 4.$

Substituting this value of x in (iii),

$$y - 12 = 9; \therefore y = 21.$$

Hence the fraction is $\frac{4}{21}$.

Ex. 2. A number of two digits is equal in value to double the product of its digits, and also equal to twelve times the excess of the unit's digit over the digit in the ten's place; find the number.

If we denote the digits by x and y, and y denote the digit in the unit's place, then the number may be represented by $10x + y$. But this is equal to double the product of the digits;

$$\therefore 10x + y = 2xy. \dotfill \text{(i)}$$

The excess of the unit's digit over the digit in the ten's place is $y - x$, and we are given that

$$12(y - x) = 2xy. \dotfill \text{(ii)}$$

Hence $\qquad 10x + y = 12y - 12x;$

$$\therefore 22x = 11y \text{ or } 2x = y. \dotfill \text{(iii)}$$

Substituting this value in (i) we get

$$5y + y = y^2;$$

$$\therefore 6y = y^2 \text{ or } y = 6;$$

and from (iii), $\qquad x = 3.$

Hence the number is 36.

Ex. 3. Find two numbers in the ratio of 2 to 3, but which are in the ratio of 5 to 7 when 4 is added to each.

Let x and y denote the two numbers.

Then the first condition that the two numbers are in the ratio of 2 to 3 is expressed by

$$\frac{x}{y} = \frac{2}{3}. \qquad \qquad \text{(i)}$$

Similarly, the latter condition, that when 4 is added to each of them the two numbers are in the ratio of 5 to 7, is expressed by

$$\frac{x+4}{y+4} = \frac{5}{7}. \qquad \qquad \text{(ii)}$$

From (i) $\qquad\qquad\qquad 3x = 2y. \qquad\qquad\qquad\text{(iii)}$

From (ii) $\qquad 7x + 28 = 5y + 20 \text{ or } 7x + 8 = 5y. \qquad \text{(iv)}$

Multiplying (iii) by 5 and we obtain $\qquad\qquad 15x = 10y$

,,   (iv) by 2   ,, $\qquad\qquad 14x + 16 = 10y$

Subtracting, $\qquad\qquad\qquad\qquad\qquad \overline{ x - 16 = 0}$

$$\therefore \; x = 16$$

From (iii) $\qquad\qquad\qquad y = \tfrac{3}{2}x = 24.$

Hence the two numbers are 16 and 24.

The unknown quantities to be found from a simultaneous equation are not necessarily expressed as x and y. It is frequently much more convenient to use other letters. Thus *pressure*, *volume*, and *temperature* may be denoted by p, v, and t respectively.

Also, *effort* and *resistance* may be indicated by the letters E and R.

It will be obvious that letters consistently used in this manner at once suggest, by mere inspection, the quantities to which they refer.

Some Applications.—It is often necessary to express the relation between two variable quantities by means of a formula, or equation. The methods by which such variable quantities are *plotted* and the law obtained are explained on p. 145, but practice in solving a simultaneous equation is necessary before any such law can be determined.

Ex. 4. The law of a machine is given by

$$R = aE + b, \qquad\qquad\qquad\qquad\text{(i)}$$

and it is found that when R is 40, E is 10, and when R is 220, E is 50; find a and b.

Substituting the given values in (i) we get

$$220 = 50a + b \quad \dotfill \text{(ii)}$$
$$40 = 10a + b \quad \dotfill \text{(iii)}$$

Subtracting, $180 = 40a$

$$\therefore \quad a = \tfrac{180}{40} = 4 \cdot 5.$$

Substituting this value in (iii),

$$b = 40 - 10 \times 4 \cdot 5 = -5.$$

Hence the required law is $R = 4 \cdot 5E - 5$.

EXERCISES. XXV.

1. If 2 be added to the numerator and denominator of a certain fraction its value will be $\frac{1}{2}$, and if 2 be subtracted from numerator and denominator its value is $\frac{1}{3}$; what is the fraction?

2. Find three numbers such that the product of the first and the sum of the second and third is 152; the product of the second and the sum of the first and third is 162; and the product of the third and the sum of the first and second is 170.

3. The area of a certain rectangle is equal to the area of a square whose side is three inches longer than one of the sides of the rectangle. If the breadth of the rectangle be decreased by one inch, and its length increased by two inches, the area is unaltered; find the lengths of the sides.

4. Of two squares of carpet, one measures 44 feet more round than the other, and 187 square feet more in area; what are their sizes?

5. There are two coins such that 15 of the first, and 14 of the second, have the same value as 35 of the first and 6 of the second; what is the ratio of the value of the first coin to that of the second?

6. If $\dfrac{4x + 5y}{3x - y} = 2$, find the ratio of x to y.

7. The volume of the first of two cylinders is to that of the second as $11 : 8$, and the height of the first is to that of the second as $3 : 4$; if the base of the first has an area of $16 \cdot 5$ square feet, what is the area of the second?

8. The first of two pictures is 1 ft. 6 in. by 2 ft., the second 2 ft. by 2 ft. 6 in.; they are to be framed in the same way. If the glass and frame of the former cost 7s. 6d., and that of the latter 11s. 2d., what is the price of the glass per square foot, and of the frame per foot of its length?

9. If the first of two numbers diminished by the reciprocal of the second equals the second number diminished by the reciprocal of the first, show that either the numbers are equal or the one is the reciprocal of the other.

10. A farmer has to pay rates amounting to 1s. 6d. an acre, but an allowance of 10 per cent. off his rent amounts to £5 more than the rates. If the rates amounted to 2s. 6d. an acre they would just be met by an allowance of 15 per cent. off the rent ; find the number of acres in the farm and the total rent.

11. If $x : y :: 11 : 15$; find what values of x and y satisfy the equation $5x + 7y = 32$.

12. The circumference of the large wheel of a carriage is $3\frac{1}{2}$ times that of the small wheel; the smaller wheel makes 10 turns more than the large wheel in running 21 yards ; find the circumference of each wheel.

13. At present B's age is to A's in the ratio of 4 to 3; but fifteen years ago it was in the ratio of 3 to 2 ; find their ages.

14. A number of two digits is equal to double the product of its digits, and also equal to four times their sum ; find the number.

15. Find a fraction in which the denominator exceeds the numerator by 3, and is equal to $\frac{1}{2}$ when 2 is added to the denominator.

16. The law of a machine is given by $E = aR + C$; it is found that when $R = 10$ E is $5\cdot46$, and when R is 100 E is $9\cdot6$; find a and b.

17. A number consisting of two digits becomes 110 when the number obtained by reversing the digits is added to it ; also the first number exceeds unity by 8 times the excess of the second number over zero ; what is the number?

18. £1000 is divided between A, B, C, and D. B gets half as much as A ; the excess of C's share over D's share is equal to one-third of A's share, and if B's share were increased by £100 he would have as much as C and D have between them ; find how much each gets.

19. The law of a machine is given by $E = aR + b$. When E is $4\cdot2$ R is 10, and when E is $7\cdot34$ R is 20 ; find a and b.

Summary.

Simultaneous Equations.—In an equation which contains two unknown quantities x and y, an indefinite number of pairs of values may be found which will satisfy the equation ; but if a second independent equation be given, only one pair can be found which will simultaneously satisfy both equations.

SECTION IV.—GRAPHIC REPRESENTATION OF VARYING QUANTITIES.

CHAPTER XVII.

USE OF SQUARED PAPER: PLOTTING. EQUATION OF A LINE. PLOTTING A CURVE.

Use of Squared Paper.—Two quantities, the results of a number of observations or experiments, which are so related that any alteration in one produces a corresponding change in the other, can be best represented by a **graphic method**, in which it is possible to ascertain by inspection the relation that one variable quantity bears to the other.

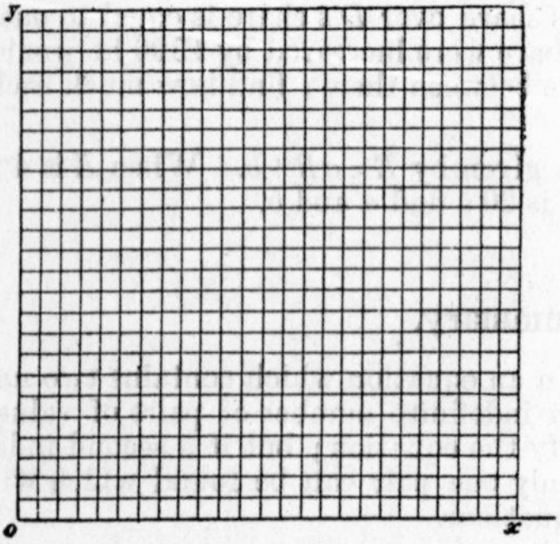

For this purpose *squared paper*—or paper having equi-distant vertical and horizontal lines $\frac{1}{10}''$, $\frac{1}{4}''$, 1 mm., etc., apart—is employed; these cover the surface of the paper with little squares (Fig. 66).

Commencing at the lowest left-hand corner of the paper, the lowest horizontal line may be taken as one axis, or line of

FIG. 66.—Squared paper

reference, and the vertical line nearest the left edge of the paper as the other axis.

The two lines ox and oy at right angles are called **axes**. The horizontal line ox is called the axis of **abscissae**; oy is the axis of **ordinates**.

One or more sides of the squares, measured along the line ox, is taken as the unit of measurement in one set of the observations; and, in a similar way, one or more sides of the squares bordered by the line oy is taken as the unit of the other set of observations.

Then for any pair of observations two points are obtained, one on ox and the other on oy.

If a vertical line is drawn upon the squared paper, from the point on ox, and a horizontal line from the point on oy, the two lines intersect, and by dealing with a number of pairs of observations a series of points may be obtained upon the squared paper; these are usually marked with a small cross or circle, and may be joined by a light line.

The line so drawn connecting the points may form a fairly uniform curve; but if, as is often the case, the line is irregular and broken, a uniform curve, lying evenly among the points, should be drawn (this may be done by bending a thin piece of wood). The curve so drawn represents the average value of the results, and serves to check errors of observation.

In the case of experimental results, the points are arranged where possible to lie as nearly as possible on a straight line. When the results are plotted as described the line which most nearly agrees with the results may be obtained by using a piece of black thread. This thread is stretched and placed on the paper, moved about as required until a good average position lying most evenly among the points is obtained.

A better plan is to use a **strip of celluloid** on which a line has been drawn, the transparency of the strip allowing the points underneath it to be clearly seen. When the position of the line is determined, two points are marked at its extremities, and the line is inserted by using a straight edge or the edge of a set square.

It should be carefully noted that the word *curve* is often used to denote *any line, whether straight or curved*, representing the relation between two quantities.

The advantage due to this method is obvious; although from

a series of numbers an average value may be obtained by the
ordinary arithmetical methods, any gradual change, and more
especially the relation of the. change to the result, is either
disregarded or may not be noticed.

The following examples will serve to illustrate the methods
used :

Ex. 1.   *To ascertain, without calculation, the number of centimetres
in a given number of inches ; or conversely, the number of inches in a
given number of centimetres.*

From p. 163 we may obtain the following list :

Inches.	Centimetres.
1	2·54
2	5·08
2½	6·4
3½	8·89

Use the vertical axis *OY* to denote inches and the horizontal
axis *OX* to denote centimetres (Fig. 67).   We read off 2·54 on the

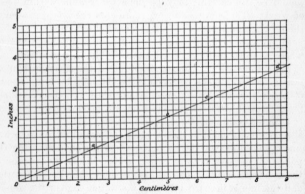

FIG. 67.—To ascertain by inspection the number of centimetres in a
given number of inches.

horizontal axis and 1 on the vertical, so obtaining point *a*.   The
point *b* is the intersection of the two lines denoting 5·08 horizontal
and 2 vertical.

In a similar manner points c and d are obtained; a fine line drawn evenly through the points enables any intermediate value to be obtained.

The equivalent value in centimetres of any given number of inches, or conversely, the equivalent in inches of any given number of centimetres, can be found by inspection by means of a curve, or line, of this kind. In a similar manner, if the divisions on the vertical or the horizontal axis are made to denote square inches and those along the other axis square centimetres the conversion from one to the other is readily made. The relation between pounds and kilograms can be obtained in a similar manner.

Equation of a Line.—In the preceding example, the position of a point a is ascertained if we proceed along the horizontal axis a distance equal to 2·54 units, and a distance of one unit parallel to the vertical axis.

The vertical distance is called the y co-ordinate, and the horizontal distance the x co-ordinate of the point.

In a similar manner the co-ordinates of another point b are $x = 5·08$, $y = 2$.

When, as in the preceding example, the relation between the two variables can be represented by a straight line, we can obtain what is called the *equation of the line*.

The equation of the line is of the form

$$y = ax + b \dots\dots\dots\dots\dots\dots \text{(i)}$$

where a and b are constants. Then, if in (i) simultaneous values of x and y are inserted, the values of a and b can be found.

Thus, when $\qquad y = 1, \quad x = 2·54$;

also when $\qquad y = 2, \quad x = 5·08.$

Substituting these values in (i) we obtain

$$2 = a \times 5·08 + b \dots\dots\dots\dots\dots\dots \text{(ii)}$$
$$1 = a \times 2·54 + b \dots\dots\dots\dots\dots\dots\text{(iii)}$$

By subtraction $\qquad \overline{1 = a \times 2·54}$

$$\therefore \ a = \frac{1}{2·54} = ·39.$$

Also substituting this value for a in (ii) or (iii) we find $b = 0$. Hence the equation of the line is $y = ·39x$.

Conversely, whenever the equation of a line is given in the form

$$y = ax + b \quad \dots\dots\dots\dots\dots\dots\dots\dots\dots\dots\dots\dots (ii)$$

by giving to x the values 1, 2, 3..., corresponding values of y are obtained which may be plotted and the line obtained.

Plotting a Line.—In a similar manner to that of the last examples, from a series of values of any two quantities which vary dependently with each other, we are able, in many cases, by plotting on squared paper, to obtain the line which lies most evenly among the points. The line so drawn will correct errors of data, or observation. Having obtained the line, we may proceed to find its equation. When the line and its equation have been found, then for any given value of one variable, the corresponding value of the other can either be obtained from the line by inspection, or from the equation by calculation.

Conversely, given the equation of a line, then by assuming a series of values for one variable, it is easy, by calculation, to find the corresponding values of the other, and to plot it. Exercises of this kind give clear notions as to the exact meaning of the two constants a and b in the equation $y = ax + b$.

It is advisable at the outset to assume definite numerical values for a and b, and to plot the line. When this has been done the constants should be altered and the line again plotted, it will be found that **the slope** or inclination of the line depends on the term a, the point at which the line, or line produced, cuts the axis of y on the term b.

The two variables are not necessarily indicated by the letters x and y, in many cases other letters may be used with advantage. Thus the forces applied to a machine called the **effort** and the **resistance** may be denoted by the letters E and R.

As R alters in value, E, which depends on R, also alters, and the "Law of the machine," as it is called, may be written in the form $E = aR + b$.

Ex. 2.   Let $y = x + 2$ be a given equation.

When $x = 0$, $y = 2$; $x = 1$, $y = 3$; $x = 2$, $y = 4$.

Corresponding values of x and y may be tabulated in two columns, thus:

Values of x	0	1	2	3	4	5	6
Values of y	2	3	4	5	6	7	8

When $x=0$, $y=2$; hence, as in Fig. 68, this gives one point in the line. When $x=1$, $y=3$; make a small dot or cross at the point of intersection of the lines 1 and 3. Again, when $x=2$, $y=4$; at the intersection of the lines through 2 and 4, make a cross or dot. Proceeding in this manner, any number of points lying on the line are obtained, and the points joined by a fine line.

Conversely, assuming that the line represents a series of plotted results of two variables E and R. To find the law connecting the two it is only necessary to substitute in the equation $E=aR+b$, the simultaneous known values of two points in the line; this will give two equations from which a and b can be determined as in the previous example.

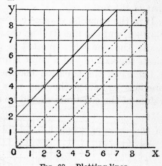

Let the values along oy represent values of E, and those along oX values of R; ∴ from the line (Fig. 68)

FIG. 68.—Plotting lines.

when E is 3, R is 1,

when E is 8, R is 6.

Substituting these values in the equation;

$$\therefore \quad 3=a\times 1+b \dots\dots\dots\dots\dots\dots (i)$$
$$8=a\times 6+b \dots\dots\dots\dots\dots\dots (ii)$$

Subtracting $5=5a$ ∴ $a=1$.

Hence from (i) $b=3-1=2$.

Substituting these values for a and b, the required equation is
$$E=R+2.$$

It will be noticed that the value of the term b gives the point in the axis of y from which the line is drawn. By altering the value of b, the term a remaining constant a series of parallel lines are obtained. Thus, let $b=0$, then the equation becomes $y=x$. ∴ when $x=0$, $y=0$, and the result obtained by plotting values of x and corresponding values of y is a line parallel to the preceding, but passing through the origin.

Again, let $b=-2$. ∴ when $x=0$, $y=-2$, and we obtain a line parallel to the preceding, intersecting the axis of y at a distance -2, or 2 units below the origin the equation is now $y=x-2$. The three lines are shown in Fig. 68.

When the term b remains unchanged, but the magnitude of a is altered, then when plotted a series of lines are obtained, all drawn from the same point, but each at a different inclination to the axis of x, or better, the **slope** of each line is different from that of the rest.

If in the equation $y=ax+b$, $a=1$, $b=2$, the equation becomes $y=x+2$, and the line (i) (Fig. 68) is obtained. When $a=0$, then $y=2$; the line when plotted is parallel to the axis of x, and meets the axis of y at a point 2 units above the origin.

Let $a=4$, the equation becomes $y=4x+2$, proceeding as in previous examples the line may readily be obtained. Other values of the constants should be assumed and the lines drawn.

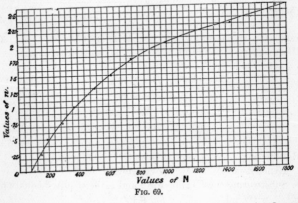

FIG. 69.

In the preceding examples it has been possible to draw a straight line through the plotted points, and to obtain an equation connecting the two variables. When, however, the plotted points lie on a curve, it would be difficult, if not impossible, to express the relation between the two variables by means of a law or an equation. In such cases a straight line may often be obtained by plotting one of the variables, and instead of the other, quantities derivable from it. The *logarithms, the reciprocals, or the squares, etc., of the given numbers.*

Thus, when a cord is passed round a fixed cylinder and a force N is applied at one end and a force M at the other, the cord remains at rest not only when N is equal to M but also when N is increased. If the increase in N is made gradually a value is obtained at which the cord just begins to slip on the cylinder. The amount by which N must be greater than M when slipping occurs is readily found by experiment, and depends not only on the surfaces in contact, but also on the fractional part of the circumference of the cylinder embraced by the cord.

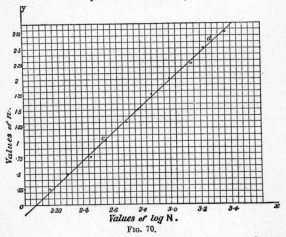

FIG. 70.

Ex. 3. Denoting by n the fractional part of the circumference of a cylinder embraced by a cord, then the following table gives a series of values of n and corresponding values of N. Find the relation between n and N.

n	·25	·5	·75	1	1·25	1·5	1·75	2	2·25	2·5	2·75
N	150	195	295	375	515	615	755	1045	1435	1735	**2335**
Log N	2·1761	2·29	2·4698	2·5740	2·7118	2·7889	2·8779	3·0191	3·1568	3·2393	3·3683

When simultaneous values of n and N are plotted, a curve lying evenly among the points (Fig. 69) can be found; but by plotting n and $\log N$ (Fig. 70) the points lie approximately on a straight line. The relation between n and $\log N$ may be expressed in the form

$$n = a \log N + b.$$

To find the numerical values of the constants a and b it is only necessary for two points on the line to substitute simultaneous values of n and $\log N$, thus obtaining two equations from which a and b can be obtained

Thus at c (Fig. 70), $n = 1$, $\log N = 2\cdot54$,

and at d, $n = 2\cdot6$, $\log N = 3\cdot28$.

Hence $2\cdot6 = a \times 3\cdot28 + b$ .... (i)

                 $1 = a \times 2\cdot54 + b$ ....(ii)

By subtraction, $1\cdot6 = a \times \quad \cdot74$

$$\therefore \quad a = \frac{1\cdot6}{\cdot74} = 2\cdot162.$$

And substituting this value for a in (i) we have

$$b = 2\cdot6 - 2\cdot162 \times 3\cdot28 = -4\cdot49.$$

Hence the relation between the variables is expressed by

$$n = 2\cdot162 \log N - 4\cdot49.$$

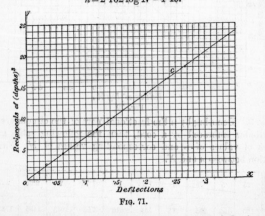

Fig. 71.

Ex. 4. The depths d, and deflections δ when loaded, of a series of beams of varying depths and constant breadths are given in the annexed table. Find the equation connecting d and δ.

d	1	·75	·625	·5	·375	·25
δ	·02	·033	·06	·118	·27	·934
$\dfrac{1}{d^3}$	1	2·37	4·1	8	18·9	64

When the variables d and δ are plotted a curve is obtained, but by plotting δ and $\dfrac{1}{d^3}$ a straight line, lying evenly among the points, can be drawn as in Fig. 71. The line passes through the origin, and its equation may be written $\delta = a \times \dfrac{1}{d^3}$.

From Fig. 71 at c, $\qquad \delta = \cdot 25$ and $\dfrac{1}{d^3} = 17$.

Hence $\qquad \cdot 25 = a \times 17$; $\quad \therefore \quad a = \dfrac{\cdot 25}{17} = \cdot 0147.$

The relation is therefore $\quad \delta = \cdot 0147 \,\dfrac{1}{d^3}.$

Ex. 5. The following table gives a series of values of the breadths b and deflections δ of a series of beams of constant depths and variable breadths ; find the equation connecting b and δ.

b	·25	·375	·5	·625	·7	1
δ	·03	·017	·014	·011	·009	·007
$\dfrac{1}{b}$	4	2·67	2	1·6	1·43	1

If the first two columns are plotted the points lie on a curve, but by plotting the second and last columns δ and $\dfrac{1}{b}$ (Fig. 72), a straight line through the points and passing through the origin may be drawn. At the point c, $\delta = \cdot 024$ and $\dfrac{1}{b} = 3 \cdot 2$. Substituting these values in the equation $\delta = a \times \dfrac{1}{b}$, the relation between the variables is found to be $\delta = \cdot 007 \times \dfrac{1}{b}.$

Simultaneous Equations.—Two general methods of solving simultaneous equations have been described on p. 132 ; another, which may be called a graphical method, is furnished by using squared paper. The method applied to the solution of a simul-

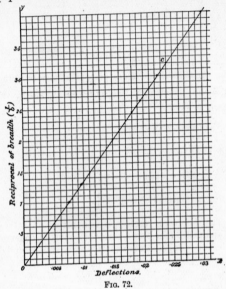

FIG. 72.

taneous equation containing two unknown quantities, consists in plotting the two lines given by the two equations. When this is done the point of intersection of the two lines is obtained. This is a point common to both lines, and as the co-ordinates of the point obviously satisfy both equations, it is the solution required.

Ex. 1. Solve the simultaneous equations

(i) $3x + 4y = 18$,   (ii) $4x - 2y = 2$.

From (i) $y = \dfrac{18 - 3x}{4}$. ....(iii)

From (ii) $y = 2x - 1$. ....(iv)

To plot the lines it is sufficient to obtain two points in each and join the points by straight lines.

In (iii) when $x = 0$, $y = 4 \cdot 5$ and when $x = 5$, $y = \cdot 75$, the first gives

point a (Fig. 73), the second point b.   Join a and b and the line
corresponding to Eq. (iii) is obtained.

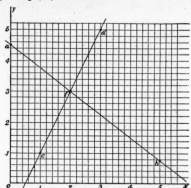

FIG. 73.—Solution of simultaneous equation.

In Eq. (iv) when $x=1$, $y=1$ and when $x=3$, $y=5$, the first gives
point c, the second gives d.   Join c and d and the two lines are
seen to cross at f. This point of intersection is a point common to
both lines, its co-ordinates are seen to be $x=2$, $y=3$ and these
values satisfy the given simultaneous equations.

  Ex. 2.   Plot the two lines given by

$$4x+3y=37, \text{ and } 6x+4\cdot5y=13,$$

and show that the two lines are parallel to each other.

EXERCISES. XXVI.

1. Graph $y=ax+b$ (i) when $b=0$, $a=1$, (ii) $b=1$, $a=1\frac{1}{2}$,
                       (iii) $b=1\frac{1}{2}$, $a=2\cdot25$,   (iv) $b=-1$, $a=1\cdot5$.

2. The following observed values of E and R are supposed to be
related by a linear law of the form $E=aR+b$.   Find by plotting the
given values of E and R the most probable values of a and b.
  (i)

E	6·5	7·75	9	10	11	12	13	14	15	16
R	14	21	28	35	42	49	56	63	70	77

(ii)

E	9·46	13·71	17·96	22·46	26·71	30·96
R	28	42	56	70	84	98

(iii)

E	1·7	2·7	3·7	4·7	5·7	6·56
R	28	42	56	70	84	98

(iv)

E	·5	·812	1·125	1·375	1·75	2·062	2·687
R	14	28	42	56	70	84	112

(v)

E	4·5	5·25	6·0	6·75	7·5	8·25	9·0	9·75	10·5	12·0	13·5	15·0	16·5
R	0	7	14	21	28	35	42	49	56	70	84	98	112

(vi)

E	6	6·5	7·07	8	9·06	10	10·98	12	13·93
R	126	138	150	171	195	217	238	261	305

3. In the following examples a series of observed values of E, R and F are given. In each case they are known to follow laws approximately represented by $E = aR + b$, $F = cR + d$; but there are errors of observation. Plot the given values on squared paper, and determine in each case the most probable values of a, b, c and d.

(i)

E	3·5	5	6·75	8·25	9·75	11·5	13·25	14·5
R	14	28	42	56	70	84	98	112
F	2·92	3·83	5·00	5·92	6·83	8·00	9·17	9·83

(ii)

E	·5	1	1·5	2	2·5	3	3·5	4
R	4	15	28	40	52	64	76	88
F	32	57	80	104	128	162	176	200

(iii)

E	3·25	4·25	5	5·75	6·75	7·5	8·5	9·25	10
R	14	21	28	35	42	49	56	63	70
F	2·68	3·39	3·86	4·32	5·04	5·5	6·22	6·68	7·14

(iv)

E	·5	1	1·5	2	2·5	3	3·5	4	4·5
R	9·5	23·5	38	51	64·5	77	89	100·5	112
F	26·2	47·8	69·0	91·6	113·5	137	160·3	184·8	209

(v)

E	3·0	3·62	4·5	5·0	6·25	6·50	7·37	8·0	9·0	10·0	12·5
R	14	21	28	35	42	49	56	63	70	84	112
F	2·41	2·75	3·33	3·54	4·5	4·45	5·04	5·37	6·08	6·5	7·83

(vi)

E	·31	·47	·59	·64	·69	·73	·78	·83	·87	·93	·97	1
R	7	9	11	12	13	14	15	16	17	18	19	20
F	·032	·112	·150	·164	·170	·175	·178	·180	·194	·208	·21	·22

(vii)

E	1·23	1·73	2·73	3·23	4·23	4·73	5·23	5·73	6·23	6·48	6·73
R	3·17	4·42	7·13	8·41	11·14	12·47	13·72	15·08	16·46	17·08	17·73
F	·112	·174	·23	·277	·319	·368	·393	·436	·454	·484	·506

(viii)

E	·875	1·375	1·875	2·375	2·875	3·37	3·87	4·37	4·87
R	9·2	23·0	37·5	51·5	65·5	79·5	94·0	107	122
F	53·8	66·0	97·5	119·5	141·5	163·5	185	208	229

4. Find the relation between n and $\log N$ from the values given in the annexed table.

n	·25	·5	·75	1·0	1·25	1·5	1·75	2·0	2·25	2·5
N	96	122	150	185	245	305	355	435	515	625
$\text{Log } N$	1·982	2·086	2·176	2·268	2·39	2·485	2·551	2·639	2·712	2·796

5. In the following tables a series of observed values of n and N are given ; find the relation between n and $\log N$.

(i)

n	·25	·5	·75	1	1·25	1·5	1·75	2	2·25	2·5	2·75
N	154	180	265	375	485	635	835	1135	1535	1835	2435

(ii)

n	·25	·5	·75	1	1·25	1·5	1·75	2·0	2·5	3·0
N	145	186	235	296	385	495	558	683	1115	1515

(iii)

N	440	445	470	480	505	515	530	545	568
n	3·14	2·82	2·54	2·25	1·87	1·57	1·25	·965	·654

If in (i) $M = 85$, in (ii) $M = 135$, (iii) $M = 610$, find in each case the relation between n and $\log \dfrac{N}{M}$.

6. In the annexed table, values of L, the length of a liquid column, and T, its time of vibration, are given. The relation between L and T^2 is given by $L = aT^2 + b$; find a and b.

L	2·4	2·8	3·0	3·2	3·4	3·6
T	1·06	1·23	1·29	1·34	1·38	1·42
T^2	1·12	1·51	1·66	1·79	1·90	2·02

Plotting a Curve.—When an equation connecting two variables is given, then it has been seen that by giving to one of the variables a series of values, corresponding values of the other can be obtained.

Ex. 1. To graph, or plot a curve, the equation of which is $4y = x^2$;

$$\therefore y = \frac{x^2}{4} \dots\dots\dots\dots\dots\dots\dots\dots\dots\dots\dots\dots(i)$$

By giving a series of values to x, 1, 2, 3, etc., we can obtain from Eq. (i) corresponding values of y.

Thus, when $x = 0$, $y = 0$,

also when $x = 1$, $y = \frac{1}{4}$.

It will be convenient to arrange the two sets of values of x and y as follows :

Values of x, - -	0	1	2	3	4	5	...	...	...
Corresponding values of y, - - - }	0	$\frac{1}{4}$	1	$2\frac{1}{4}$	4	$6\frac{1}{4}$	...	...	..

As y is 0 when x is 0, the curve passes through the origin (or point of intersection of the axes). Plotting the values of x and y from the two columns, as shown in Fig. 74, a series of points are obtained.

A curve can be drawn through the plotted points either freehand or by bending a thin slip of wood.

It is sometimes difficult to draw a fairly uniform curve through plotted points, but when a curve has been drawn improvements may be made, or faults detected, by simply holding the paper on which the curve is drawn at the level of the eye, and looking along the curve. Some such simple device should always be used.

The curve plotted is of the form $y = ax^2$, and is known to be a **parabola**.

As the square of either a positive or a negative number is necessarily positive, it follows that two values of x, equal in magnitude but opposite in sign, correspond to each value found for y. By using positive values of x, the curve shown on the right of the line oy is obtained. The negative values give the corresponding curve on the left.

The constant a has been assumed to be positive, and equal to $\frac{1}{4}$.

If the constant a be negative, its numerical value remaining the same, then the equation becomes $y = -\frac{1}{4}x^2$; this when plotted will be found to be another parabola below the axis of x (Fig. 74).

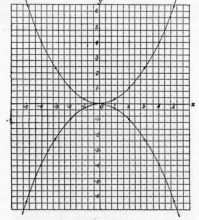

Fig. 74.—Graph of $4y = x^2$.

The space described by a body moving with uniform acceleration f is known to be given by the equation $s = \frac{1}{2}ft^2$.

Ex. 2. Plot the curve $s = \frac{1}{2}ft^2$; (a) assuming $f = \pm 4$, (b) $f = \pm 8$; (c) $f = \pm 32$ (values of t can be set off along ox, and corresponding values of s along oy).

Ex. 4.   Plot the curve $x^2 + y^2 = 20$.

First transpose and get $y^2 = 20 - x^2$;

$$\therefore \quad y = \pm \sqrt{20 - x^2}. \quad\text{.......................................(i)}$$

Putting in (i) $x = 0, 1, 2, 3$, etc., corresponding values of y can be obtained.

Thus let $x = 1$, then $y = \pm \sqrt{20 - 1} = \pm \sqrt{19} = \pm 4 \cdot 36$.

,,　　$x = 2$,　,,　$y = \pm \sqrt{20 - 4} = \pm 4$.

Proceeding in this manner the numbers in the following table are obtained.

(1)	x	0	1	2	3	4	4·47
(2)	y	4·47	4·36	4	3·32	2	0

As the square of a quantity, whether the quantity be negative or positive, is necessarily positive, it follows that corresponding to each value of x there are two values for y, equal in magnitude, but opposite in sign.   Thus when $x = 2$, $y = +4$ and $y = -4$.

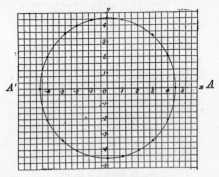

Fig. 75.—Graph of $x^2 + y^2 = 20$.

In a similar manner, whether $x = +2$ or -2, its square will be $+4$; thus the numbers in the rows (1) and (2) are to be taken as both positive and negative, *i.e.*, values of x are set off both along OA and along OA', and corresponding values of y are set off both above and below the line $A'A$.

Again, when $x=0$, $y=4\cdot47$, and when $y=0$, $x=4\cdot47$; and the maximum values of both x and y are equal, each being the radius of the circle (Fig. 75). Thus, the curve passing through the plotted points is found to be a circle, centre O, radius $4\cdot47$.

Ex. 4. Plot the curve $\dfrac{x^2}{3}+\dfrac{y^2}{4}=1$.

$$\therefore \ y=\pm4\sqrt{1-\frac{x^2}{3}}.$$

As in the last example, a table giving corresponding values of x and y can be made. Each value of x and y being positive and negative, the curve when plotted will be found to be an ellipse.

Another important curve is the **rectangular hyperbola** ; its equation is of the form $xy=c$, where c is a constant.

Let the equation be $xy=8$;

$$\therefore \ y=\frac{8}{x}\ \dotfill\text{(i)}$$

From (i), when x is 1, $y=8$. When x is $\frac{1}{2}$, $y=16$; when x is $\frac{1}{1000}$, $y=8000$, or, in other words, as the value of x is diminished, the corresponding value of y is increased.

It will be seen that when $x=0$, $y=\dfrac{8}{0}$, or is infinite in value.

In other words, the curve gets nearer and nearer to the line oy as the value of x is diminished, but does not reach the axis at any finite distance from the origin. This is expressed by the symbols $y=\infty$ when $x=0$.

As equation (i) can be written $x=\dfrac{8}{y}$, it follows, as before, that when $y=0$, $x=\infty$.

The two lines or axes OX and OY are called **asymptotes**, and are said to meet (or touch) the curve at an infinite distance from the origin.

Arranging, as before, in two columns the series of values of x and y obtained from Eq. (i), we obtain :

Values of x, - -	0	1	3	4	5	6	7	8	...
Corresponding values of y, - -	∞	8	$\frac{8}{3}$	2	$\frac{8}{5}$	$\frac{8}{6}$	$\frac{8}{7}$	1	...

The curve obtained is of the utmost importance; it is shown in Fig. 76, and should be carefully plotted, also using different values for the constant c.

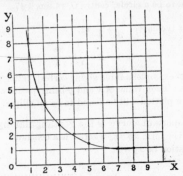

FIG. 76.—Graph of $xy=8$. A rectangular hyperbola.

The rectangular hyperbola is the curve of expansion for a gas such as air, and is often taken to represent the curve of expansion of superheated or saturated steam.

If p and v denote the *pressure* and *volume* respectively of a gas, the equation becomes $pv=$ constant $=c$.

MISCELLANEOUS EXERCISES. XXVII.

Plot the following :

1. $y=\frac{3}{2}x+2.$ **2.** $y=\frac{3}{2}x+4.$ **3.** $y=\frac{3}{2}x-2.$

4. (i) $E=\cdot26R+\cdot15$; (ii) $F=1\cdot76R+1\cdot47.$

5. (i) $E=\cdot3R+\cdot7$;   (ii) $F=\cdot3R+2\cdot5.$

6. $x^2+y^2=25.$ **7.** $\dfrac{x^2}{3}+\dfrac{y^2}{4}=25.$ **8.** $y=\cdot2x^2.$

9. $y=5x^{\frac{1}{3}}.$ **10.** $y=2x^5.$ **11.** $y=4x^{-1}$, or $xy=4.$

12. In the equation $y=x^n$, plot the curves obtained when n has the values 1, 2, 3, $\frac{1}{2}$, $\frac{1}{3}$, i.e., (i) $y=x$, (ii) $y=x^2$, (iii) $y=x^3$, (iv) $y=x^{\frac{1}{2}}$, (v) $y=x^{\frac{1}{3}}.$

13. $y^2=5x.$ **14.** $y=\dfrac{x^2}{5}.$

15. The following table gives some sizes of Whitworth bolts and nuts:

d = Diameter of bolt in inches, -	$\frac{1}{4}$	$\frac{3}{8}$	$\frac{1}{2}$	$\frac{5}{8}$	$\frac{3}{4}$	$\frac{7}{8}$	$1''$	$1\frac{1}{8}$	$1\frac{1}{4}$	$1\frac{1}{2}$
w = Width of nut and bolt - head across the flat sides, -	·52	·70	·91	1·09	1·30	1·48	1·67	1·86	2·05	2·22
W = Width across the corners, -	·62	·81	1·06	1·26	1·5	1·70	1·95	2·16	2·36	2·78
d_1 = Diameter of bolt at bottom of thread, -	·19	·29	·39	·51	·62	·73	·84	·94	1·07	1·29

(i) Plot d and w, and obtain the relation between d and w in the form $w = ad + b$, and find the constants a and b.

(ii) Plot d and W, and find the constants a and b in the relation
$$d = aW + b.$$

(iii) Plot d and d_1, and find the constants a and b in the relation
$$d = ad_1 + b.$$

(iv) Plot the results obtained from the usual rules and compare with those already drawn;

i.e. $w = 1\frac{1}{2}d + \frac{1}{8}''$, $W = 2d$.

16. The following table gives some prices of steam stop valves:

Diameter of valve in inches, -	$1\frac{1}{2}$	4	8
Price, - - -	26s. 6d.	70s.	180s.

Plot these values, and find the probable prices of valves 3 inches and 6 inches diameter respectively.

17. Some particulars of riveted lap joints are given in the following table:

$t=$Thickness of plate,	$\frac{3}{8}$	$\frac{1}{2}$	$\frac{5}{8}$	$\frac{3}{4}$	$\frac{7}{8}$	$1''$
$d=$Diameter of rivet,	$\frac{3}{4}$	$\frac{7}{8}$	$1\frac{5}{16}$	$1\frac{7}{16}$	$\frac{9}{8}$	$\frac{5}{4}$
$p_1=$Pitch of rivets (*single riveted*), -	2·06	2·25	2·3	2·37	2·40	2·63
$p_2=$Pitch of rivets (*double riveted*), -	3·33	3·58	3·60	3·63	3·63	3·95

Plot d and $\sqrt{t}$, and obtain the value of the constant a in the relation $d=a\sqrt{t}$. Using the same values for t, plot the line $d=1\cdot2\sqrt{t}$. Compare the results obtained from the two lines. Find values of d when t is $\frac{5}{16}$, $\frac{7}{16}$, and $\frac{9}{16}$. Also plot d and p_1, and d and p_2, and obtain the b and c in the relations $p_1=d+b$; $p_2=d+c$.

18. The population of a country is as follows:

Year, -	1830	1840	1850	1860	1870	1880	1890
Population (millions),	20	23·5	29·0	34·2	41·0	49·4	57·7

Find by plotting the probable population in 1835, 1865, and in 1895.

19. In a price list, the following prices occur:

12 pint kettle, price 68 pence ;
6   ,,   ,,   50   ,,
2   ,,   ,,   22   ,,

Find by plotting the probably correct prices of 4 and 8 pint sizes.

MISCELLANEOUS EXERCISES XXVIII.

Section I. Multiplication and Division.

Compute

1. (i) $8 \cdot 102 \times 35 \cdot 14$.   (ii) $254 \cdot 3 \div 0 \cdot 09027$.

2. (i) $12 \cdot 39 \times 5 \cdot 024$.   (ii) $5 \cdot 024 \div 12 \cdot 39$.

3. (i) $3 \cdot 405 \times 9 \cdot 123$.   (ii) $3 \cdot 405 \div 9 \cdot 123$.

4. (i) $0 \cdot 03056 \times 0 \cdot 4105$.   (ii) $30 \cdot 56 \div 4 \cdot 105$.

5. (i) $23 \cdot 07 \times 0 \cdot 1354$.   (ii) $2307 \div 1 \cdot 354$.

6. (i) $168 \cdot 3 \times 2 \cdot 476$.   (ii) $16 \cdot 83 \div 24 \cdot 76$.

7. (i) $0 \cdot 1683 \div 0 \cdot 002476$.

8. Why are the logarithms of two or more numbers added to obtain the logarithm of their product?

9. Why are the logarithms of two numbers subtracted to obtain the logarithm of their quotient?

10. Write down the values of : $\log_{10} 153 \cdot 4$, $\log_e 153 \cdot 4$.

Compute

11. (i) $30 \cdot 56 \div 4 \cdot 105$.   (ii) $0 \cdot 03056 \times 0 \cdot 4105$.

12. (i) $0 \cdot 9415 \times 0 \cdot 5024$.   (ii) $0 \cdot 1239 \div 50 \cdot 24$.

13. (i) $0 \cdot 5624 \times 0 \cdot 2471$.   (ii) $4 \cdot 326 \div 0 \cdot 003457$.

14. $87 \cdot 35 \div (0 \cdot 3524 \times 3 \cdot 501)$.

Section II. Involution and Evolution by Logarithms.

Compute

1. $4 \cdot 105^{1 \cdot 23}$, $0 \cdot 04105^{-2 \cdot 3}$.   2. $2 \cdot 307^{0 \cdot 65}$, $23 \cdot 07^{-1 \cdot 25}$.

3. $\sqrt[3]{37 \cdot 24}$, $\sqrt[3]{3 \cdot 724}$.   4. $372 \cdot 4^{2 \cdot 43}$, $0 \cdot 3724^{-2 \cdot 43}$.

5. The value of a ruby is said to be proportional to the 1½ power of its weight. If one ruby is exactly of the same shape as another, but of 2·2 times its linear dimensions, of how many times the value is it?

[NOTE. The weights of similar things are as the cubes of their linear dimensions.]

6. In any class of turbine if P is the power of the waterfall and H the height of the fall, and n the rate of revolution, then it is known that for any particular class of turbines of all sizes

$$n \propto H^{1·25} P^{-0·5}.$$

In the list of a particular maker I take a turbine at random for a fall of 6 feet, 100 horse-power, 50 revolutions per minute. By means of this I find I can calculate n for all the other turbines of the list. Find n for a fall of 20 feet and 75 horse-power.

7. Why is the logarithm of a number divided by 3 to obtain the logarithm of its cube root?

Why is log a multiplied by b to obtain the logarithm of a^b?

8. Compute

(i) $(1·683)^{3·65}$, (ii) $(0·01683)^{-0·26}$.

9. $97·43 \div (0·3524 \times 6·321)^{2·56}$.

10. If

$$\frac{rA}{100a} = \left(1 + \frac{r}{100}\right)^n - 1,$$

find n when $r=3$ and $A=20a$.

11. Find the value of

(i) $(1·342 \times 0·01731 \div 0·00274)^{0·317}$,

(ii) $(1·342 \times 0·01731 \div 0·0274)^{0·317}$.

12. $\sqrt{2·607}$, $26·07^{1·13}$, $26·07^{-1·13}$.

13. If $p_1 v_1^{1·13} = p_2 v_2^{1·13}$ and if v_2/v_1 be called r.

If $p_2 = 6$, find r if $p_1 = 150$.

Compute

14. $\sqrt[3]{2·354 \times 1·607}$, $(32·15)^{1·52}$.

15. Given $F = EI\pi^2 \div 4l^2$,

where $I = bt^3 \div 12$, $E = 3 \times 10^7$, $\pi = 3·142$, $l = 62$, $b = 2$, $t = 0·5$; find F.

16. Given $P = cd^{5·5}n^{3·5}$, where P denotes the horse-power wasted in air friction when a disc d feet in diameter is revolving at n revolutions per minute.

If $P = 0·1$, when $d = 4$ and $n = 500$, find the constant c. Now find P when d is 9 and n is 400.

17. If H is proportional to $D^{\frac{2}{3}}v^3$, and if D is 1810 and v is 10 when H is 620, find H if D is 2100 and v is 13.

18. If
$$\frac{T}{T_1} = \sqrt{\frac{I_0}{I_0 + I_1}},$$
find the ratio of I_1 to I_0 when $T = 2\cdot54$, $T_1 = 3\cdot27$.

19. Find the fifth root of $76\cdot52 \times 0\cdot254$.

20. Find the tenth power and the tenth root of $0\cdot7$.

21. If $m = (a^3 + 2a^2b + s^{-0\cdot345})^{\frac{3}{2}} \div (a^2b^2)^5$, find m if $a = 0\cdot504$, $b = 0\cdot309$, $s = 1\cdot567$.

22. Assuming that the squares of the periodic times of the planets vary as the cubes of the semi-major axes of their orbits, determine the semi-major axis of the orbit of Mars about the Sun from the following data :

Periodic time of Earth = 365 days.
,,   ,,   Mars = 687 ,,
Semi-major axis of Earth's orbit = 93×10^6 miles.

Section III. Area.

1. Find the area of a circle of radius $1\cdot4$ ft.

2. Find the slant height and curved surface of a right cone, the radius of the base being $1\cdot4$ ft. and the height 10 ft.

3. Find the surface of a sphere of radius $1\cdot4$ ft.

4. The ordinates of an irregular plane figure 1 inch apart are in inches as follows : $29\cdot05$, $28\cdot95$, $28\cdot45$, $28\cdot04$, $28\cdot62$, $29\cdot0$, $29\cdot95$.
Find the area of the figure, (i) using the mean of the given numbers ; (ii) using Simpson's rule.

5. The sides of a triangle are 13, 14, and 15 feet.
Find its area to the nearest square foot.

6. Find the length and weight of a wrought iron flat bar, 1 in. thick and 3 in. wide, required to make a hoop 6 ft. diameter, allowing 2 in. as overlap at the welded joint.

7. The external dimensions of a rectangular cistern are : length 6 ft. $4\frac{3}{4}$ inches, width 4 ft. $3\frac{3}{4}$ inches, and depth 5 ft. $6\frac{3}{8}$ inches. The mean thickness of the material is $\frac{3}{8}$ inch. Find the internal surface and cost of lining it with lead weighing 6 lbs. per sq. ft. and costing 3d. per lb.

8. The areas of a square and a rectangular field are equal, the lengths of the sides of the latter being $135\cdot5$ and $103\cdot8$ metres respectively. Find the cost of enclosing the square field by a fence at $2\cdot5$ francs per metre.

9. A circular lawn has an area of $\frac{1}{4}$ acre. What is its diameter ? There is a path round the lawn 6 ft. wide. What is the area of the path ?

10. A boiler contains 500 smoke tubes, each $2\frac{1}{4}$ inches internal diameter. Find the total area for draught through them.

11. The area of a square field falls short of 10 acres by 440 square yards. Find the length of each side.

12. The diameter of a circular lawn is 14 yards, and it is surrounded by a gravel path 10 ft. wide. What is the area of the gravel paths?

13. A cylinder 20 ft. long and 5 ft. in diameter is capped at one end by a hemisphere and at the other by a cone 6 ft. in altitude. Find the cost of painting the whole surface at 6d. per square yard.

14. The ordinates of a curve 1 in. apart are 4·60, 4·70, 4·92, 5·14, 4·84, 4·42, 4·20.
Find the area between the curve, the axis of x, and the first and last of the given ordinates, (i) by the Trapezoidal rule; (ii) by Simpson's rule.

15. A rectangular field contains $1\frac{3}{4}$ acres; if it were 11 yds. longer and 7 yds. narrower than it is, its area would be unaltered; find its length and breadth.

16. A circle and an equilateral triangle have each a perimeter of 12 ft. Find their areas.

17. In a rectangular field of 5 acres the length is to the breadth as 4 to 3. Find the length.

18. A plot of land measures 300 acres and is in the form of a rectangle having its length three times its breadth.
Find to the nearest yard the length of fence which would be required to enclose it.

Section IV. Volume.

1. Find the volume of a circular cylinder—radius of base 8 ft., length 14 ft.

2. Find the volume of a sphere, radius 1·4 ft.

3. A volume of 9·702 cubic feet of lead is divided into two equal parts. One part is formed into a solid sphere, the other into a cone, the radius of the base being equal to the radius of the sphere. Find the radius of the sphere and the height of the cone.

4. A hollow cylinder, radius 2 ft., contains water to a height of 1 ft. If a heavy sphere, radius 1 ft., is placed inside the cylinder, what will be the height of the water?

5. A plate of metal is 106·6 in. long, 14·6 in. wide, and 2 in. thick. Supposing it to be melted and cast into an exact cube, what would be the edge of the cube?

6. A cubic foot of copper weighs 560 lbs. It is rolled into a square bar 40 ft. long. An exact cube is cut from the bar; find its weight.

7. The edges of a rectangular box are $16\frac{2}{3}$ in., $10\frac{2}{3}$ in., and $1\frac{2}{3}$ in.; find the edge of a cubical box of the same volume, and compare the areas of the surfaces of the two boxes.

8. A lake, whose area is 5 acres, is covered with ice of a uniform thickness of 3 in.; find the weight of the ice in tons, if a cubic foot of it weighs 56 lbs.

9. Find the weight in kilograms of a cubical block of metal each of whose edges is 1·02 metres long, having given that a cubic centimetre of the metal weighs 8·95 grams.

Find also to the nearest centimetre the length of a diagonal of a face of the block.

10. A rectangular beam of wood is 5·4 metres long, 0·35 metre wide, and 0·28 metre thick. Find the weight in kilograms if the wood is three-quarters as heavy as an equal volume of water.

11. A log of timber is 36 ft. long, the areas of the cross section at equal distances of 6 feet are 8·57, 5·81, 4·05, 2·86, 2·13, 1·54, 1·05. Find the volume by the Trapezoidal and Simpson's rules.

12. Find the volume of a spherical shell, the internal and external radii being 8 ins. and 10 ins. respectively.

13. The rim of a cast-iron fly-wheel, of 10 ft. mean diameter, is 8 ins. wide and 4 ins. thick; find its weight.

14. A tube of copper (0·32 lb. per cubic inch) is 12 ft. long and 3 ins. inside diameter; it weighs 100 lbs. Find its outer diameter, and the area of its curved outer surface.

15. A cast-iron fly-wheel weighs 13,700 lbs. The rim is of rectangular section; the thickness radially is x, and its size the other way 1·6x. The inside radius of the rim is $14x$. Find the actual sizes.

16. Assuming the earth to be a sphere, if its circumference is 360×60 nautical miles, what is the circumference of the parallel of latitude 56°? What is the length there of a degree of longitude? If a small map is to be drawn in this latitude, with north and south and east and west distances to the same scale, and if a degree of latitude (which is 60 miles) is shown as 10 inches, what distance will represent a degree of longitude?

17. A brass tube, 8 feet long, has an outside diameter 3 inches, inside 2·8 inches. What is the volume of the brass in cubic inches? If a cubic inch of brass weighs 0·3 lb., what is the weight of the tube?

18. A circle is 3 inches diameter, its centre is 4 inches from a line in its plane. The circle revolves about the line as an axis and so generates a ring. Find the volume of the ring, also its surface area.

19. Two men measure a rectangular box; one finds its length, breadth, and depth in inches to be 5·32, 4·15, 3·29. The other finds them to be 5·35, 4·17, 3·33. Calculate the volume in each case; what is the mean of the two, what is the percentage difference of either from the mean?

20. A box open at the top has externally the form of a cube, each edge of which is 20 inches long; it is made up of five plates each an inch thick. Find the volume of the material in cubic inches, and show that it is nearly three-tenths of the internal volume of the box.

21. Find the surface and volume of a cylindrical anchor ring, the diameter of the cross section being 9 inches and inner diameter 32 inches.

22. A right circular cone was measured in such a way that the diameter of the base is known to be between 16·2 and 16·3 inches, and the height between 27·5 and 27·6 inches. Find the volume of the cone, using (i) the smaller, (ii) the greater dimensions.

23. A circular lake, the area of which is $\frac{1}{2}$ acre, is covered with ice of an average thickness of 2 inches; find the weight of the ice in tons if a cubic foot of it weighs 56 lbs.
Find the cost of enclosing the lake by a fence at 2s. 6d. per yard.

24. The external and internal diameters of a hollow steel cylindrical shaft are 16 and 8 inches respectively; find the area of a cross section.
If the length of such a shaft is 4 yards, find its weight.

25. The internal dimensions of a wrought-iron cylinder, with hemispherical ends, are : diameter 4 feet, total length 8 feet. How many cubic feet of water will it hold?

26. What is the weight of the metal forming the cylinder in the preceding question, if the thickness is $\frac{1}{2}$ inch?

27. The rainfall at a particular place is 29·2 inches in a year. To how many gallons per acre is this equivalent? [1 gallon = 0·1605 cub. ft.]

28. Find the number required, and the cost of the bricks needed, to build a wall 30 yards long, 6 feet high, and 13$\frac{1}{2}$ inches thick. Each brick may be taken to fill a space 9 in. long, 4$\frac{1}{2}$ in. wide and 3 in. deep, and 1000 bricks cost 25s.

29. The section of a stream is 10 ft. wide and 10 in. deep. Find the number of gallons which flow through the section in 24 hours, assuming the mean flow of water through the section is 3 miles per hour. [1 gallon = 0·1605 cub. ft.]

30. If 648 boxes are stowed close together on board a ship, find the total cost of freightage at 1s. 2d. per cubic yard, when each box measures $4\frac{1}{2}$ ft. long, 3 ft. wide, and $2\frac{1}{4}$ ft. deep.

If all the boxes are piled in the form of a cube, what is the length of an edge of the cube?

31. Find how many cwts. of lead will be required to cover an area 50 ft. long and 37 ft. 4 in. wide with a sheet of lead one-tenth of an inch thick.

32. The length and breadth of a rectangular reservoir with vertical sides are 12 ft. 3 in. and 8 ft. 4 in. respectively; its contents are 38·28 cubic yards; find its depth.

Find also the depth of a cubical reservoir of equal contents.

33. Each edge of a cube of zinc increases by 0·003 of its length for a rise of temperature of 100 degrees centigrade. If the volume of such a cube is originally 125 cubic inches, find the increase in volume when the temperature of the cube has been raised through 100°. Find also the corresponding increase in the surface of the cube.

34. A hollow cast-iron cylinder is 4·32 inches long, its external and internal diameters are 3·15 and 1·724 inches respectively. Find its volume, its weight, and the sum of the areas of its two curved surfaces.

35. A circular anchor ring has a volume 930 cub. in. and an area 620 sq. in. Find its dimensions.

36. A path 6 ft. wide is to be made on the outside of a circular lawn 30 ft. in diameter. What will be the cost of covering the path with gravel to an average depth of 3 inches, if gravel costs 3s. per cub. yard?

37. The external dimensions of a cistern are: length 6 ft. $4\frac{3}{4}$ in., width 4 ft. $3\frac{3}{4}$ in., and depth 5 ft. $6\frac{3}{8}$ in. The mean thickness of the material is $\frac{3}{8}$ in. What is the weight and the number of gallons of water which the cistern can hold?

38. A piece of copper (specific gravity 8·9) 1 ft. long, 4 in. wide, and $\frac{1}{2}$ in. thick, is drawn out into wire of uniform diameter $\frac{1}{16}$ in. Find the length and the weight of the wire.

39. A roof flat 48 ft. long and 32 ft. wide is to be covered with lead $\frac{1}{12}$ in. thick. Allowing 5 per cent. for roll joints, find the weight of lead required. [1 cub. ft. lead = 712 lbs.]

40. A cylindrical gasometer with a flat top is required to hold two million cubic feet of gas, and is 200 feet in diameter:

(i) find its height;

(ii) determine its weight in tons, assuming the average weight of the iron plate and frame to be $7\frac{1}{2}$ lbs. per square foot of surface.

41. A boiler contains 500 smoke tubes, each $2\frac{1}{4}$ inches internal diameter. Find the total weight of the tubes if the thickness of metal is $\frac{1}{8}$ in., length 7 ft., and specific gravity of the material 7·8.

Section V. Symbolic Notation, etc.

1. There are two quantities, a and b. The square of a is to be multiplied by the sum of the squares of a and b; add 3, extract the cube root, divide by the product of a and the square root of b. Write down these steps and the final result algebraically.

2. Let x be multiplied by the square of y and subtracted from the cube of z; the cube root of the whole is taken and is then squared. This is then divided by the sum of x, y, and z. Write all this down algebraically.

3. Write down algebraically: Three times the square of x, multiplied by the square root of y; from this subtract a times the Napierean logarithm of x; again, subtract b times the sine of cx; divide the result by the sum of the cube of x and the square of y.

4. Write down algebraically: Square a, divide by the square of b, add 1, extract the square root, multiply by w, and divide by the square of n.

5. Represent the following algebraically: The sum of the cubes of two numbers divided by their sum equals the sum of the squares of the same numbers diminished by their product.

6. Represent algebraically: The nth power of a exceeds the nth root of the number by the qth root of its pth power.

Resolve into factors:

7. $x^2 + 7x + 12.$ **8.** $x^2 + x - 12.$

9. $x^2 + 11x + 30.$ **10.** $x^2 - x - 30.$

11. $x^2 + 0·4x - 4·37.$ **12.** $12x^2 - 11x - 15.$

13. $a^2 + 4ax + 4x^2 - y^2 - 6y - 9.$

14. Simplify $\dfrac{x+8}{(x-15)(x-17)} + \dfrac{x+15}{(x-8)(x-17)} - \dfrac{x+17}{(x-8)(x-15)}.$

15. $\dfrac{x^4 - 8x^2y^2 + 16y^4}{x^3 - 6x^2y + 12xy^2 - 8y^3}.$

16. Simplify $\dfrac{x^2 - x - 2}{x^2 - 3x + 2} + \dfrac{2x^2 + x - 3}{2x^2 + 5x + 3} - 2,$

and find its value to three significant figures, when $x = 1 + \sqrt{3}$.

Show that $(x^2 - 7x + 12)(x - 1) - (x^2 - 4x + 3)$ is the product of three factors.

If x stands for a positive whole number, show that the three factors are either three consecutive even numbers or three consecutive odd numbers.

Section VI. Simple Equations.

Solve the equations :

1. $2x + 3 - \dfrac{x}{3} = x + 5.$

2. $\dfrac{x}{2} - 1 + 3x = \dfrac{5x}{2} + 3.$

3. $\dfrac{2x - \frac{1}{3}}{5} - \dfrac{x + \frac{2}{3}}{3} + \dfrac{4}{15} = 0.$

4. $\dfrac{x}{6} - \dfrac{x - \frac{1}{2}}{3} - \dfrac{1}{3}\left(\dfrac{2}{5} - \dfrac{x}{3}\right) = 0.$

5. $\dfrac{(2x - 1)(3x + 2)}{7} - \dfrac{5x^2 + 4}{14} = \dfrac{x^2}{2}.$

6. $\dfrac{x - 1}{7} - \dfrac{x - 23}{5} = 7 - \dfrac{x + 4}{4}.$

7. $(2 - 3x)\left(4 - \dfrac{5}{x}\right) = (3 - 2x)\left(6 - \dfrac{7}{x}\right).$

8. $13\frac{3}{4} - \dfrac{x}{2} = 2x - 8\frac{3}{4}.$

9. $\frac{1}{2}(x + 11) + \dfrac{x + 2}{3} = 19 - \dfrac{5x - 7}{4}.$

10. $x - \dfrac{x - 2}{3} = \dfrac{23}{4} - \dfrac{x + 10}{5} + \dfrac{x}{4}.$

11. $(x + 3)(x + 7) = (x - 3)(x - 8).$

12. $\dfrac{3x + 1}{4} = \dfrac{9x + 8}{12} - \dfrac{x + 1}{x + 8}.$

13. $\dfrac{3x + 4}{5} - \dfrac{7}{10} = \dfrac{2(x - 1)}{5} - \dfrac{x - 2}{2}.$

14. $\dfrac{a}{x - a} + \dfrac{x + a}{a} = \dfrac{x - b}{a}.$

15. $\dfrac{2x + a}{a} - \dfrac{x - b}{a} = \dfrac{3ax + (a - b)^2}{ab}.$

16. $a - \dfrac{a + x}{b} = b - \dfrac{b + x}{a}.$

17. $\dfrac{a}{bx} + \dfrac{b}{ax} = a^2 + b^2.$

18. $\dfrac{6x + a}{4x + b} = \dfrac{3x - b}{2x - a}.$

19. $\dfrac{a - x}{b - a} - \dfrac{b - x}{a - b} = \dfrac{b^2 + a^2}{b^2 - a^2}.$

20. $ax + b^2 = \dfrac{a(x^2 + c^2)}{a + x}.$

21. $\dfrac{a}{a^2 - x} + \dfrac{b}{b^2 - x} = 0.$

22. $\dfrac{x + a}{x - b} + \dfrac{x + b}{x - a} = 2.$

23. $x - \dfrac{x - a}{b + 1} = a - \dfrac{x}{b + 1}.$

24. $\dfrac{2x + a}{b} - \dfrac{x - b}{a} = \dfrac{3ax + (a - b)^2}{ab}.$

Section VII. Simultaneous Equations.

1. If $z = ax - by^3 x^{\frac{1}{2}}.$

If $z = 1\cdot32$ when $x = 1$ and $y = 2$, and if $z = 8\cdot58$ when $x = 4$ and $y = 1$, find a and b ; also find z when $x = 2$ and $y = 0.$

2. If $y = ax^{\frac{1}{2}} + bxz^2.$

If $y = 62\cdot3$ when $x = 4$ and $z = 2$, and $y = 187\cdot2$ when $x = 1$ and $z = 1\cdot46$, find a and b ; also find the value of y when x is 9 and z is $0\cdot5.$

3. If $t - p = 2b$ and $t + p = \dfrac{2a}{r^2}$, find the values of t and p when $r = 4\cdot25$, $a = 318\cdot3$, $b = 4\cdot85$.

4. Solve the equations :

$$\frac{5}{y} - \frac{2}{x} = \frac{7}{6} \; ; \; \frac{36}{x} - \frac{24}{y} = 1.$$

5. $5x + 2y = 3\frac{1}{3}, \quad 6x - 9y = 4.$

6. $5x - 2y = 5, \quad 6y - 2x = 11.$

7. $2x + \dfrac{y-2}{5} = 21, \quad 4y + \dfrac{x-4}{6} = 29.$

8. $\dfrac{2}{x} + 3y = 7, \quad \dfrac{3}{x} - 5y = 1.$

9. $x + 0\cdot2y = 0\cdot4, \quad 1\cdot7x - 0\cdot01y = 0\cdot015.$

10. $5x - 3y + z = a, \quad 2x + 5y - z = 2a, \quad 2x + 3y + z = a.$

11. $3x + 2y - z = -2, \quad 3y - x + z = 15, \quad 5x - y + 2z = 34\frac{2}{3}.$

12. $ax - by = a^2, \quad (b - a)x + ay = b^2.$

13. $2x + \dfrac{3}{y} = 59, \quad 3x + \dfrac{2}{y} = 61.$

14. $2x - \dfrac{y+2}{5} = 21, \quad \dfrac{x-4}{6} - 4y = 29.$

Section VIII. Problems.

1. Divide £4. 2s. 6d. amongst three persons A, B, and C, so that A's share may be $\frac{2}{3}$ths of B's and B's share $1\frac{1}{2}$ of C's.

2. Divide 279 into two parts such that one-third of the first part is less by 15 than one-fifth of the second part.

3. Find a number such that, when diminished by 3, one-fourth of the remainder may be greater by 2 than one-fifth of the original number.

4. Divide £3. 18s. 4d. among three persons A, B, C, so that B may receive seven-eighths as much as A and C and five shillings more than B.

5. The numerator of a certain fraction is 4 less than the denominator ; if 10 be subtracted from the numerator, or if 30 be added to the denominator, the resulting fractions would be equal ; find the original fraction.

6. A crew which can pull at the rate of 6 miles an hour finds that it takes twice as long to come up a river as to go down ; at what rate does the river flow ?

7. The electrical resistance of a copper wire is proportional to its length divided by its cross section. Show that the resistance of a pound of wire of circular section all in one length is inversely proportional to the fourth power of the diameter of the wire.

8. Some men agree to pay equally for the use of a boat, and each pays 15 pence. If there had been two more men in the party, each would have paid 10 pence. How many men were there, and how much was the hire of the boat?

9. The total cost C of a ship per hour (including interest, wages, coals, etc.) is $C = a + bs^3$, where s is the speed in knots per hour.

> When s is 10, C is found to be £5·2;
>   ,, s is 15, C ,,   ,,   ,,   £7·375.

Calculate a and b. What is C when s is 12?

How many hours are spent in a passage of 300 nautical miles at a speed of 12 knots (or nautical miles per hour), and what is the total cost of the passage?

10. The sum of two numbers is 76, and their difference is equal to one-third of the greater; find them.

11. A majority against a certain motion is equal to $6\frac{3}{4}$ per cent. of the total number voting. If twelve of those who voted against the motion had voted for it, the motion would have been carried by a single vote. Find the numbers voting on each side.

12. The sum of two numbers is 12·54, and the sum of their squares is 81·56; find the numbers.

13. The net yearly profit P of a railway may be represented by

$$P = bx + cy,$$

where x is the gross yearly receipt from passengers, and y from goods; b and c being constant numbers. When $x = 520000$ and $y = 220000$, P was 330000; and at a later period, when $x = 902000$ and $y = 700000$, P was 603000. What will probably be the value of P when $x = 1000000$ and when $y = 800000$?

14. The ages of a man and his wife added together amount to 72·36 years; fifteen years ago the man's age was 2·3 times that of his wife; what are their ages now?

15. A rectangular garden has one side 28 yds. longer than the other; if the smaller side were increased by 40 yds. and the greater diminished by 34 yds., the area would remain unaltered; what are the lengths of the sides?

16. A certain resolution was carried in a debating society by a majority which was equal to one-third of the number of votes given on the losing side; but if with the same number of votes 10 more votes had been given to the losing side, the resolution would only have been carried by a majority of one. Find the number of votes given on each side.

17. A certain piece of work can be completed by x men in y days. If, however, $x+5$ men were employed the work could be done in $y-6$ days, while if only $x-5$ men were employed the work would take $y+12$ days. In how many days could the work be done by 24 men?

18. Find two consecutive numbers such that $\lceil$the difference of their squares is 49.

Section IX.   Squared Paper.

1. If $y = \dfrac{2}{x} + 5\log_{10}x - 2\cdot70$, find the values of y when x has the values 2, 2·5, 3.

Plot the values of y and x on squared paper, and draw the probable curve in which these points lie. State approximately what value of x would cause y to be 0.

2. x and t are the distance in miles and the time in hours of a train from a railway station. Plot on squared paper. Describe why it is that the *slope* of the curve shows the speed; where is the speed greatest and where is it least?

x	0	0·12	0·50	1·52	2·50	2·92	3·05	3·17	3·50	3·82	4·15
t	0·00	0·05	0·10	0·15	0·20	0·25	0·30	0·35	0·40	0·45	0·50

3. A vessel is shaped like the frustum of a cone, the circular base is 10 inches diameter, the top is 5 inches diameter, the vertical axial height is 8 inches. By drawing, find the axial height to the imaginary vertex of the cone. If x is the height of the surface of a liquid from the bottom, plot a curve, to any scales you please, showing for any value of x the area of the horizonal section there. Three points of the curve will be enough to find.

4. A feed pump of variable stroke driven by an electro-motor at constant speed; the following experimental results were obtained:

Electrical Horse Power.	Power given to Water.
3·12	1·19
4·5	2·21
7·5	4·26
10·74	6·44

Plot on squared paper, and state the probable electrical power when the power given to the water was 5.

5. Mr. Scott Russell found that at the following speeds of a canal-boat the tow-rope pull was as follows :

Speed in miles per hour, - -	6·19	7·57	8·52	9·04
Tow-rope pull in pounds, - -	250	500	400	280

What was the probable pull when the speed was 8 miles per hour? There was reason to believe that the pull was at its maximum at 8 miles per hour, because this was the natural speed of a long wave in that canal.

6. Given $y = 3x^2 - 20 \log_{10} x - 7·077$, find the values of y when x is 1·5, 2, 2·3. Plot the values of x and y on squared paper and draw the probable curve in which these points lie. What value of x would cause y to be 0 ?

7. If $y = 2x + \dfrac{1·5}{x}$ for various values of x, calculate y ; plot on squared paper ; state approximately the value of x which causes y to be of its smallest value.

8. Find to three significant figures a value of x which satisfies the equation

$$2x^2 - 10 \log_{10} x - 3·25 = 0.$$

9. It is thought that the following observed quantities, in which there are probably errors of observation, follow a law like

$$y = ae^{bx}.$$

Test if this is so, and find the most probable values of a and b.

x	2·30	3·10	4·00	4·92	5·91	7·20
y	33·0	39·1	50·3	67·2	85·6	125·0

10.   Plot $3y = 4·8x + 0·9$
                      Plot $y = 2·24 - 0·7x$.

Find the point where they cross. What angle does each of them make with the axis of x? At what angle do they meet ?

11. Plot the curve

$$y = 8x^3 - 6x + 1$$

for values of x between -1 and 1. Find the least positive value of x which satisfies the equation.

12. Find one value of x for which

$$5 \log_{10} x + \frac{2}{x} - 2·7 = 0.$$

13. Find the values of x which satisfy the equation

$$e^x = 3 \cdot 5x$$

by drawing in one figure the curves

$$y = 3 \cdot 5x \text{ and } y = e^x.$$

14. Find by squared paper the values of x and y which satisfy simultaneously the equations

$$x^2 + y^2 - 2x - 9 = 0, \ x - 2y + 4 = 0.$$

15. An army of 5000 men costs a country £800,000 per annum to maintain it, an army of 10,000 men costs £1,300,000 per annum to maintain it ; what is the annual cost of an army of 8000 ? Take the simplest law which is consistent with the figures given. Use squared paper or not, as you please.

16. At the following draughts in sea water a particular vessel has the following displacements :

Draught h feet ·	15	12	9	6·3
Displacement T tons	2098	1512	1018	586

What are the probable displacements when the draughts are 11 and 13 feet respectively ?

17. The keeper of a restaurant finds that when he has G guests a day his total daily profit (the difference between his actual receipts and expenditure including rent, taxes, wages, wear and tear, food and drink) is P pounds, the following numbers being averages obtained by comparison of many days' accounts ; what simple law seems to connect P and G ?

G	P
210	−0·9
270	+1·8
320	+4·8
360	+6·4

For what number of guests would he just have no profit ?

18. An examiner has given marks to papers ; the highest number of marks is 185, the lowest 42. He desires to change all his marks according to a linear law, converting the highest number of marks into 250 and the lowest into 100 ; show how he may do this, and state the converted marks for papers already marked 60, 100, 150.

Use squared paper, or algebra, as you please.

19. A is the horizontal sectional area of a vessel in square feet at the water level, h being the vertical draught in feet.

A	14,850	14,400	13,780	13,150
h	23·6	20·35	17·1	14·6

Plot on squared paper and read off and tabulate A for values of h, 23, 20, 16.

If the vessel changes in draught from 20·5 to 19·5, what is the diminution of its displacement in cubic feet?

20. Find a value of x which satisfies the equation

$$x^2 - 5\log_{10}x - 2\cdot531 = 0.$$

21. If $x = a(\phi - \sin \phi)$ and $y = a(1 - \cos \phi)$, and if $a = 5$; taking various values of ϕ between 0 and, say, 1·5, calculate x and y and plot this part of the curve.

22. If x be the depth to which a floating sphere of radius r and density ρ sinks in water, it is found that $x^3 - 3rx^2 + 4r^3\rho = 0$.

By squared paper determine approximately the depth to which a sphere of radius 10 inches and density 0·65 will sink in water.

23. The following numbers relate to the flow of water over a triangular notch:

H	1·2	1·4	1·6	1·8	2·0	2·4
Q	4·2	6·1	8·5	11·5	14·9	23·5

H denotes the head of water (in feet) and Q the quantity (in cubic feet) of water flowing per second. Show that Q and H are connected by the formula $Q = cH^n$, and determine the values of n and c. Find the value of Q when $H = 2\cdot2$.

24. In the formula for a hollow shaft,

$$\frac{D^4 - d^4}{D} = \frac{16T}{f\pi}.$$

Given $d = 3$ in., $T = 280$, $f = 7$, find D.

25. A series of soundings taken across a river channel is given by the following table, x feet being distance from one shore and y feet the corresponding depth. Draw the section. Find its area.

x	0	10	16	23	30	38	43	50	55	60	70	75	80
y	5	10	13	14	15	16	14	12	8	6	4	3	0

26. h is the height in feet of the atmospheric surface of the water in a reservoir above the lowest point of the bottom ; A is the area of the surface in square feet.

When the reservoir was filled to various heights the areas were measured and found to be :

Values of h	0	13	23	33	47	62	78	91	104	120
Values of A	0	21,000	27,500	33,600	39,200	44,700	50,400	54,700	60,800	69,300

How many cubic feet of water leave the reservoir when h alters from 113 to 65?

27. In a table of values of x and y I find the following entries :

x	10	11	12	13
y	0·1115	0·1128	0·1150	0·1202

What is the probable value of y when x is 11·5?
What is the probable value of x when y is 0·1165?

28. The cross-section of a tree (A sq. in.), at distance x from one end, is as follows :

x	10	30	50	70	90	110	130	150
A	120	123	129	129	131	135	142	156

What is the volume of the tree, its total length being 13 ft. 4 in.?

29. If $y = x^3 + 5x - 11$, calculate y for various values of x from 1 to 2, and plot on squared paper. For what value of x is $y=0$?

30. If $y = 2 \cdot 5 \log x + \dfrac{x^2}{100} - 6 \cdot 35$, find y for a number of values of x between 15 and 20, and plot on squared paper. For what value of x is $y=0$?

CHAPTER XVIII.

MEASUREMENT OF ANGLES IN DEGREES AND RAD-
IANS. TRIGONOMETRICAL RATIOS AND TABLES.
RIGHT-ANGLED TRIANGLES. SOLUTION OF TRI-
ANGLES.

If AC is a line, movable about a centre A, and in the opposite
direction to the hands of a clock, then any angle such as BAC
may be measured in either
degrees or radians (Fig. 77).

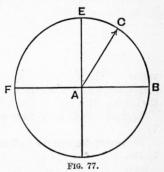

FIG. 77.

Unit Angle.—If the circumference of a circle be
divided into 360 equal parts,
then the straight lines joining
any two consecutive points
to the centre of the circle
will enclose an angle of **one
degree**, written 1°. A degree
is subdivided into 60 equal
parts each a **minute**, and a
minute into 60 equal parts
each a second. Thus an angle of 25 degrees, 15 minutes and
30 seconds, is written 25° 15′ 30″, or 25° 15·5′.

Radian Measure.—If the arc BC be made equal to the radius
AB (Fig. 77), then the angle BAC is **one radian** $= 57·296°$ or
57·3°. If AC be rotated until C coincides with E then the angle
is 90° or $\dfrac{\pi}{2}$ radians. When C coincides with F the angle is **180°**
or π radians, at B the angle is 360° or 2π radians.

A radian is the angle subtended at the centre of a circle by an arc equal to the radius, and the **circular measure** of an angle is given by the number of radians it contains. If an arc of a circle of radius r subtends an angle θ at the centre, then arc $= r\theta$.

An angle of 1 radian may be set out as follows : Draw a circle of any convenient size, radius AB (Fig. 78). On a strip of tracing paper draw a straight line equal to the radius. Put one end of the line at B and a small portion of the line to coincide with the curve. Insert a needle point at that position of the line where it leaves the curve.

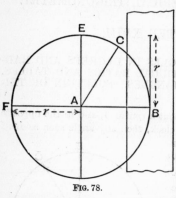

Rotate the tracing paper about this point as centre until the line coincides with another short length of the arc. In this manner a length of arc BC (Fig. 78) is obtained equal to the radius r. The angle BAC is found to be $57 \cdot 3°$.

FIG. 78.

It is frequently necessary to convert from one set of units to the other. This may be effected as follows :

To convert **radians to degrees.** Multiply by 180 and divide by π.

To convert **degrees to radians.** Multiply by π and divide by 180.

Ex. 1. Express in radians, 30°, 45°, 60°, 90°, 180°, 360°.

$$30 \times \frac{\pi}{180} = \frac{\pi}{6}; \quad 45 \times \frac{\pi}{180} = \frac{\pi}{4}; \quad 60 \times \frac{\pi}{180} = \frac{\pi}{3};$$

$$90 \times \frac{\pi}{180} = \frac{\pi}{2}; \quad 180 \times \frac{\pi}{180} = \pi.$$

Ex. 2. Express in degrees, 3·5, 2·38, 6·45, 1·386 radians.

$$3 \cdot 5 \times \frac{180}{3 \cdot 142} = 200 \cdot 5°; \quad 2 \cdot 38 \times \frac{180}{3 \cdot 142} = 136 \cdot 3°;$$

$$6 \cdot 45 \times \frac{180}{3 \cdot 142} = 369 \cdot 6°; \quad 1 \cdot 386 \times \frac{180}{\pi} = 79 \cdot 4°.$$

Ex. 3. A wheel is rotating at 76 rev. per min. Through what angle does one of the spokes turn in one second ?

Angle $= \frac{76}{60} \times 360 = 456°$, or $\frac{76}{60} \times 2\pi = 7.958$ radians.

Ex. 4. Find the distance between two places on the same meridian of the earth's surface, if the difference of latitude is 25°, assuming the radius of the earth to be 4000 miles.

Distance $= 25 \times \dfrac{\pi}{180} \times 4000 = 1746$ miles.

EXERCISES. XXIX.

1. Express in radians the following :
  20°, 25·6°, 40°, 45·5°, 61·4°, 70° 48', 85°, 87° 42'.

2. The following angles are in radians; express them in degrees and minutes :
  ·1815, ·2705, ·5672, ·9477, 1·227, 1·2863, 1·5656.

3. An arc 10 ft. long subtends an angle of 71° at the centre of a circle. Find the radius.

4. Find the radian measure of an angle 37° 15'. Find the length of arc which subtends this angle at the centre of a circle of radius 105 ft.

5. Find the number of degrees and minutes in an angle of $\frac{2}{3}$ radian.

6. Find the radian measure of an angle of 112° 42', and length of an arc which subtends an angle of 112° 42' at the centre of a circle radius 153 ft.

7. Express in degrees the angles $\dfrac{\pi}{6}$ and 1·2 radians.

8. A circular racing track has a radius of 320 yds. A cyclist travels on it at a speed of 18 miles per hour. Through what angle does he turn in 10 seconds ?   [U.E.I.]

9. Find the angle between two radii of a circle of 3·5 ft. radius which intercept an arc 3·5 ft. in length.

10. A wheel 30 in. diameter makes 400 rev. per min. Find speed of rim in feet per second.

11. A flywheel has a diameter of 3 ft. 6 in. A point on its rim is moving at 2200 ft. per min. What is its angular velocity in (i) radians, (ii) in degrees, per sec.   [N.U.T.]

12. Given that the earth is a sphere 7920 miles diameter. Find the distance between two places on the same meridian if difference in latitude is 2° 6'.   [U.E.I.]

13. Find the angle at the centre of a circle of radius 4 ft., subtended by an arc 5½ ft. long.   [U.E.I.]

14. Find approximately the diameter of the sun if it subtends an angle of 32′ at the earth, given that its distance from the earth is 93,000,000 miles.

15. Find approximately the diameter of the moon if it subtends an angle of 32′ at the earth, given that its distance from the earth is 240,000 miles.

Ratios of an Angle.—Another method of estimating the magnitude of the angle between two lines which intersect at a point A is as follows :

From any point B in one line AB draw BC perpendicular to AC (Fig. 79). This determines the three sides of a right-angled

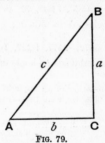

FIG. 79.

triangle. The angles are denoted by the letters A, B, C, and the lengths of the sides opposite by a, b, c.

The ratio $\dfrac{BC}{AB}$ or $\dfrac{\text{opposite side}}{\text{hypotenuse}}$ is the **sine** of A.

The ratio $\dfrac{AC}{AB}$ or $\dfrac{\text{adjacent side}}{\text{hypotenuse}}$ is the **cosine** of A.

The ratio $\dfrac{BC}{AC}$ or $\dfrac{\text{opposite side}}{\text{adjacent side}}$ is the **tangent** of A.

The preceding ratios are abbreviated into :

$$\sin A = \frac{BC}{AB} = \frac{a}{c}\; ;\quad \cos A = \frac{AC}{AB} = \frac{b}{c}\; ;\quad \tan A = \frac{BC}{AC} = \frac{a}{b} = \frac{\sin A}{\cos A}.$$

These three ratios together with three ratios formed by their reciprocals are called the **trigonometrical ratios**. The reciprocals are :

$$\text{cosecant } A = \frac{AB}{BC}, \quad \text{secant } A = \frac{AB}{AC}, \quad \text{cotangent } A = \frac{AC}{BC}.$$

These are abbreviated into the following :

$$\operatorname{cosec} A = \frac{c}{a}, \quad \sec A = \frac{c}{b}, \quad \cot A = \frac{\cos A}{\sin A} = \frac{b}{a}.$$

As the hypotenuse is the greatest side, it follows that the sine and cosine of any angle cannot be greater than unity ; the tangent may have any numerical value.

Ex. 4. Draw angles of 30° and 60° and find by measurement and calculation the sines, cosines and tangents of the angles.

Draw a horizontal line AD as base and by means of a protractor, or by construction, set out the required angles. With A as centre and radius, say, 10 units (Fig. 80), describe an arc of a circle DB. With the

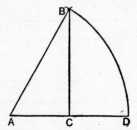

FIG. 80.—Construction of an angle of 60°.

same radius and centre D, describe an arc intersecting the former at B. Join A to B, then $DAB = 60°$.

Draw BC perpendicular to AD. Measure the lengths of $BC = 8.66$ and $AC = 5$;

$$\sin 60° = \frac{BC}{AB} = \frac{8.66}{10} = .866 ; \quad \cos 60° = \frac{AC}{AB} = \frac{5}{10} = .5 ;$$

$$\tan 60° = \frac{BC}{AC} = \frac{8.66}{5} = 1.732.$$

As the angle at $C = 90°$, the angle $ABC = 30°$;

$$\therefore \sin 30° = \frac{AC}{AB} = .5 ; \quad \cos 30° = \frac{BC}{AB} = .866, \quad \tan 30° = \frac{5}{8.66} = .5774.$$

Complementary Angles.—It will be seen from the above that $\sin 30° = \cos 60°$; $\cos 30° = \sin 60°$. These properties always hold for complementary angles, *i.e.* angles whose sum $= 90°$. Thus $\cos 37° 30' = \sin 52° 30'$.

Ex. 5. Construct an angle whose sine is $\frac{3}{5}$, or ·6. Measure the angle and find the cosine and tangent.

Draw a horizontal line AC and at C draw CB perpendicular and equal 6 units. With B as centre, radius 10, describe an arc cutting AC at A (Fig. 81). Join B to A.

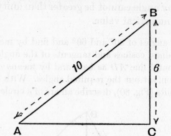

FIG. 81.—To construct an angle whose sine is ·6.

The angle at A is found to be 37°.

$$AC = 8, \text{ hence } \cos A = ·8, \ \tan A = ·75.$$

Ex. 6. Construct an angle whose cosine is ·89.

Draw a horizontal line $AC = 8·9$ units (to scale, or by using squared paper).

Draw CB perpendicular and with A as centre, radius 10, describe an arc cutting CB at B. Join B to A (Fig. 82). Measure the angle at $A = 27°$.

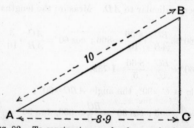

FIG. 82.—To construct an angle whose cosine is ·89.

Ex. 7. Construct an angle whose tangent is 1·8 and find the sine and cosine of the angle.

Draw $AC = 10$ and CB perpendicular to $AC = 18$.

Join B to A (Fig. 83), then the length $BA = 20\cdot6$,

$$A = 61°, \quad \sin A = \cdot87, \quad \cos A = \cdot48.$$

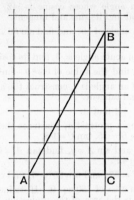

FIG. 83.—To construct an angle whose tangent is $1\cdot8$.

Projection of a Line or Area.—Let AB (Fig. 84) represent a line or edge view of an area inclined at an angle BAC to the horizon.

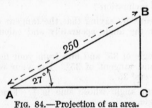

FIG. 84.—Projection of an area.

Draw CB perpendicular to AC; then AC is the plan or projection of AB; $\quad \therefore \quad AC = AB \cos A.$

Ex. 8. Part of a roof has an area of 250 sq. ft. What is the area of its projection, or plan, if its inclination to the horizon is 27°. Given $\cos 27° = \cdot891$.

At A (Fig. 84) make the angle $BAC = 27°$ and $AB = 250$. Draw BC perpendicular to AC. Then AC is found to be $222\cdot7$.

$$\text{Or area} = 250 \cos 27° = 250 \times \cdot891$$
$$= 222\cdot7 \text{ sq. ft.}$$

EXERCISES. XXX.

1. If the sine of an angle is $\frac{7}{11}$, find its cosine and tangent.

2. Construct an angle whose cosine is ·42. Measure the angle from your figure and find its sine and tangent.

3. Construct an angle of 50° and find sin 50°, cos 50°, tan 50° and $\sin^2 50° + \cos^2 50°$.

4. The sine of an acute angle is ·3, find its cosine and tangent.

5. If $\tan \theta = \frac{8}{15}$, find the value of $\cos^2 \theta - \sin^2 \theta$.

6. The cosine of an angle is $\frac{3}{7}$, construct the angle and measure it. Calculate its sine and tangent.

7. Given $\sin A = \frac{16}{28}$, find A.

8. Without using a protractor, construct the angles A, B and C, given $\sin A = ·3$, $\cos B = ·15$, $\tan C = 1·8$.

9. If $\cos A = x$, and $\sin A = y$, find $\tan A$. Given $\cos 42° = ·743$, $\tan 42° = ·9$, find $\sin 42°$.

10. Given $\sin 35° = ·574$ and $\tan 35° = ·7$, find $\cos 35°$.

11. A roof has an area of 150 sq. ft. If its inclination to the horizontal is 37°, what is the area of the projection?

12. In a certain district the surface of the ground is known to be 3·246 sq. miles; it is shown on a map as 2·875 sq. miles. At what angle is it inclined?

13. The plan of part of a roof is 600 sq. ft. If the real area is 800 sq. ft., what is its inclination?

14. What is meant by saying that the tangent of a certain angle is $\frac{13}{10}$? Construct the angle accurately and calculate its sine and cosine? [N.U.T.]

15. Draw an angle of 35° and find from your figure the values of the sine, cosine and tangent of 35°. Use your results to find the value of $\sin^2 35° + \cos^2 35°$. [N.U.T.]

16. Construct an angle whose sine is $\frac{1}{2}$. Find the cosine and tangent of the angle. [U.E.I.]

17. A path slopes upward at 18° to the horizon. What vertical height will a man ascend when he walks 450 yds. along the path? [U.E.I.]

18. Draw the angle C when angle $C = (\text{angle } A + \text{angle } B)$. Given $\sin A = ·7$, $\tan B = ·6$. Measure the angle in degrees. [U.E.I.]

Tables of Natural Sines, Cosines, etc.—Referring to Table V., it will be found that the various ratios of an angle are given for all angles from 0° to 90° at intervals of 1°. The values from 0° to 45° are found at the extreme left reading downwards; for 45° to 90° reading upwards.

In four-figure tables the values of the sine, cosine, tangent, etc., are given for all angles between 0° and 90° at intervals of 6 minutes or ·1°. Difference columns are provided for angles of 1, 2, 3, 4 and 5 minutes, enabling the angle to be read off to the nearest minute.*

These fractional parts may be obtained by calculation from Table V. as follows :

Ex. 9.   Find the sine, cosine and tangent of 32° 27′.

From Table V.

$$\begin{aligned} \sin 33° &= ·5446 \\ \sin 32° &= ·5299 \\ \hline &\ 147 \end{aligned} \qquad\qquad \frac{147 \times 27}{60} = 66$$

$$\begin{aligned} \sin 32° &= ·5299 \\ \text{Diff. for } 27′ =&\ \ \ 66 \ \text{(to be added)} \\ \hline \therefore\ \sin 32° \ 27′ &= ·5365 \end{aligned}$$

$$\begin{aligned} \cos 32° &= ·8480 \\ \cos 33° &= ·8387 \\ \hline &\ \ 93 \end{aligned} \qquad\qquad \frac{93 \times 27}{60} = 42$$

$$\begin{aligned} \cos 32° &= ·8480 \\ \text{Diff. for } 27′ =&\ \ \ 42 \ \text{(to be subtracted)} \\ \hline \therefore\ \cos 32° \ 27′ &= ·8438 \end{aligned}$$

$$\begin{aligned} \tan 33° &= ·6494 \\ \tan 32° &= ·6249 \\ \hline \text{Diff. for } 60′ =&\ \ 245 \end{aligned} \qquad\qquad \frac{245 \times 27}{60} = 110$$

$$\begin{aligned} \tan 32° &= ·6249 \\ \text{Diff. for } 27′ =&\ \ 110 \ \text{(to be added)} \\ \hline \therefore\ \tan 32° \ 27′ &= ·6359 \end{aligned}$$

Table V. can also be used to find the angle when the value of the sine, cosine or tangent is given.

Ex. 10.   Find the angle whose sine is ·7381

$$\begin{aligned} \sin 48° &= ·7431 \\ \sin 47° &= ·7314 \\ \hline \text{Diff. for } 60′ =&\ \ 117 \end{aligned} \qquad\qquad \begin{aligned} \text{Given value} &= ·7381 \\ \sin 47° &= ·7314 \\ \hline &\ \ 67 \end{aligned}$$

$$\therefore\ \frac{67 \times 60}{117} = 34.$$

Hence the angle is 47° 34′.

* *Logarithms and other Tables for Schools,* by F. Castle (Macmillan).

Ex. 11. Find the angle whose cosine is ·5976.

cos 53° = ·6018	cos 53° = ·6018
cos 54° = ·5878	Given value = ·5976
Diff. for 60′ = 140	42

$$\therefore \frac{42 \times 60}{140} = 18.$$

Hence the angle is 53° 18′.

Ex. 12. If tan A = 1·3048, find angle A.

tan 53° = 1·3270	Given value = 1·3048
tan 52° = 1·2799	tan 52° = 1·2799
Diff. for 60′ = 471	249

Hence

$$\frac{249 \times 60}{471} = 32 ;$$

$$\therefore A = 52° 32′.$$

Angles greater than 90°.—In Fig. 85 AC is assumed to be a line which can be rotated in the direction of the arrow. Thus

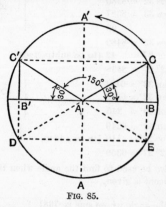

FIG. 85.

if BAC be a given angle, then using AC as radius and A as centre a circle can be described.

Making $B'C' = BC$ and joining C' to A, the angle $B'AC' = BAC$, and sin BAC = sin $B'AC'$ or sin A = sin $(180° - A)$.

In addition to the convention that all angles are measured anti-clockwise, all lines measured in an upward direction from BB' are positive, those measured downwards are negative ; all lines measured from AA' towards B are positive, those from AA' to B' negative. The radius AC is always positive. Hence as BC and $B'C'$ are both measured in an upward direction,

$$\sin (180° - A) = \sin A \; ;$$

AB and AB' are measured in opposite directions; hence

$$\cos (180° - A) = - \cos A.$$

If $C'B'$ be produced to D, the angle $DAB' = 180° + A$; hence $\sin (180° + A) = - \sin A$; also $\cos (180° + A) = - \cos A$.

Similarly, for the angle EAB, $\sin (360° - A) = - \sin A$ and $\cos (360° - A) = \cos A$.

As the tangent is $\dfrac{\text{sine}}{\text{cosine}}$, its sign, positive or negative, will depend upon the sine and cosine of the angle; when they are alike the tangent is positive, and negative when they are unlike.

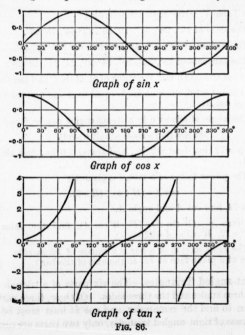

Graph of sin x

Graph of cos x

Graph of tan x

Fig. 86.

The graphs of sin x, cos x and tan x can be drawn on squared paper, as in Fig. 86. Using the values in Table V. as follows:

x	0°	30°	60°	90°	120°	150°	180°
sin x	0	·5 ½	·87	1	·87	·5	0
cos x	1	·87	·5	0	− ·5	− ·87	− 1
tan x	0	·58	1·7	∞	−1·7	− ·58	0

x	210°	240°	270°	300°	330°	360°	
sin x	− ·5	− ·87	− 1	− ·87	− ·5	0	
cos x	− ·87	− ·5	0	·5	·87	1	
tan x	·58	1·7	∞	−1·7	− ·58	0	

EXERCISES. XXXI.

From Table V. write down the following:

1. The sines of 17°, 28°, 47°, 19° 36′, 33° 44′, 75° 27′.

2. The cosines of 29°, 37°, 44°, 48° 24′, 61° 38′, 73° 45′.

3. The tangents of 25°, 36°, 70°, 14° 50′, 24° 34′, 42° 28′.

4. If cos $C = ·8387$, find the value of C, of sin C and tan C.

5. If tan $A = 1·6$, draw an angle equal to A and find the values of sin A and cos A.

6. The angle of advance in a steam engine can be found from

$$\sin A = (\text{lap} + \text{lead}) \div (\text{half travel}).$$

If lap $= ·72$ in., lead ·12 in., and travel 3·6 in., find sin A and angle A.　　　　　　　　　　　　　　　　　　　　　　　[U.E.I.]

7. The power factor of a motor is given by

$$\cos A = (H + 4) \div (H + 5).$$

If $H = 4·78$, find cos A and angle A.　　　　　　　　　[U.E.I.]

8. Given $m = (W \sin A) \div (P + W \cos A)$, find the value of m, when $P = 12$, $W = 35$, $A = 32°$.　　　　　　　　　　[N.U.T.)

9. The cross-section of a bar is a square of 3·5 in. side. What is the area of a plane face at 72° to the axis of the bar?　　(U.E.I.]

Right-angled Triangles.—The six parts of a triangle consist of the three angles and the three sides. Of these, three parts must be given to find the remainder, and one at least must be a side; in the case of right-angled triangles, only two parts are necessary,

.e. (i) two sides, (ii) one side and one angle. If the sides a and b are given (Fig. 87), then the value of c could be found from

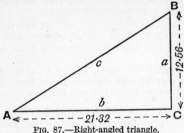

FIG. 87.—Right-angled triangle.

$=\sqrt{a^2+b^2}$, but this method is in some cases rather tedious; the difficulty is removed by using the trigonometrical functions.

Ex. 13. Find the remaining parts when $c=9\cdot82$, $A=28°$, $C=90°$.

$$a=c \sin A$$
$$=9\cdot82 \times \cdot4695$$
$$=4\cdot612.$$

	No.	log.
	9·82	0·9921
	0·4695	$\bar{1}$·6717
	4·612	0·6638

$$b=c \cos 28°$$
$$=9\cdot82 \times \cdot8829$$
$$=8\cdot67. \qquad B=62°.$$

	No.	log.
	9·82	0·9921
	0·8829	$\bar{1}$·9459
	8·67	0·9380

Ex. 14. Solve the triangle in which $a=12\cdot56$, $b=21\cdot32$, $C=90°$.

$$\tan A = \frac{a}{b} = \frac{12\cdot56}{21\cdot32} = \cdot5889 ;$$

$$\therefore \ A=30° \ 30', \ B=59° \ 30' ;$$

$$c=\frac{a}{\sin A}=\frac{12\cdot56}{0\cdot5075}=24\cdot75,$$

	No.	log.
	12·56	1·0989
	21·32	1·3288
	$\tan A$	$\bar{1}$·7701

or $\quad c=\sqrt{12\cdot56^2+21\cdot32^2}=24\cdot75.$

EXERCISES. XXXII.

In the following exercises the angle $C=90°$. Find in each case the remaining parts and the area.

1. $b=4$ in., $A=40°$.
2. $a=12\cdot4$ ft., $A=65°$.
3. $a=4$ in., $c=4\cdot5$ in.
4. $c=6\cdot2$ in., $A=56°$.
5. $c=2\cdot5$ ft., $B=49°$.
6. $c=9\cdot82$ in., $A=28°$.
7. If $c=2\cdot75$ in., $a=1\cdot625$, find $\sin B$, $\cos B$ and $\tan B$.

8. If B is 90°, A is 56°, $a = 10$ in., find b and c.

9. A ladder 40 ft. long leans against a vertical wall; the foot of th ladder 6 ft. from the wall. How high does the ladder reach, an what is its inclination to the ground ?

10. The blades of a pair of shears measure 16·5 in. What is th distance between the points if the angle between them is 25° ?

11. If a ship sails 25 miles on a course 40° E. of N, how far I and N. has she run ?

12. The lower edge of a square picture frame is 18 in. long an rests against a vertical wall, the upper edge $5\frac{1}{2}$ in. from the wal Find the angle between the picture and the wall.   [N.U.T

Angles of Elevation and Depression.—If A is a point observation and B an object above (Fig. 88), then BAC is called the angl of elevation.

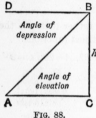

If B is the point of observation and A a object below B, then the angle DBA (Fig. 88 is called the **angle of depression.**

As DB (representing the horizon) parallel to AC, the angle
$$DBA = BAC.$$

Angle of depression

Angle of elevation

FIG. 88.

To avoid unnecessary repetition, it i assumed in the following pages that the point of observation an the object are either in the same or in a parallel horizontal plan

Ex. 15. At 5 feet above ground and at a distance of 60 ft. th angle of elevation of the top of a tower is 38°. Find the height.

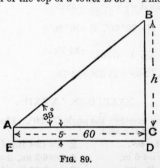

FIG. 89.

Draw, to any convenient scale (or on squared paper), the lin $AC = 60$, and ED parallel to AC and 5 from it (Fig. 89).

Draw AB at 38° to AC, intersecting a perpendicular CB at B.
Measure $CB = 46\cdot88$ ft., or by calculation

$$\frac{h}{60} = \tan 38°, \text{ or } h = 60 \times \tan 38° ;$$

$$\therefore \ h = 60 \times \cdot7813 = 46\cdot88 \text{ ft.}$$

$$\text{Height} = 46\cdot88 + 5 = 51\cdot88 \text{ ft.}$$

Ex. 16.   An observer on a cliff 220 ft. above sea level finds the
angle of depression of a boat to be 35°. Find the distance of the
boat from the observer and from the foot of the cliff.

Draw a horizontal line DB and AC parallel to it and 220 from it.

Make the angle $DBA = 35°$, cutting CA at A (Fig. 90).   Measure

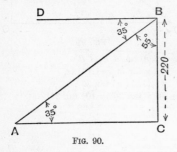

FIG. 90.

the lengths of BA and AC: these are found to be 383·5 and 314·2
respectively.

The angle $ABC = 55°$.

Hence

$$AC = 220 \tan 55° = 220 \times 1\cdot4281$$

$$= 314\cdot2 \text{ ft.}$$

$$AB = 220 \div \sin 35° = 220 \div \cdot5736$$

$$= 383\cdot5 \text{ ft.}$$

In many cases it is neither practical nor possible to measure a
distance from the point C.   (The point C may lie in the interior of a
building or other inaccessible position.)   In all such cases the height
of an object can be ascertained by taking two observations in the
horizontal plane and at a known distance apart.

Ex. 17.   A tower on one bank of a river subtends an angle of 50°
at a place A on the opposite bank, and 36° at a place D 100 ft. from A.
Find the height of the tower and the breadth of the river.

Draw a horizontal line DC and to any convenient scale make
$DA = 100$.   Draw DB and AB at 36° and 50° respectively to DC:

intersecting in B, draw BC perpendicular to DC (Fig. 91). Measure the length of BC and AC.

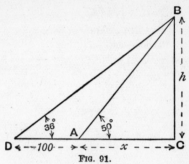

FIG. 91.

Let

$$x = AC \text{ and } h = CB,$$
$$h = x \tan 50° = 1·1918x,$$
$$h = (100 + x) \tan 36°.$$
$$x(\tan 50° - \tan 36°) = 100 \tan 36° = 100 × ·7265 ;$$
$$\therefore \ x = \frac{72·65}{·4653} = 156·7,$$

$$\dot{h} = x \tan 50° = 2 × ·5959 × 156·7 ;$$
$$\therefore \ h = 186·7.$$

No.	log.
72·65	1·8612
0·4635	$\bar{1}$·6661
156·7	2·1951
2	0·3010
0·5959	$\bar{1}$·7752
186·7	2·2713

EXERCISES. XXXIII.

1. An observer at a distance a from the foot of a tower observes the angle of elevation. Find the height of the tower under the following conditions :

(i) Distance of a from foot = 200·5 ft., angle of elevation 40°.

(ii)   ,,   ,,   ,,   = 85 ft.   ,,   ,,   ,,   35°.

(iii)   ,,   ,,   ,,   = 350 ft.   ,,   ,,   ,,   20° 10′.

(iv)   ,,   ,,   ,,   = 420 ft.   ,,   ,,   ,,   16° 14′.

2. What will be the distance of a boat from the foot of a vertical cliff and from the observer if :

(i) Height of cliff = 350·6 ft., angle of depression = 20°.

(ii)   ,,   ,,   = 500 ft.   ,,   ,,   = 30°.

(iii)   ,,   ,,   = 150·4 ft.   ,,   ,,   = 67°.

(iv)   ,,   ,,   = 75·6 ft.   ,,   ,,   = 32° 21′.

3. Find the height of a tree if the angle of elevation of its top is 57° at a point 50 ft. from the foot of the tree.

4. At 80 ft. from the foot of a tower the angle of elevation of the top is 51°, and top of flagstaff 57°. Find height of tower and flagstaff.

5. By walking towards a chimney a distance of 75 ft., the angle of elevation of its top changes from 43° to 60°. Find the height.

6. From a place in a horizontal plane through the foot of a tower the angle of elevation of its summit is 12° and from a place 100 yards nearer 18°. Find the height.

7. The angle of elevation of the top of an unfinished chimney at a place distant 100 ft. is 42°. How much higher must the chimney be raised for the angle of elevation to be 58° ?

8. A man walking in the direction of a captive balloon observes its elevation to be 30°, and after walking 1 mile nearer the elevation is 60°. How much further must he walk until he is directly underneath, and what is the height of the balloon ?

9. From a place immediately across a river the angle of elevation of a tree on the opposite bank is 35°. From a second place 150 yards from the bank the angle is 25°. Calculate the height of the tree and the breadth of the river.

10. From the top of a cliff 300 ft. high the angle of depression of a steamer is 18°. Find the distance of the steamer from the base of the cliff.

11. From a point A the angle of elevation of the top of a chimney is 29°, from a point B, 100 ft. from A, the angle is 16°. Find the height. [U.E.I.]

12. The angle of elevation of an aeroplane is 50°, its horizontal distance from point of observer is 1000 ft. Find the height. [U.E.I.]

13. A guy rope, 30 ft. long, from the top of a vertical pole makes an angle of $22\frac{1}{2}$° with the pole. What is the height of the pole ? [U.E.I.]

14. From the roof of a warehouse 50 ft. high the angle of elevation of the top of a steeple is 35°, from the basement the elevation is 50°. Find the height. [L.C.U.]

15. A factory chimney subtends an angle of 30°; at a place 100 ft. nearer the chimney the angle is 45°. Find its height. [U.E.I.]

16. By observations on a lighthouse L from two stations P and Q, 1250 yds. apart on the shore of the mainland, the angle LPQ is found to be 62° and angle LQP, 51°. If the shore between P and Q is straight, what are the distances PL and QL, and the shortest distance to the lighthouse from the shore ? [N.U.T.]

17. The shadow of a tree on a horizontal road is 37 ft. long when the elevation of the sun is 39°. What is the height of the tree ? [U.E.I.]

18. At a point B in the horizontal plane through the base of a tower the angle of elevation of the top is 58°, at a distance of 125 ft. from B the angle is 28°.   Find the height of the tower.   [L.C.U.]

19. A ladder 30 ft. long leans against a tower, its upper end 30 ft. from the top of the tower.   At the foot of the ladder the elevation of the top of the tower is 60°.   Find the height of the tower.   [U.E.I.]

20. A balloon rises vertically from a point P.   After an interval the angle of elevation 24° is observed from a point A, where $AP = 450$ ft.   What is the height ?   What will be the angle of elevation when it has risen to three times that height ?

Solution of Triangles.—The remaining parts of a triangle may be found either by construction or calculation when the given data consist of : (*a*) the three sides, (*b*) two sides and the included angle, (*c*) two angles and a side.   When formulae is used the proofs of the formulae may be obtained from other books on the subject.*

Ex. 18.   The three sides of a triangle are $a = 9$ ft., $b = 11$ ft., $c = 14$ ft. Find the angles and the area of the triangle.

(i) Draw $AB = 14$ on any convenient scale.   With A as centre radius 11, and B as centre radius 9, describe arcs intersecting in C. Join A and B to C (Fig. 92).

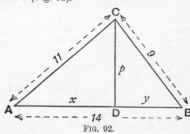

FIG. 92.

Measure the angles $A = 40°$, $B = 51°\ 46'$, $C = 88°\ 14'$.
Draw CD perpendicular and measure its length, then the area is
$$\tfrac{1}{2}(AB \times CD) = 49.5 \text{ sq. ft.}$$

(ii) The following formulae may be used :

$$\tan \frac{A}{2} = \sqrt{\frac{(s-b)(s-c)}{s(s-a)}} \; ; \quad \tan \frac{B}{2} = \sqrt{\frac{(s-a)(s-c)}{s(s-b)}} \; ;$$

$$\tan \frac{C}{2} = \sqrt{\frac{(s-a)(s-b)}{s(s-c)}} ,$$

* See *Manual of Practical Mathematics*, by F. Castle (Messrs. Macmillan and Co. Ltd.).

where $\quad s = \frac{1}{2}(a+b+c)$,

$\qquad s = \frac{1}{2}(9+11+14) = 17.$

$\qquad s-a=8,$

$\qquad s-b=6, \qquad \therefore \tan \frac{A}{2} = \sqrt{\frac{6 \times 3}{17 \times 8}} = \cdot 3639.$

$\qquad s-c=3.$

$$\frac{A}{2} = 19° \ 59' ; \quad \therefore \ A = 39° \ 58'.$$

$$\tan \frac{B}{2} = \sqrt{\frac{8 \times 3}{17 \times 6}} = \cdot 4851.$$

$$\frac{B}{2} = 25° \ 53' ; \quad \therefore \ B = 51° \ 46'.$$

$$C = 180° - (39° \ 58' + 51° \ 46') = 88° \ 16'.$$

$$\text{Area} = \sqrt{s(s-a)(s-b)(s-c)}$$

$$= \sqrt{17 \times 8 \times 6 \times 3} = 49 \cdot 5 \text{ sq. ft.}$$

In Fig. 92 the line CD divides the triangle into two right-angled triangles. Let x denote the segment AD and y the segment DB, and p the length of CD.

In the triangle ADC, $\qquad x^2 + p^2 = 11^2.$

„ „ BDC, $\qquad y^2 + p^2 = 9^2.$

By subtraction, $\qquad x^2 - y^2 = 11^2 - 9^2 = 40,$

$$x - y = \frac{40}{x+y} = \frac{40}{14} = 2 \cdot 858,$$

$$x + y = 14 ;$$

$$\therefore \ x = 8 \cdot 429, \ y = 5 \cdot 571.$$

$$\cos A = \frac{8 \cdot 429}{11} = \cdot 7663 ;$$

$$\therefore \ A = 39° \ 58',$$

$$\cos B = \frac{5 \cdot 571}{9} = 51° \ 46'.$$

The angles can also be obtained from the following :

$$\cos A = \frac{b^2 + c^2 - a^2}{2bc} ; \ \cos B = \frac{a^2 + c^2 - b^2}{2ac} ; \ \cos C = \frac{a^2 + b^2 - c^2}{2ab}.$$

As these are not adapted for use with logarithms, they are troublesome when the lengths of the sides consist of three or more figures.

Ex. 19. The sides of a triangle are $a=4$, $b=7$, $c=9$. Find (a) the angles, (b) the sine of the smallest angle, (c) the cosine of the greatest angle.

(a) $$\cos A = \frac{7^2 + 9^2 - 4^2}{2 \times 7 \times 9} = \cdot 9048 ; \quad \therefore \ A = 25° \ 12'.$$

$$\cos B = \frac{4^2 + 9^2 - 7^2}{2 \times 4 \times 9} = \cdot 6667 ; \quad \therefore \ B = 48° \ 11 \ .$$

$$C = 180° - (25° \ 12' + 48° \ 11') = 106° \ 37'.$$

(b) $$\sin A = \sin 25° \ 12' = \cdot 4258.$$

(c) $$\cos C = \cos 106° \ 37' = -\cos 73° \ 23' = - \cdot 2860.$$

(ii) **Two Sides and an Angle.**—The data may be two sides and included angle, or two sides and the angle opposite one side.

Ex. 20. In a triangle ABC, $a = 5 \cdot 6$ in., $b = 7$ in. and $C = 46°$. Find the remaining parts and area.

Draw $CA = 7$, at C make the angle $ACB = 46°$ and $CB = 5 \cdot 6$ in. Join B to A; at B draw BD perpendicular to CA. Measure the angle $A = 52° \ 20'$ and length $AB = 5 \cdot 2$ in. (Fig. 93).

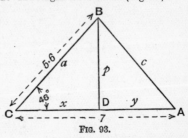

FIG. 93.

Let x denote the distance CD, y the distance DA and p the length BD.

$$x = 5 \cdot 6 \cos 46° = 5 \cdot 6 \times \cdot 6947 = 3 \cdot 89 ;$$

$$\therefore \ y = 7 - 3 \cdot 89 = 3 \cdot 11,$$

$$p = 5 \cdot 6 \sin 46° = 4 \cdot 028,$$

$$\tan A = \frac{4 \cdot 028}{3 \cdot 11} = 1 \cdot 295,$$

$$A = 52° \ 20',$$

$$B = 180° - (46° + 52° \ 20') = 81° \ 40',$$

$$\sin A = p \div c ; \quad \therefore \ c = \frac{4 \cdot 028}{\sin 52° \ 20'} = 5 \cdot 089 \text{ in.}$$

$$\text{Area} = \tfrac{1}{2}(AC \times DB) = \tfrac{1}{2}ab \sin C = \tfrac{1}{2} \times (5 \cdot 6 \times 7) \sin 46°$$

$$= 14 \cdot 1 \text{ sq. in.}$$

(iii) **Two Angles and a Side.**—Referring to Fig. 93, we obtain

$$\frac{p}{a} = \sin C \text{ and } \frac{p}{c} = \sin A \ ;$$

$$\therefore \ a \sin C = c \sin A \ ;$$

or

$$\frac{a}{\sin A} = \frac{c}{\sin C} \ ;$$

and by drawing a perpendicular from A to BC, we can obtain

$$\frac{c}{\sin C} = \frac{b}{\sin B}.$$

Hence $\dfrac{a}{\sin A} = \dfrac{b}{\sin B} = \dfrac{c}{\sin C} =$ diameter of circumscribing circle of triangle or *circum-circle* (Fig. 94).

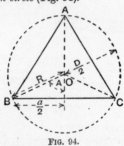

FIG. 94.

Ex. 21. In a triangle ABC, $A = 55°$, $B = 42°$, $a = 10$ in. Find the remaining parts, the area and the diameter of the circum-circle.

$$C = 180° - (55° + 42°) = 83°,$$

$$\frac{b}{a} = \frac{\sin B}{\sin A} \quad \text{or} \quad b = \frac{a \sin B}{\sin A},$$

$$b = \frac{10 \times \cdot 6691}{\cdot 8192} = 8 \cdot 168,$$

$$c = \frac{a \sin C}{\sin A}$$

$$= \frac{10 \times \cdot 9925}{\cdot 8192} = 12 \cdot 12.$$

$$\text{Area} = \tfrac{1}{2}(10 \times 8 \cdot 168 \sin 83°)$$

$$= 40 \cdot 53 \text{ sq. in.}$$

$$\text{Diameter} = \frac{10}{\sin 55°} = \frac{10}{\cdot 8192} = 12 \cdot 2 \text{ in.}$$

No.	log.
6·6910	0·8255
0·8192	$\overline{1}$·9134
8·168	0·9121
9·925	0·9967
0·8192	$\overline{1}$·9134
12·12	1·0833
5	0·6990
8·168	0·9121
sin 83°	$\overline{1}$·9967
40·54	1·6078

EXERCISES. XXXIV.

Solve the following triangles. Find the area in each case. Verify your results by using squared paper, or drawing to scale (dimensions in feet).

1. (i) $a=3$, $b=4$, $c=6$;   (ii) $a=3$, $b=5$, $c=7$;
   (iii) $a=8\cdot3$, $b=4\cdot2$, $c=5\cdot7$; (iv) $a=47\cdot5$, $b=51\cdot4$, $c=39\cdot4$;
   (v) $a=17\cdot58$, $b=13\cdot86$, $c=22$;
   (vi) $a=1061$, $b=909$, $c=698$.

2. (i) $a=37$, $b=42\cdot9$, $C=74°$; (ii) $a=30$, $b=40$, $C=52°$.
   (iii) $b=81$, $c=52$, $A=60°$; (iv) $a=91$, $b=62$, $C=48°\ 12'$;
   (v) $b=123$, $c=62$, $A=77°\ 20'$;
   (vi) $a=36\cdot5$, $b=27\cdot8$, $C=37°\ 36'$.

3. (i) $A=53°\ 8'$, $B=71°\ 34'$, $c=13$;
   (ii) $A=66°\ 2'$, $B=77°\ 6'$, $c=9\cdot849$;
   (iii) $A=47°\ 30'$, $C=52°$, $b=4$;
   (iv) $A=21°\ 48'$, $C=38°\ 13'$, $b=7$.

4. In a triangular field ABC, $a=300$ ft., $B=35°$, $A=75°$. Find the remaining parts, the area and value of turf at 1s. 6d. per sq. yd.

5. What is the angle of elevation of the sun when the length of the shadow of a post is 6 times the height of the post ?

6. A and B 300 yds. apart, are two places on the straight bank of a canal, C a place on the opposite bank, the angles CBA and BCA are found to be $35°$ and $75°$. Find the distance of C from A and B and from the nearest point on the bank.   [U.E.I.]

7. The angles of elevation of an airship at a certain instant from two stations A and B, 1200 yds. apart, are $70°$ and $45°$. Find the height of the airship.   [L.C.U.]

8. Resultant R of two forces P and Q inclined at an angle θ is given by

$$R=\sqrt{P^2+Q^2+2PQ\cos\theta}.$$

Find values of R (i) when $\theta=68°$, (ii) when $\theta=0°$.   [L.C.U.]

9. Perimeter of a triangle is 12 in. The sides are in the ratio $4:5:6$. Construct the triangle and find the angles and the area.
                    [U.E.I.]

10. The sides of a triangle are 3 in., 4 in., and 5 in. Find the three angles, the area, and diameter of circum-circle.   [N.U.T.]

11. At a certain point the angle of elevation of a tower is $14°$. From another point 60 yds. nearer the tower the elevation is $24°$. Find the height of the tower.   [U.E.I.]

12. An aeroplane flying 3000 ft. above ground makes a signal when exactly over an enemy. If a man in our own lines finds the angle of elevation is $15°$, how far is he from the enemy ?   [U.E.I.]

MATHEMATICAL TABLES.

TABLE I. IMPORTANT DATA.

$\pi = 3\cdot1416 = 3\cdot142$ or $\frac{22}{7}$.

$\pi^2 = 9\cdot87$.

$g = 32\cdot2$.

$\log \pi = \cdot4972$.

,, $2\cdot718 = \cdot4343$.

,, $\cdot7854 = \bar{1}\cdot8951$.

,, $62\cdot3 = 1\cdot7945$.

,, $1728 = 3\cdot2375$.

1 inch $= 2\cdot54$ centimetres.

1 mile $= 5280$ ft. $= 1760$ yards.

1 cubic foot of water $= 62\cdot3$ lbs.

1 gallon of water $= 10$ lbs. $= 277\cdot3$ cub. in.

$5\frac{1}{2}$ yards $= 1$ rod, pole, or perch.

100 links $= 1$ linear chain $= 22$ yards.

$30\frac{1}{4}$ sq. yards $= 1$ sq. rod.

10 sq. chains $= 1$ acre $= 4840$ sq. yards.

1 horse-power $= 33,000$ ft.-lbs. per min. $= 746$ watts.

Volts $\times$ amperes $=$ watts.

1 atmosphere $= 14\cdot7$ lbs. per sq. in.; corresponds to the pressure due to a column of water 34 ft. high, or a column of mercury 760 mm.

1 radian $= 57\cdot3$ degrees.

The base of Naperian logarithms is $\epsilon = 2\cdot718$.

To convert common into Naperian logarithms multiply by $2\cdot3026$.

TABLE II. RELATIVE WEIGHTS.

NAME.	Weight of Unit Volume in pounds.		Relative Density, or Specific Gravity.
	Cub. ft.	Cub. in.	
Water, - - - -	$62\cdot3$	$\cdot036$	1
Cast Iron, - - -	450	$\cdot26$	$7\cdot22$
Wrought Iron, - -	480	$\cdot28$	$7\cdot698$
Steel, - - - -	490	$\cdot29$	$7\cdot85$
Brass, - - - -	515	$\cdot298$	$8\cdot25$
Copper, - - - -	552	$\cdot319$	$8\cdot9$
Lead, - - - -	712	$\cdot414$	$11\cdot418$

TABLE III. LOGARITHMS.

	0	1	2	3	4	5	6	7	8	9	1 2 3	4 5 6	7 8
10	0000	0043	0086	0128	0170						4 9 13	17 21 26	30 34
						0212	0253	0294	0334	0374	4 8 12	16 20 24	28 32
11	0414	0453	0492	0531	0569						4 8 12	15 19 23	27 31
						0607	0645	0682	0719	0755	4 7 11	15 19 22	26 30
12	0792	0828	0864	0899	0934						3 7 11	14 18 21	25 28
						0969	1004	1038	1072	1106	3 7 10	14 17 20	24 27
13	1139	1173	1206	1239	1271						3 7 10	13 16 20	23 26
						1303	1335	1367	1399	1430	3 7 10	13 16 19	22 25
14	1461	1492	1523	1553	1584						3 6 9	12 15 19	22 25
						1614	1644	1673	1703	1732	3 6 9	12 15 17	20 23
15	1761	1790	1818	1847	1875						3 6 9	11 14 17	20 23
						1903	1931	1959	1987	2014	3 6 8	11 14 17	19 22
16	2041	2068	2095	2122	2148						3 6 8	11 14 16	19 22
						2175	2201	2227	2253	2279	3 5 8	10 13 16	18 21
17	2304	2330	2355	2380	2405						3 5 8	10 13 15	18 20
						2430	2455	2480	2504	2529	2 5 7	10 12 15	17 20
18	2553	2577	2601	2625	2648						2 5 7	9 12 14	16 19
						2672	2695	2718	2742	2765	2 5 7	9 11 14	16 18
19	2788	2810	2833	2856	2878						2 4 7	9 11 13	16 18
						2900	2923	2945	2967	2989	2 4 6	8 11 13	15 17
20	3010	3032	3054	3075	3096	3118	3139	3160	3181	3201	2 4 6	8 11 13	15 17
21	3222	3243	3263	3284	3304	3324	3345	3365	3385	3404	2 4 6	8 10 12	14 16
22	3424	3444	3464	3483	3502	3522	3541	3560	3579	3598	2 4 6	8 10 12	14 15
23	3617	3636	3655	3674	3692	3711	3729	3747	3766	3784	2 4 6	7 9 11	13 15
24	3802	3820	3838	3856	3874	3892	3909	3927	3945	3962	2 4 5	7 9 11	12 14
25	3979	3997	4014	4031	4048	4065	4082	4099	4116	4133	2 3 5	7 9 10	12 14
26	4150	4166	4183	4200	4216	4232	4249	4265	4281	4298	2 3 5	7 8 10	11 13
27	4314	4330	4346	4362	4378	4393	4409	4425	4440	4456	2 3 5	6 8 9	11 13
28	4472	4487	4502	4518	4533	4548	4564	4579	4594	4609	2 3 5	6 8 9	11 12
29	4624	4639	4654	4669	4683	4698	4713	4728	4742	4757	1 3 4	6 7 9	10 12
30	4771	4786	4800	4814	4829	4843	4857	4871	4886	4900	1 3 4	6 7 9	10 11
31	4914	4928	4942	4955	4969	4983	4997	5011	5024	5038	1 3 4	6 7 8	10 11
32	5051	5065	5079	5092	5105	5119	5132	5145	5159	5172	1 3 4	5 7 8	9 11
33	5185	5198	5211	5224	5237	5250	5263	5276	5289	5302	1 3 4	5 6 8	9 10
34	5315	5328	5340	5353	5366	5378	5391	5403	5416	5428	1 3 4	5 6 8	9 10
35	5441	5453	5465	5478	5490	5502	5514	5527	5539	5551	1 2 4	5 6 7	9 10
36	5563	5575	5587	5599	5611	5623	5635	5647	5658	5670	1 2 4	5 6 7	8 10
37	5682	5694	5705	5717	5729	5740	5752	5763	5775	5786	1 2 3	5 6 7	8 9
38	5798	5809	5821	5832	5843	5855	5866	5877	5888	5899	1 2 3	5 6 7	8 9
39	5911	5922	5933	5944	5955	5966	5977	5988	5999	6010	1 2 3	4 5 7	8 9
40	6021	6031	6042	6053	6064	6075	6085	6096	6107	6117	1 2 3	4 5 6	8 9
41	6128	6138	6149	6160	6170	6180	6191	6201	6212	6222	1 2 3	4 5 6	7 8
42	6232	6243	6253	6263	6274	6284	6294	6304	6314	6325	1 2 3	4 5 6	7 8
43	6335	6345	6355	6365	6375	6385	6395	6405	6415	6425	1 2 3	4 5 6	7 8
44	6435	6444	6454	6464	6474	6484	6493	6503	6513	6522	1 2 3	4 5 6	7 8
45	6532	6542	6551	6561	6571	6580	6590	6599	6609	6618	1 2 3	4 5 6	7 8
46	6628	6637	6646	6656	6665	6675	6684	6693	6702	6712	1 2 3	4 5 6	7 7
47	6721	6730	6739	6749	6758	6767	6776	6785	6794	6803	1 2 3	4 5 5	6 7
48	6812	6821	6830	6839	6848	6857	6866	6875	6884	6893	1 2 3	4 5 5	6 7
49	6902	6911	6920	6928	6937	6946	6955	6964	6972	6981	1 2 3	4 4 5	6 7

TABLE III. LOGARITHMS.

	0	1	2	3	4	5	6	7	8	9	1 2 3	4 5 6	7 8 9
50	6990	6998	7007	7016	7024	7033	7042	7050	7059	7067	1 2 3	3 4 5	6 7 8
51	7076	7084	7093	7101	7110	7118	7126	7135	7143	7152	1 2 3	3 4 5	6 7 8
52	7160	7168	7177	7185	7193	7202	7210	7218	7226	7235	1 2 2	3 4 5	6 7 7
53	7243	7251	7259	7267	7275	7284	7292	7300	7308	7316	1 2 2	3 4 5	6 6 7
54	7324	7332	7340	7348	7356	7364	7372	7380	7388	7396	1 2 2	3 4 5	6 6 7
55	7404	7412	7419	7427	7435	7443	7451	7459	7466	7474	1 2 2	3 4 5	5 6 7
56	7482	7490	7497	7505	7513	7520	7528	7536	7543	7551	1 2 2	3 4 5	5 6 7
57	7559	7566	7574	7582	7589	7597	7604	7612	7619	7627	1 2 2	3 4 5	5 6 7
58	7634	7642	7649	7657	7664	7672	7679	7686	7694	7701	1 1 2	3 4 4	5 6 7
59	7709	7716	7723	7731	7738	7745	7752	7760	7767	7774	1 1 2	3 4 4	5 6 7
60	7782	7789	7796	7803	7810	7818	7825	7832	7839	7846	1 1 2	3 4 4	5 6 6
61	7853	7860	7868	7875	7882	7889	7896	7903	7910	7917	1 1 2	3 4 4	5 6 6
62	7924	7931	7938	7945	7952	7959	7966	7973	7980	7987	1 1 2	3 3 4	5 6 6
63	7993	8000	8007	8014	8021	8028	8035	8041	8048	8055	1 1 2	3 3 4	5 5 6
64	8062	8069	8075	8082	8089	8096	8102	8109	8116	8122	1 1 2	3 3 4	5 5 6
65	8129	8136	8142	8149	8156	8162	8169	8176	8182	8189	1 1 2	3 3 4	5 5 6
66	8195	8202	8209	8215	8222	8228	8235	8241	8248	8254	1 1 2	3 3 4	5 5 6
67	8261	8267	8274	8280	8287	8293	8299	8306	8312	8319	1 1 2	3 3 4	5 5 6
68	8325	8331	8338	8344	8351	8357	8363	8370	8376	8382	1 1 2	3 3 4	4 5 6
69	8388	8395	8401	8407	8414	8420	8426	8432	8439	8445	1 1 2	2 3 4	4 5 6
70	8451	8457	8463	8470	8476	8482	8488	8494	8500	8506	1 1 2	2 3 4	4 5 6
71	8513	8519	8525	8531	8537	8543	8549	8555	8561	8567	1 1 2	2 3 4	4 5 5
72	8573	8579	8585	8591	8597	8603	8609	8615	8621	8627	1 1 2	2 3 4	4 5 5
73	8633	8639	8645	8651	8657	8663	8669	8675	8681	8686	1 1 2	2 3 4	4 5 5
74	8692	8698	8704	8710	8716	8722	8727	8733	8739	8745	1 1 2	2 3 4	4 5 5
75	8751	8756	8762	8768	8774	8779	8785	8791	8797	8802	1 1 2	2 3 3	4 5 5
76	8808	8814	8820	8825	8831	8837	8842	8848	8854	8859	1 1 2	2 3 3	4 5 5
77	8865	8871	8876	8882	8887	8893	8899	8904	8910	8915	1 1 2	2 3 3	4 4 5
78	8921	8927	8932	8938	8943	8949	8954	8960	8965	8971	1 1 2	2 3 3	4 4 5
79	8976	8982	8987	8993	8998	9004	9009	9015	9020	9025	1 1 2	2 3 3	4 4 5
80	9031	9036	9042	9047	9053	9058	9063	9069	9074	9079	1 1 2	2 3 3	4 4 5
81	9085	9090	9096	9101	9106	9112	9117	9122	9128	9133	1 1 2	2 3 3	4 4 5
82	9138	9143	9149	9154	9159	9165	9170	9175	9180	9186	1 1 2	2 3 3	4 4 5
83	9191	9196	9201	9206	9212	9217	9222	9227	9232	9238	1 1 2	2 3 3	4 4 5
84	9243	9248	9253	9258	9263	9269	9274	9279	9284	9289	1 1 2	2 3 3	4 4 5
85	9294	9299	9304	9309	9315	9320	9325	9330	9335	9340	1 1 2	2 3 3	4 4 5
86	9345	9350	9355	9360	9365	9370	9375	9380	9385	9390	1 1 2	2 3 3	4 4 5
87	9395	9400	9405	9410	9415	9420	9425	9430	9435	9440	0 1 1	2 2 3	3 4 4
88	9445	9450	9455	9460	9465	9469	9474	9479	9484	9489	0 1 1	2 2 3	3 4 4
89	9494	9499	9504	9509	9513	9518	9523	9528	9533	9538	0 1 1	2 2 3	3 4 4
90	9542	9547	9552	9557	9562	9566	9571	9576	9581	9586	0 1 1	2 2 3	3 4 4
91	9590	9595	9600	9605	9609	9614	9619	9624	9628	9633	0 1 1	2 2 3	3 4 4
92	9638	9643	9647	9652	9657	9661	9666	9671	9675	9680	0 1 1	2 2 3	3 4 4
93	9685	9689	9694	9699	9703	9708	9713	9717	9722	9727	0 1 1	2 2 3	3 4 4
94	9731	9736	9741	9745	9750	9754	9759	9763	9768	9773	0 1 1	2 2 3	3 4 4
95	9777	9782	9786	9791	9795	9800	9805	9809	9814	9818	0 1 1	2 2 3	3 4 4
96	9823	9827	9832	9836	9841	9845	9850	9854	9859	9863	0 1 1	2 2 3	3 4 4
97	9868	9872	9877	9881	9886	9890	9894	9899	9903	9908	0 1 1	2 2 3	3 4 4
98	9912	9917	9921	9926	9930	9934	9939	9943	9948	9952	0 1 1	2 2 3	3 4 4
99	9956	9961	9965	9969	9974	9978	9983	9987	9991	9996	0 1 1	2 2 3	3 3 4

TABLE IV. ANTILOGARITHMS.

	0	1	2	3	4	5	6	7	8	9	1 2 3	4 5 6	7 8 9
·00	1000	1002	1005	1007	1009	1012	1014	1016	1019	1021	0 0 1	1 1 1	2 2 2
·01	1023	1026	1028	1030	1033	1035	1038	1040	1042	1045	0 0 1	1 1 1	2 2 2
·02	1047	1050	1052	1054	1057	1059	1062	1064	1067	1069	0 0 1	1 1 1	2 2 2
·03	1072	1074	1076	1079	1081	1084	1086	1089	1091	1094	0 0 1	1 1 1	2 2 2
·04	1096	1099	1102	1104	1107	1109	1112	1114	1117	1119	0 1 1	1 1 2	2 2 2
·05	1122	1125	1127	1130	1132	1135	1138	1140	1143	1146	0 1 1	1 1 2	2 2 2
·06	1148	1151	1153	1156	1159	1161	1164	1167	1169	1172	0 1 1	1 1 2	2 2 2
·07	1175	1178	1180	1183	1186	1189	1191	1194	1197	1199	0 1 1	1 1 2	2 2 2
·08	1202	1205	1208	1211	1213	1216	1219	1222	1225	1227	0 1 1	1 1 2	2 2 2
·09	1230	1233	1236	1239	1242	1245	1247	1250	1253	1256	0 1 1	1 1 2	2 2 3
·10	1259	1262	1265	1268	1271	1274	1276	1279	1282	1285	0 1 1	1 1 2	2 2 3
·11	1288	1291	1294	1297	1300	1303	1306	1309	1312	1315	0 1 1	1 2 2	2 2 3
·12	1318	1321	1324	1327	1330	1334	1337	1340	1343	1346	0 1 1	1 2 2	2 2 3
·13	1349	1352	1355	1358	1361	1365	1368	1371	1374	1377	0 1 1	1 2 2	2 3 3
·14	1380	1384	1387	1390	1393	1396	1400	1403	1406	1409	0 1 1	1 2 2	2 3 3
·15	1413	1416	1419	1422	1426	1429	1432	1435	1439	1442	0 1 1	1 2 2	2 3 3
·16	1445	1449	1452	1455	1459	1462	1466	1469	1472	1476	0 1 1	1 2 2	3 3 3
·17	1479	1483	1486	1489	1493	1496	1500	1503	1507	1510	0 1 1	1 2 2	2 3 3
·18	1514	1517	1521	1524	1528	1531	1535	1538	1542	1545	0 1 1	1 2 2	2 3 3
·19	1549	1552	1556	1560	1563	1567	1570	1574	1578	1581	0 1 1	1 2 2	3 3 3
·20	1585	1589	1592	1596	1600	1603	1607	1611	1614	1618	0 1 1	1 2 2	3 3 3
21	1622	1626	1629	1633	1637	1641	1644	1648	1652	1656	0 1 1	2 2 2	3 3 3
·22	1660	1663	1667	1671	1675	1679	1683	1687	1690	1694	0 1 1	2 2 2	3 3 3
·23	1698	1702	1706	1710	1714	1718	1722	1726	1730	1734	0 1 1	2 2 2	3 3 4
·24	1738	1742	1746	1750	1754	1758	1762	1766	1770	1774	0 1 1	2 2 2	3 3 4
·25	1778	1782	1786	1791	1795	1799	1803	1807	1811	1816	0 1 1	2 2 2	3 3 4
·26	1820	1824	1828	1832	1837	1841	1845	1849	1854	1858	0 1 1	2 2 3	3 3 4
·27	1862	1866	1871	1875	1879	1884	1888	1892	1897	1901	0 1 1	2 2 3	3 3 4
·28	1905	1910	1914	1919	1923	1928	1932	1936	1941	1945	0 1 1	2 2 3	3 4 4
·29	1950	1954	1959	1963	1968	1972	1977	1982	1986	1991	0 1 1	2 2 3	3 4 4
·30	1995	2000	2004	2009	2014	2018	2023	2028	2032	2037	0 1 1	2 2 3	3 4 4
·31	2042	2046	2051	2056	2061	2065	2070	2075	2080	2084	0 1 1	2 2 3	3 4 4
·32	2089	2094	2099	2104	2109	2113	2118	2123	2128	2133	0 1 1	2 2 3	3 4 4
·33	2138	2143	2148	2153	2158	2163	2168	2173	2178	2183	0 1 1	2 2 3	3 4 4
·34	2188	2193	2198	2203	2208	2213	2218	2223	2228	2234	1 1 2	2 3 3	4 4 5
·35	2239	2244	2249	2254	2259	2265	2270	2275	2280	2286	1 1 2	2 3 3	4 4 5
·36	2291	2296	2301	2307	2312	2317	2323	2328	2333	2339	1 1 2	2 3 3	4 4 5
·37	2344	2350	2355	2360	2366	2371	2377	2382	2388	2393	1 1 2	2 3 3	4 4 5
·38	2399	2404	2410	2415	2421	2427	2432	2438	2443	2449	1 1 2	2 3 3	4 5 5
·39	2455	2460	2466	2472	2477	2483	2489	2495	2500	2506	1 1 2	2 3 3	4 5 5
·40	2512	2518	2523	2529	2535	2541	2547	2553	2559	2564	1 1 2	2 3 4	4 5 5
·41	2570	2576	2582	2588	2594	2600	2606	2612	2618	2624	1 1 2	2 3 4	4 5 5
·42	2630	2636	2642	2649	2655	2661	2667	2673	2679	2685	1 1 2	2 3 4	4 5 6
·43	2692	2698	2704	2710	2716	2723	2729	2735	2742	2748	1 1 2	3 3 4	4 5 6
·44	2754	2761	2767	2773	2780	2786	2793	2799	2805	2812	1 1 2	3 3 4	4 5 6
·45	2818	2825	2831	2838	2844	2851	2858	2864	2871	2877	1 1 2	3 3 4	5 5 6
·46	2884	2891	2897	2904	2911	2917	2924	2931	2938	2944	1 1 2	3 3 4	5 5 6
·47	2951	2958	2965	2972	2979	2985	2992	2999	3006	3013	1 1 2	3 3 4	5 5 6
·48	3020	3027	3034	3041	3048	3055	3062	3069	3076	3083	1 1 2	3 4 4	5 6 6
·49	3090	3097	3105	3112	3119	3126	3133	3141	3148	3155	1 1 2	3 4 4	5 6 6

TABLE IV. ANTILOGARITHMS.

0	1	2	3	4	5	6	7	8	9	1 2 3	4 5 6	7 8 9
3162	3170	3177	3184	3192	3199	3206	3214	3221	3228	1 1 2	3 4 4	5 6 7
3236	3243	3251	3258	3266	3273	3281	3289	3296	3304	1 2 2	3 4 5	5 6 7
3311	3319	3327	3334	3342	3350	3357	3365	3373	3381	1 2 2	3 4 5	5 6 7
3388	3396	3404	3412	3420	3428	3436	3443	3451	3459	1 2 2	3 4 5	6 6 7
3467	3475	3483	3491	3499	3508	3516	3524	3532	3540	1 2 2	3 4 5	6 6 7
3548	3556	3565	3573	3581	3589	3597	3606	3614	3622	1 2 2	3 4 5	6 7 7
3631	3639	3648	3656	3664	3673	3681	3690	3698	3707	1 2 3	3 4 5	6 7 8
3715	3724	3733	3741	3750	3758	3767	3776	3784	3793	1 2 3	3 4 5	6 7 8
3802	3811	3819	3828	3837	3846	3855	3864	3873	3882	1 2 3	4 4 5	6 7 8
3890	3899	3908	3917	3926	3936	3945	3954	3963	3972	1 2 3	4 5 5	6 7 8
3981	3990	3999	4009	4018	4027	4036	4046	4055	4064	1 2 3	4 5 6	6 7 8
4074	4083	4093	4102	4111	4121	4130	4140	4150	4159	1 2 3	4 5 6	7 8 9
4169	4178	4188	4198	4207	4217	4227	4236	4246	4256	1 2 3	4 5 6	7 8 9
4266	4276	4285	4295	4305	4315	4325	4335	4345	4355	1 2 3	4 5 6	7 8 9
4365	4375	4385	4395	4406	4416	4426	4436	4446	4457	1 2 3	4 5 6	7 8 9
4467	4477	4487	4498	4508	4519	4529	4539	4550	4560	1 2 3	4 5 6	7 8 9
4571	4581	4592	4603	4613	4624	4634	4645	4656	4667	1 2 3	4 5 6	7 9 10
4677	4688	4699	4710	4721	4732	4742	4753	4764	4775	1 2 3	4 5 7	8 9 10
4786	4797	4808	4819	4831	4842	4853	4864	4875	4887	1 2 3	4 6 7	8 9 10
4898	4909	4920	4932	4943	4955	4966	4977	4989	5000	1 2 3	5 6 7	8 9 10
5012	5023	5035	5047	5058	5070	5082	5093	5105	5117	1 2 4	5 6 7	8 9 11
5129	5140	5152	5164	5176	5188	5200	5212	5224	5236	1 2 4	5 6 7	8 10 11
5248	5260	5272	5284	5297	5309	5321	5333	5346	5358	1 2 4	5 6 7	9 10 11
5370	5383	5395	5408	5420	5433	5445	5458	5470	5483	1 3 4	5 6 8	9 10 11
5495	5508	5521	5534	5546	5559	5572	5585	5598	5610	1 3 4	5 6 8	9 10 12
5623	5636	5649	5662	5675	5689	5702	5715	5728	5741	1 3 4	5 7 8	9 10 12
5754	5768	5781	5794	5808	5821	5834	5848	5861	5875	1 3 4	5 7 8	9 11 12
5888	5902	5916	5929	5943	5957	5970	5984	5998	6012	1 3 4	5 7 8	10 11 12
6026	6039	6053	6067	6081	6095	6109	6124	6138	6152	1 3 4	6 7 8	10 11 13
6166	6180	6194	6209	6223	6237	6252	6266	6281	6295	1 3 4	6 7 9	10 11 13
6310	6324	6339	6353	6368	6383	6397	6412	6427	6442	1 3 4	6 7 9	10 12 13
6457	6471	6486	6501	6516	6531	6546	6561	6577	6592	2 3 5	6 8 9	11 12 14
6607	6622	6637	6653	6668	6683	6699	6714	6730	6745	2 3 5	6 8 9	11 12 14
6761	6776	6792	6808	6823	6839	6855	6871	6887	6902	2 3 5	6 8 9	11 13 14
6918	6934	6950	6966	6982	6998	7015	7031	7047	7063	2 3 5	6 8 10	11 13 15
7079	7096	7112	7129	7145	7161	7178	7194	7211	7228	2 3 5	7 8 10	12 13 15
7244	7261	7278	7295	7311	7328	7345	7362	7379	7396	2 3 5	7 8 10	12 13 15
7413	7430	7447	7464	7482	7499	7516	7534	7551	7568	2 3 5	7 9 10	12 14 16
7586	7603	7621	7638	7656	7674	7691	7709	7727	7745	2 4 5	7 9 11	12 14 16
7762	7780	7798	7816	7834	7852	7870	7889	7907	7925	2 4 5	7 9 11	13 14 16
7943	7962	7980	7998	8017	8035	8054	8072	8091	8110	2 4 6	7 9 11	13 15 17
8128	8147	8166	8185	8204	8222	8241	8260	8279	8299	2 4 6	8 9 11	13 15 17
8318	8337	8356	8375	8395	8414	8433	8453	8472	8492	2 4 6	8 10 12	14 15 17
8511	8531	8551	8570	8590	8610	8630	8650	8670	8690	2 4 6	8 10 12	14 16 18
8710	8730	8750	8770	8790	8810	8831	8851	8872	8892	2 4 6	8 10 12	14 16 18
8913	8933	8954	8974	8995	9016	9036	9057	9078	9099	2 4 6	8 10 12	15 17 19
9120	9141	9162	9183	9204	9226	9247	9268	9290	9311	2 4 6	8 11 13	15 17 19
9333	9354	9376	9397	9419	9441	9462	9484	9506	9528	2 4 7	9 11 13	15 17 20
9550	9572	9594	9616	9638	9661	9683	9705	9727	9750	2 4 7	9 11 13	16 18 20
9772	9795	9817	9840	9863	9886	9908	9931	9954	9977	2 5 7	9 11 14	16 18 20

TABLE V.

Deg.	Radians.	Chords.	Sine.	Tangent.	Cotangent.	Cosine.			
0°	0	0	0	0	∞	1	1·414	1·5708	90°
1	·0175	·017	·0175	·0175	57·2900	·9998	1·402	1·5533	89
2	·0349	·035	·0349	·0349	28·6363	·9994	1·389	1·5359	88
3	·0524	·052	·0523	·0524	19·0811	·9986	1·377	1·5184	87
4	·0698	·070	·0698	·0699	14·3006	·9976	1·364	1·5010	86
5	·0873	·087	·0872	·0875	11·4301	·9962	1·351	1·4835	85
6	·1047	·105	·1045	·1051	9·5144	·9945	1·338	1·4661	84
7	·1222	·122	·1219	·1228	8·1443	·9925	1·325	1·4486	83
8	·1396	·139	·1392	·1405	7·1154	·9903	1·312	1·4312	82
9	·1571	·157	·1564	·1584	6·3138	·9877	1·299	1·4137	81
10	·1745	·174	·1736	·1763	5·6713	·9848	1·286	1·3963	80
11	·1920	·192	·1908	·1944	5·1446	·9816	1·272	1·3788	79
12	·2094	·209	·2079	·2126	4·7046	·9781	1·259	1·3614	78
13	·2269	·226	·2250	·2309	4·3315	·9744	1·245	1·3439	77
14	·2443	·244	·2419	·2493	4·0108	·9703	1·231	1·3265	76
15	·2618	·261	·2588	·2679	3·7321	·9659	1·217	1·3090	75
16	·2793	·278	·2756	·2867	3·4874	·9613	1·204	1·2915	74
17	·2967	·296	·2924	·3057	3·2709	·9563	1·190	1·2741	73
18	·3142	·313	·3090	·3249	3·0777	·9511	1·176	1·2566	72
19	·3316	·330	·3256	·3443	2·9042	·9455	1·161	1·2392	71
20	·3491	·347	·3420	·3640	2·7475	·9397	1·147	1·2217	70
21	·3665	·364	·3584	·3839	2·6051	·9336	1·133	1·2043	69
22	·3840	·382	·3746	·4040	2·4751	·9272	1·118	1·1868	68
23	·4014	·399	·3907	·4245	2·3559	·9205	1·104	1·1694	67
24	·4189	·416	·4067	·4452	2·2460	·9135	1·089	1·1519	66
25	·4363	·433	·4226	·4663	2·1445	·9063	1·075	1·1345	65
26	·4538	·450	·4384	·4877	2·0503	·8988	1·060	1·1170	64
27	·4712	·467	·4540	·5095	1·9626	·8910	1·045	1·0996	63
28	·4887	·484	·4695	·5317	1·8807	·8829	1·030	1·0821	62
29	·5061	·501	·4848	·5543	1·8040	·8746	1·015	1·0647	61
30	·5236	·518	·5000	·5774	1·7321	·8660	1·000	1·0472	60
31	·5411	·534	·5150	·6009	1·6643	·8572	·985	1·0297	59
32	·5585	·551	·5299	·6249	1·6003	·8480	·970	1·0123	58
33	·5760	·568	·5446	·6494	1·5399	·8387	·954	·9948	57
34	·5934	·585	·5592	·6745	1·4826	·8290	·939	·9774	56
35	·6109	·601	·5736	·7002	1·4281	·8192	·923	·9599	55
36	·6283	·618	·5878	·7265	1·3764	·8090	·908	·9425	54
37	·6458	·635	·6018	·7536	1·3270	·7986	·892	·9250	53
38	·6632	·651	·6157	·7813	1·2799	·7880	·877	·9076	52
39	·6807	·668	·6293	·8098	1·2349	·7771	·861	·8901	51
40	·6981	·684	·6428	·8391	1·1918	·7660	·845	·8727	50
41	·7156	·700	·6561	·8693	1·1504	·7547	·829	·8552	49
42	·7330	·717	·6691	·9004	1·1106	·7431	·813	·8378	48
43	·7505	·733	·6820	·9325	1·0724	·7314	·797	·8203	47
44	·7679	·749	·6947	·9657	1·0355	·7193	·781	·8029	46
45	·7854	·765	·7071	1·0000	1·0000	·7071	·765	·7854	45
			Cosine.	Cotangent.	Tangent.	Sine.	Chords.	Radians.	Deg.
								Angle.	

ANSWERS.

PART II.

Exercises I., p. 4.

1. 43 sq. ft. 6′ 6″, or 43 sq. ft. 78 sq. in. **2.** 198·75 sq. ft.

3. 12 sq. ft. 81 sq. in. **4.** 103 sq. ft. 2′ 5″ 3‴ 6^{iv}.

5. 300 cub. ft. 368 cub. in. **6.** 6696·969 cub. ft.

7. 139 cub. ft. 519 cub. in. **8.** 334 cub. ft. 4′ 11″ 6‴.

9. 5 cub. ft. 192 cub. in. **10.** 11 cub. yds. 6 cub. ft. 1123 cub. in.

11. 99·65 cub. ft. **12.** 105 cub. ft. 339·5138 cub. in.

13. 50 cub. ft. 946$\frac{7}{8}$ cub. in. **14.** 8 cub. ft. 656·375 cub. in.

15. 38 cub. ft. 432 cub. in. ; 54 sq. ft. 70·6 sq. in.

16. 11 sq. ft. 80·6 sq. in. **17.** 456·2 sq. ft.

Exercises II., p. 10.

1. 714·1. **2.** 1·176. **3.** 48·55. **4.** 853·1.

5. ·07993. **6.** 1065. **7.** 984·2. **8.** 287·4.

9. 6·474. **10.** (i) 24·18 ; (ii) 750·2. **11.** ·1233.

12. ·07186. **13.** ·01561. **14.** 148·9. **15.** ·2531.

16. ·04682. **17.** 507·6. **18.** ·00917. **19.** 2·396.

20. ·05398. **21.** 9·088. **22.** ·08935. **23.** 183·7.

24. ·01614. **25.** (i) ·04246 ; (ii) 248·8. **26.** (i) ·8722 ; (ii) ·2346.

27. ·1097. **28.** 973·6. **29.** ·09761. **30.** ·00007381.

31. (i) ·7625 ; (ii) ·07391 ; (iii) 78·38 ; (iv) 6·25.

Exercises III., p. 11.

1. ·0031. **2.** ·03458. **3.** 7850. **4.** 40000.

5. ·012. **6.** ·04369. **7.** ·07087. **8.** 53·32.

9. 204. **10.** ·4006. **11.** 2551. **12.** ·0006398

13. 12000. **14.** ·02665. **15.** ·04619. **16.** ·3607.

17. 108·8. **18.** ·005803. **19.** ·06039. **20.** ·1072.

21. 3·736. **22.** (i) ·0177 ; (ii) 2·44. **23.** 76·93.

24. 1·285. **25.** ·0000008389.

Miscellaneous Exercises IV., p. 12.

1. (i) 1·2 ; (ii) ·1099.   2. (i) 1265 ; (ii) 736.
3. (i) ·02932 ; (ii) 1551.   4. (i) 33·29 ; (ii) 28·39.
5. (i) ·3001 ; (ii) 736.   6. (i) 1100 ; (ii) 27070.
7. (i) 7499 ; (ii) 3·74.   8. (i) ·01447 ; (ii) 76·9.   9. 1·285.
10. 1·06.   11. (i) 50·67 ; (ii) ·0004511 ; (iii) 24·4.   12. 171·4.
13. (i) 630, 64·4 ;   (ii) 973·6, 181·3 ;   (iii) ·000002074, 37·56 ;
   (iv) ·00007381, 2·44 ;   (v) 937·8, 45·34 ;
   (vi) 1·03, 736 ;   (vii) 15800, 32·94.

Exercises V., p. 17.

1. ·04062.   2. ·5195.   3. (i) 3·009 ; (ii) ·4441.   4. 503·4.
5. 2·06.   6. ·08502.   7. 1·162.   8. (i) 3·267 ; (ii) ·5919.
9. ·1601.   10. ·0001129.   11. ·153.   12. 2·696.
13. (i) 8·87 ; (ii) 5·723 ; (iii) ·8333.   14. 3·981.   15. ·5409.
16. ·03465.   17. 21·59.   18. 6·401.   19. 13·32.

Miscellaneous Exercises VI., p. 20.

1. ·0001344.   2. ·1246.   4. 3.   5. 2296.
6. ·0001352.   7. 3·873.   8. 5·7356 ; 2·7356 ; 5̄·7356.
9. 8287.   10. ·3221.   11. 10640.   12. 2̄·4807.
13. 1·162.   14. ·00007474.   15. 10·4.   16. 1·708.
17. ·02191.   18. 1783.   19. 31·1.   20. 4873.
21. 1119.   22. 1·816.   23. 1297.   24. (ii) ·6142.
25. 2·8.   26. ·3271.   27. ·2928.   28. ·008004.
29. 43·46.   30. ·05733.   31. ·4677.   32. 5887.
33. 1·078.   34. 4851.   35. 2·56.   36. 3·39×10⁶.
37. (i) ·1246, 1146 ; (ii) ·0001344, ·005466 ; (iii) 0001404, 3·021.
38. 1·703 ; ·001107.   39. ·06714.   40. (i) 18·38 ; (ii) 22·3 ; (iii) 11·8.
41. (a) 87·22 ; (b) 0·9042 ; (c) 8·127.
42. (a) 0·2418 ; (b) 0 5598 ; (c) 39·07.
43. (a) 538 9 ; (b) 2·062 ; (c) 2·253 ; (d) 0·09101 ; (e) 2048.
44. 20 87 ; 19 ; 3·415.   45. 6 725.
46. 295·2 ; 1·627×10⁻¹¹ ; x=5·906.   47. 800·2.   48. 3·681.
49. x=40·66.   50. (a) v=2·495 ; (b) x=7 544   51. 1·854.

Exercises VII., p. 29.

1. 3·14, 7, 12·6, 28·3, 4·15, 8·04, 13·85, 30·2.
2. 623·4.   3. 5 in.

Exercises VIII., p. 33.

1. 46.	2. 151·582 inches.	3. 15·71 ft.
4. 24857·9 miles.	5. 2? ft. 7·4 in.	6. 4965.
7. 26400 ; 6·365 ft.	8. 63·05 ; 58·75.	9. 396.
10. 640.	11. 5¾ miles.	12. 13 ft.
13. 180.	14. 1·91 ft. ; 2·228 ft.	15. 5712 ft.
16. 43·98 in.	17. 34·7 ; 31·825.	18. 78·5 in.
19. 47·744 in.; 11·936 in.	20. 98·97 in.	21. 32·99 in.
22. 1206·36 sq. in.	23. 57° 17′ 45″ or 57°·3.	24. ·434°.
25. 12·5664 in.	26. ·2286 radians.	27. 691 yds.
28. 7918 miles.	29. 4·52 in.	30. 183° 20′ 47″.
31. 435·7.	32. 4° 20′ 13″.	33. 25 in.

Exercises IX., p. 41.

1. 17 in.	2. 5·046 sq. in.	3. 9·499 in.	4. 159·7 sq. ft.
5. 200 yds.	6. (i) 3 ; (ii) ·004 ; (iii) ·02 ; (iv) ·2.		
7. (i) ·003217 ; (ii) ·00933 ; (iii) 8·553.		8. £2. 18s. 10·2d.	
9. 140·3 sq. ft.	10. 11393 624 sq. ft.	11. 539·375 sq. ft.	
12. 20·6 sq. ft.	13. 42·774.	14. £27. 9s. 9d.	
15. 1 : 3·78.	16. 82·47 sq. ft.	17. 489 sq. ft.; 64 ft.	
18. ·982 sq. ft.	19. 525 sq. in.	20. 1472·625.	
21. 20·106 sq. ft.	22. 15·187 ft.	23. 13·352 sq. in.	
24. 7·658 sq. in.	25. 43·5 in.	26. 22·8 in.	
27. 2618 sq. yds.	28. 157·08 yds. ; 1884·96 sq. yds.		
29. 43·98 ft. : 150·797 sq. ft.	30. 2748·9 sq. ft.	31. 339·2928 sq. in.	
32. 6454 sq. ft.	33. 4·094 in.		

Exercises X., p. 59.

3. 144 ; 142.	4. 2720 lbs.	5. 80·2 sq. yds.	6. 236 lbs.
7. 339·7 sq. ft.	8. 12800 cub. ft.	9. 248 72 cub. ft. ; 8678 ibs.	
10. 1704 sq. ft.	11. 286 sq. ft.	12. 52·32 ; 52·8 ; 52·8.	
13. 61·01 ; 59·26 ; 58·66.	14. 32·778 ; 32·598.	15. 31053·6 cub. ft.	
16. 12·4 tons	17. £991. 10s.	18. £17. 15s. 2d.	
19. 596 9 cub. in., 21·49. lbs.	20. 61·1, 10279·5.	21. 2375⅓ sq. yds.	

Exercises XI., p. 68.

1. 28·316.	2. 1157.	4. 30350.	5. 2181·3.	6. 1018 ; 15·432.
7. 200 lbs.	8. 1226 grams.	9. 11·007 ; 216·5.	10. 56·793.
11. 49·978.	12. 54431·12.	13. 1543·235 ; 220·36.	14. 163·2.
15. 64968·75.	16. 0·4898.	17. 14·29 c.c.	18. 35·23.	19. 7·3
20. 13·9. cub in.	21. 3 pts.	22. Gold 452·3 silver 147·7 grams.
23. Hollow, cavity 1 c.c.	24. 13 cub. in.		

Exercises XII., p. 79.

1. 1008 cub. in.   **2.** 64 cub. ft. 398·72.

3. 13 cub. ft.; 81; 810 lbs.   **4.** 6·191 ft.

5. 3000 kilos.   **6.** 2359.

7. 11·51; 9·245 cub. ft.   **8.** 15 ft. 7 in.; £18. 5s. 2·8d.

9. £2. 15s. 5·7d.   **10.** 86·4 in.   **11.** 4·87.

12. 343.   **13.** 4984 lbs.   **14.** 1s. 4d.

15. 421·875 cub. ft.   **16.** 472 sq. ft.   **17.** 9 sq. in.

18. 10 ft. 8 in.; 1½ in.   **19.** 7980 cub. in.; 9s. 2d.

20. 1·542 cub. ft.; 12·66 tons. **21.** 1·091 ft.   **22.** £1. 2s. 6d.

23. 216 cub. ft.   **24.** 280 lbs.   **25.** 158·48 lbs.

26. £90.   **27.** 4·099 ft. **28.** 6885 cub. in.; 230·8 lbs.

29. 7921 cub. in.; 151·4 lbs.   **30.** 3·569 tons.   **31.** 33·47 tons.

32. 32·5 lbs.   **33.** 8·596 rods.

34. 34 lbs.   **35.** 2798 lbs. **36.** 1330 lbs.

37. 2·23 cub. ft.; 0.45 tons.   **38.** 7·764 cub. ft.; 3493·8 lbs.

39. (a) 3·056 cub. ft.; 190·4 lbs.   (b) 1632 cub. in.; 424·3 lbs.

40. 500,000.   **41.** 8 ft. 0·45 in.

42. (a) 3·55 xyz; (b) (i) $2(xz+yz)$; (ii) $\sqrt{x^2+y^2}$; (iii) $\sqrt{x^2+y^2+z^2}$.

43. 17010 cub. ft.   **44.** 10 in.   **45.** 2·156 lb.

Exercises XIII., p. 87.

1. 402·124 sq. ft.; 1608·48 cub. ft.   **2.** 95·14 sq. ft.; 70·93 cub. ft.

3. 7·979 in.   **4.** 4084 sq. in.

5. 21·48 sq. ft.; 3092·5 sq. in. **6.** 2262 cub. in.; 674·2 lbs.

7. 1·57 cub. ft.   **8.** 237·9 lbs.   **9.** 5497·8 cub. ft.; 152·95 tons.

10. 100·53 lbs.   **11.** 2·45 inches per min.

12. 10 ft.   **13.** £32. 19s. 6d.   **14.** 1352·4 cub. in.

15. 30580 lbs.   **16.** 4·6735 lbs. **17.** 960·25 lbs.

18. 1508 lbs.   **19.** 2222 lbs.   **20.** 26·54 sq. yds.; 4353 lbs.

21. 39·5 in.   **22.** 14·9 tons.   **23.** 2·012 lbs.

24. 21·21.   **25.** 49·48 sq. ft.; 43·3 cub. ft.; 19450 lbs.

26. 2029·5 cub. in.; 527·4 lbs. **27.** 6 ft.; £10. 14s. 6d.

28. 1434 lbs.; £10. 4s. 8·9d.   **29.** 6896 lbs.   **30.** 17·04 tons.

31. ·274 ft.   **32.** 6·446 in.   **33.** 405·2 lbs.   **34.** 355 lbs.

35. 17s. 10·2d.   **36.** ·025 in.   **37.** 10 mill. cub. ft.; 239 tons.

38. 512·9 lbs.   **39.** 40·8 lbs.   **40.** 67 lbs.; 726 lbs.

41. 1½ in.   **42.** 9350.   **43.** 1 hr. 21·9 min.

Exercises XIV., p. 96.

1. 500 sq. ft.; 645·3 cub. ft.   **2.** 6·534 lbs.

3. 66·59 sq. ft.; 32 cub. ft.   **4.** 47·124 cub. ft.; 54·95 sq. ft.

5. 33·4 lbs.; 53·11 lbs.   **6.** 3·22 lbs.   **7.** 249·4 cub. ft.

8. 23·6 inches.   **9.** 532·2 cub. ft.

10. 32·567 yds.   **11.** 763·3 ft.; 3458987 cub. yds.

12. $128\frac{5}{8}$ cub. in.; $2\frac{1}{24}$ cub. in.; 177·4 sq. in.   **13.** 3466145 cub. yds.

14. 70·1 ft.   **15.** 263·1 ft.   **16.** 38·5 sq. in.; 9·629 sq. in.

17. 36382 cub. in.   **18.** 206·5 cub. ft.   **19.** 117285 cub. ft.

20. 22·75 sq. in.   **21.** 11·8 in.   **22.** 12·57 cub. in.

23. (a) 204·2 sq. in.; (b) 314·2 cub. in.

24. (a) 6·648 in.; (b) 37·4 cub. in.; (c) 50·13 sq. in.

25. (a) 241·3 cub. ft.; (b) 11·09 ft.; (c) 167·2 sq. ft.

26. 0·994 : 1.   **27.** 357·7 sq. in.; 56·9°.

28. 17880 grs.   **29.** 1·815.

Exercises XV., p. 101.

1. 6636 cub. in.; 1725·36 lbs.   **2.** 3327 lbs.

3. 631·9 sq. in.; 631·9 cub. in.; 176 9 lbs.   **4.** 7843 lbs.

5. 3·5 in.   **6.** 9·8 in.   **7.** 128·03 cub. ft

Exercises XVI., p. 104.

1. 154 sq. in.; 46·72 lbs.   **2.** 8·088 in.   **3.** 8·306 in.; 12·98 in.

4. 16·875 in.   **5.** 8014·9; 12·625.   **6.** 4·044 in.

7. 4 hours 32 min.   **8.** 4·1888 cub. ft.   **9.** 7·445 in.; 3·385 in.

10. 11·62 in.   **11.** 49·8.   **12.** 655·8 lbs.   **13.** 2264 lbs.

14. 66·42 lbs.   **15.** £29. 13s. 7½d.   **16.** 12·98 in.

Miscellaneous Exercises XVII., p. 105.

1. 1233 lbs.   **2.** 133·74 ft.   **3.** 1033·849 lbs.

4. 96 cub. in.; 138·528 sq. in.   **5.** 1891·32 sq. ft.   **6.** 1 ft.

7. 151·7 cub. ft.   **8.** 4·083 in.   **9.** ·79 lb.

11. 4r (where r = rad. of sphere).   **12.** 1232 cub. ft.

13. 9·048 in.   **14.** 3·2 ft.   **15.** 33·47 tons.

16. 188·496 cub. in.   **17.** 140900.   **18.** 14·6 in.

19. 7595 lbs.   **20.** 568 ; 426.   **21.** 2324·7 sq. ft.

22. 216.   **23.** 1·084 : 1.   **24.** 10·9 min.

25. £1. 17s. 3d.   **26.** 16 ft. 2·4 in.   **27.** ½ in.

28. 1256·63 sq. ft.   **29.** 31·37 min.   **30.** 4·43 ft.; 249700.

31. 493·3 lbs.   **32.** £136.   **33.** 1309 lbs.

Exercises XVIII., p. 111.

1. $(x+3)(x-19)$.   **2.** $(10x-1)(x+8)$.   **3.** $(x+5)(x-17)$.

4. $(11x-2)(x+7)$.   **5.** $(2x+1)(5x-2)$.   **6.** $(x+2+2y)(x+2-2y)$.

7. $(a-b+c)(a^2-2ab-ac+b^2+bc+c^2)$.   **8.** b^2.

9. (i) $(x-11)(x+4)$; (ii) $(x+6)(x-17)$.   **10.** $(2x-3y)(7x-2y)$.

11. $(x+2)(x-7)$.   **12.** $y(x-3y)(x-12y)$.   **13.** $5(c-a)(7a+6b-c)$.

14. (i) $(3x-2y)(2x+3y)$;   (ii) $x(x-6y)(x-7y)$;

  (iii) $(3a+4b+c)(-a+5c)$; (iv) $(9x^2+25y^2)(3x+5y)(3x-5y)$.

15. $(3x-4y)(7x+5y)$.   **16.** $(x-y)(x^2-5xy+7y^2)$.

17. $(x^2+2xy+4y^2)(x^4-4x^2y^2+16y^4)$.   **18.** $(11x-2)(x+7)$.

Exercises XIX., p. 114.

4. a^{pq+qr}.   **5.** a^{2q-2r}.   **6.** b^{4p+4q}.   **7.** x^{3a+3b}.

8. $x^{\frac{1}{4}}(a^2+4ax^{\frac{1}{2}}+16x)$.   **9.** $a^{\frac{1}{6}}x^{\frac{1}{3}}(81a^{\frac{5}{3}}+36a^{\frac{5}{6}}x+16x^2)$.

10. (i) $5a^2b\sqrt{3ab}$; (ii) $3\sqrt[3]{5}$; (iii) $a^{\frac{1}{q^2-p^2}}$.   **11.** $a^{-\frac{1}{6}}b^{-\frac{3}{10}}$.

12. $\frac{1}{6}$.   **13.** $a^5b^5c^3$.   **14.** $(xy^2)^n$.   **15.** $2c\sqrt[3]{a^2b}$.

Miscellaneous Exercises XX., p. 115.

1. $2x^2-4xz+2z^2-2y^2$.   **2.** (i) $x^6-4x^4+2x^3-x^2+1$; (ii) $x-2$.

3. x^2-1.   **4.** $\dfrac{x^2+1}{x^2+2}$.   **5.** $2x^7-7x^2+5$.

6. $a^4-3a^3b+6a^2b^2-3ab^3+b^4$.   **7.** x^2+ax+a^2.

8. $13\cdot86$.   **9.** $5\cdot44$.   **10.** $8ab$.

11. (i) x^2+ax+a^2; (ii) $x^4+a^2x^2+a^4$.   **13.** $4x-5$.

14. $(3x+y)(9x^2-3xy+y^2)$.

15. (i) $x^4+x^3-a^2x^3+\dfrac{x^2}{a^2}+a^2x-x+1$; (ii) $x^2+(n+3)ax+3a^2$.

17. $a-2b+2c-d$; 1.   **19.** $x=\dfrac{a^2+b^2}{a+b}$, $y=-\dfrac{a^2+b^2}{a+b}$.   **20.** a.

21. $\left(\dfrac{a}{b}\right)^{mn}$.   **23.** $(2a+3b)(2a-3b)$; $(2a-3b)^2$; $(4a-b)(a-2b)$.

24. (a) $(2a+3b)(4a^2-6ab+9b^2)$; (b) $x(x+2)(2x+7)$.

25. (a) $6p^2+5pq-6q^2$; (b) $4p^2-12pq+9q^2$;

  (c) $9q^2-4p^2$: $(x+2)(x+3)$; $(x+6)(x-1)$.

26. (a) $1672+70$; (b) $(a+b)(c+d)$; (c) $(x-y)(x+y-xy)$.

27. $(a+b)(x-y)$; $(x-1)(x-2)$.

28. $(x+12\cdot35)(x-11\cdot65)$; $(x+11\cdot123)(x+2\cdot877)$; $(x+3)(x^2-3x+9)$.

29. $-1\frac{3}{4}$.   **30.** $1\cdot586$.

Exercises XXI., p. 121.

1. $\dfrac{x-1}{x+5}$.   2. $\dfrac{x-4}{x+4}$.   3. $\dfrac{3a+x}{a+x}$.   4. $\dfrac{x-3y}{x+3y}$.   5. $\dfrac{2x-a}{x+a}$.

6. $\dfrac{x+1}{x-5}$.   7. $\dfrac{x-4}{(x-2)(x-3)}$.   8. $-\dfrac{5ab(3a^2+4b^2)}{a^4-16b^4}$.

9. $\dfrac{x^2+y^2}{(x+y)^2}$.   10. $\dfrac{34xy}{y^2-16x^2}$.   11. $\dfrac{x-1}{x-4}$.   12. $\dfrac{2xy^2}{x+3y}$.

13. $\dfrac{x^2}{y^2}$.   14. $\dfrac{f^2+fg+g^2}{fg}$.   15. $\dfrac{1}{x^2-2xy-3y^2}$.

16. 0.   17. 0.   18. $-\dfrac{(x+y-z)^2}{2yz}$.

19. $x+y+z$.   20. 0.   21. $\dfrac{x^2+1}{x^2+2}$.   22. $-\dfrac{2a^2-ab-b^2}{a^2-b^2}$.

23. $\dfrac{1}{x^2-y^2}$.   24. $\dfrac{x}{x+a}$.   25. $\dfrac{2}{x^4-5x^2+4}$.   26. x^5.

27. $\dfrac{x^3y^3}{2xy(x+2y)}$.   28. $1\cdot008$; $0\cdot000012$.   29. (a) 2920; (b) $\dfrac{6a}{b}$; (c) $\dfrac{24y^3}{15x}$.

30. (a) $4x+2y-5z$; (b) $10+4y-2z$; (c) $y-3x-z$; (d) $5x-3y+6z$;
$18\cdot5$; 27 ; $-10\cdot25$; $18\cdot75$.

Exercises XXII., p. 125.

1. 6.   2. 15.   3. 21.   4. 48.   5. 14.

6. $\dfrac{a^2}{b-a}$.   7. $\dfrac{3ac-bc}{2b}$.   8. 11.   9. 2.   10. $\dfrac{a+c}{2}$.

11. $\dfrac{2}{3}$.   12. $\dfrac{20}{27}$.   13. $1\frac{1}{2}$.   14. $1\frac{3}{4}$.   15. $-\frac{4}{5}$.

16. 12.   17. $\dfrac{1}{21}$.   18. $\dfrac{ab}{a+b}$.   19. $\cdot12$.   20. $13\frac{6}{7}$.

21. a^2-c^2.   22. 5.   23. $-\frac{2}{5}$.   24. 2.   25. 1.   26. $\frac{1}{9}$.

27. -21.   28. $\frac{15}{7}$.   29. abc.   30. $\dfrac{2ab}{a+b}$.   31. $\frac{7}{2}$.   32. 1.

Exercises XXIII., p. 128.

1. 25 and 35.   2. 21 ; 18.   3. 78 yds. ; 58 yds.   4. 6 yds. ; 1 yd.

5. £166. 13s. 4d. ; £833. 6s. 8d.   6. $2\frac{1}{2}$ minutes.

7. A's is £32. 5s., B's £43, C's £15. 1s. 0d.   8. £660 ; £340.

9. 71 ; 51.   10. 216 ; 378.   11. 77, 66.   12. $10\frac{10}{11}$ mins. to 4.

13. 18 ; 24.   14. A, 22s.; B, 26s.   15. $16\frac{4}{11}$ past 6 ; $49\frac{1}{11}$ past 6.

16. 34.   17. 10.   18. 1470.   19. 30, $7\frac{1}{2}$, 6.

20. 20.   21. 4 days.   22. $\frac{5}{18}$.   23. $\cdot0542$ amperes.

24. £1. 15s. ; 7s. 6d.   25. 15 per cent. decrease.

26. £18. 8s. ; £14. 14s. ; £13. 16s.

Exercises XXIV., p. 134.

1. $x=4,\quad y=3.$ 2. $x=3,\quad y=1.$ 3. $x=\frac{1}{7},\quad y=\frac{1}{5}.$

4. $x=\frac{1}{7},\quad y=-\frac{1}{3}.$ 5. $x=15,\ y=16.$ 6. $x=10,\ y=12.$

7. $x=-\frac{1}{11},\ y=\frac{1}{5}.$ 8. $x=16,\ y=-4.$ 9. $x=12,\ y=-2$

10. $x=36,\ y=40.$ 11. $x=40,\ y=30.$ 12. $x=13,\ y=17.$

13. $x=\frac{1}{7},\quad y=\frac{1}{4}.$ 14. $x=-1,\ y=1,\ z=1.$

15. $x=\frac{1}{2}(a+b),\ y=\frac{1}{2}(a-b).$ 16. $x=1,\ y=-1$

17. $x=\dfrac{a^2+ab+b^2}{a+b},\ y=\dfrac{ab}{a+b}.$ 18. $x=7\frac{2}{11},\ y=3.$

19. $x=2\frac{5}{21},\ y=\frac{15}{10}.$ 20. $x=2b-a,\ y=2a-b.$

21. $x=\dfrac{2}{a},\quad y=3b.$ 22. $x=1,\ y=-1.$ 23. $x=4,\ y=\frac{1}{2}.$

24. $x=10,\ y=7.$ 25. $x=\frac{1}{4},\ y=\frac{1}{5}.$ 26. $x=3,\ y=6.$

27. $x=\dfrac{ac+b^2}{a^2+bc},\ y=\dfrac{c^2-ab}{a^2+bc}.$ 28. $x=2\frac{2}{3},\ y=3\frac{2}{3}.$

Exercises XXV., p. 138.

1. $\frac{6}{14}.$ 2. 8, 9, and 10.   3. 9 ; 16.

4. 3 and 14 ft. sides.   5. $2:5.$ 6. $\dfrac{x}{y}=\dfrac{7}{2}.$

7. 9 sq. ft.   8. 1s. 4d. per sq. ft. ; 6d.   10. 600, £500.

11. $2\frac{1}{5}$; 3.   12. $1\frac{1}{2}$; $5\frac{1}{4}$ yds.   13. 60 ; 45.   14. 36.

15. $\frac{5}{8}.$ 16. $E=\cdot046R+5.$ 17. 91.

18. £450 ; £225 ; £87. 10s. ; £237. 10s.   19. $E=\cdot313R+1\cdot08.$

Exercises XXVI., p. 151.

2. (i) $E=\cdot142R+5$;   (ii) $E=\cdot307R+\cdot91$;
    (iii) $E=\cdot0714R-\cdot299$;   (iv) $E=\cdot023R+\cdot12$;
    (v) $E=\cdot119R+4\cdot5,\ R=8\cdot4E-37$;
    (vi) $E=\cdot044R+\cdot456.$

3. (i) $E=\cdot115R+1\cdot9,$ $F=\cdot0736R+1\cdot83$;
    (ii) $E=\cdot042R+\cdot35,$ $F=2R+25$;
    (iii) $E=\cdot118R+1\cdot75,$ $F=\cdot077R+1\cdot75$;
    (iv) $E=\cdot0386R+\cdot08,$ $F=1\cdot75R+5$;
    (v) $E=\cdot1R+1\cdot75,$ $F=\cdot05R+2\cdot88$;
    (vi) $E=\cdot023R+\cdot4,$ $F=\cdot0057R+\cdot1$;
    (vii) $E=\cdot38R+\cdot06,$ $F=\cdot026R+\cdot04$;
    (viii) $E=\cdot0354R+\cdot57,$ $F=1\cdot69R+27.$

4. $n = 2 \cdot 7 \log N - 5 \cdot 1$.

5. (i) $n = 2 \cdot 045 \log N - 4 \cdot 192$, $\quad n = 2 \cdot 04 \log \dfrac{N}{M} - \cdot 264$;

   (ii) $n = 2 \cdot 97 \log N - 5 \cdot 9$, $\qquad n = 2 \cdot 86 \log \dfrac{N}{M} + 1 \cdot 87$;

   (iii) $\log \dfrac{N}{M} = \cdot 104 n$.

6. $L = 1 \cdot 49 T^2 + \cdot 537$.

MISCELLANEOUS EXERCISES.

Section I. Multiplication and Division, p. 163.

1. (i) 284·7, (ii) 2817.
2. (i) 62·25, (ii) 0·4056.
3. (i) 31·06, (ii) 0·3732.
4. (i) 0·01254, (ii) 7·446.
5. (i) 3·123, (ii) 1704.
6. (i) 416·8, (ii) 0·6797.
7. 67·97.
10. 2·1858, 5·033.
11. (i) 7·446, (ii) 0·01254.
12. (i) 0·4730, (ii) 0·002466.
13. (i) 0·1390, (ii) 1251.
14. 70·79.

Section II. Involution and Evolution, p. 163.

1. 5·68, 1546.
2. 1·722, 0·0198.
3. 6·102, 1·55.
4. 1768000, 11·03.
5. 34·73 : 1.
6. 260.
8. (i) 6·686, (ii) 2·892.
9. 12·53.
10. 15·94.
11. (i) 1·969, (ii) 0·9491.
12. 1·614, 39·82, 0·02511.
13. 17·26.
14. 1·558, 195·4.
15. 401·3.
16. $c = 1 \cdot 747 \times 10^{-14}$, $P = 3 \cdot 959$.
17. 1503.
18. 0·6575.
19. 1·810.
20. 0·02825, 0·9649.
21. $1 \cdot 362 \times 10^8$.
22. $14 \cdot 18 \times 10^7$.

Section III. Area, p. 165.

1. 6·158 sq. ft.
2. 10·09 ft., 44·41 sq. ft.
3. 24·63 sq. ft.
4. (i) 173·15, (ii) 172·37.
5. 84 sq. ft.
6. 231·4 in., 194·4 lbs.
7. 143·3 sq. ft., £10. 15s. 0d.
8. 1186 francs.
9. 39·24 yds., 259·1 sq. yds.
10. 13·81 sq. ft.
11. 219 yds.
12. 1634 sq. ft.

13. £1. 2s. 5·64d.　　　　**14.** (i) 28·42 sq. in., (ii) 28·45 sq. in.
15. 110, 77 yds.　　　　　　**16.** 6·928, 11·46 sq. ft.
17. 179·6 yds.　　　　　　　**18.** 5565 yds.

Section IV. Volume, p. 166.

1. 2815 cub. ft.　　　　　　**2.** 11·94 cub. ft.
3. 1·05 ft., 4·2 ft.　　　　**4.** 16 ins.
5. 14·6.　　　　　　　　　**6.** 2·2 lbs.
7. 6·652, 1·675 : 1.　　　　**8.** 1361 tons.
9. 9497 kilog.　　　　　　　**10.** 397.
11. 127·2, 125·64 cub. ft.　　**12.** 2045 cub. in.
13. 1·4 tons.　　　　　　　　**14.** 3·43 ins., 1552 sq. in.
15. $x = 7 \cdot 124$ in., width 11·4 in., inside radius 99·7 in.
16. 12080 miles, 33·55, 5·592 in.　**17.** 87·46 cub. in., 26·24 lbs.
18. 177·7 cub. in., 236·9 sq. in.
19. 72·636, 74·292, mean 73·464, 1 per cent.
20. 2000 cub in., internal volume 5508 cub. in.
21. 3642 sq. in., 8196 cub. in.　**22.** (i) 1889, (ii) 1920.
23. 90·74 tons, £21. 16s. 0d.　**24.** 150·8 sq. in., 2·727 tons.
25. 83·79 cub. ft.　　　　　　**26.** 2059 lbs.
27. 660400.　　　　　　　　**28.** 8640, £10. 16s.
29. 19730000.　　　　　　　**30.** £42. 10s. 4·8d., 9 yds.
31. 99·4.　　　　　　　　　**32.** 3·375, 3·367 yds.
33. 1·1 cub. in., 0·9 sq. in.
34. 23·58 cub. in., 6·27 lbs., 66·16 sq. in.
35. Dia. of section 6 in., mean rad. of ring 5·2 in.
36. 18s. 10·2d.　　　　　　　**37.** 9223 lbs., 922·3.
38. $217\frac{7}{33}$ yds., 7·701 lbs.　**39.** $7974\frac{2}{3}$ lbs.
40. (i) 63·65 ft., 134 tons.　　**41.** 11020 lbs.

Section V. Algebra, p. 170.

1. $\dfrac{\sqrt[3]{a^2(a^2+b^2)}+3}{a\sqrt{b}}$.

2. $\dfrac{(z^3-xy^2)^{\frac{2}{3}}}{x+y+z}$.

3. $\dfrac{3x^2\sqrt{y}-a\log_e x-b\sin cx}{x^3+y^2}$.

4. $\sqrt{\left(\dfrac{a^2}{b^2}+1\right)\dfrac{w}{n^2}}$.

5. $\dfrac{x^3+y^3}{x+y}=x^2+y^2-xy$.

6. $a^n - \sqrt[n]{a} = \sqrt[q]{a^p}$.

7. $(x+3)(x+4)$.
8. $(x-3)(x+4)$.
9. $(x+5)(x+6)$.
10. $(x+5)(x-6)$.
11. $(x-1\cdot9)(x+2\cdot3)$.
12. $(3x-5)(4x+3)$.
13. $(2x+y+a+3)(2x-y+a-3)$.
14. $\dfrac{x^2}{(x-8)(x-15)(x-17)}$.
15. $\dfrac{(x+2y)^2}{x-2y}$.
16. $\dfrac{4}{x^2-1}$, $0\cdot619$.
17. $(x-1)(x-3)(x-5)$.

Section VI. Simple Equations, p. 171.

1. 3. 2. 4. 3. $\frac{1}{3}$. 4. $\frac{3}{5}$.
5. 4. 6. 8. 7. $1\frac{2}{9}$. 8. 9.
9. 7. 10. 5. 11. $\frac{1}{7}$. 12. 4.
13. $\frac{5}{7}$. 14. $\dfrac{ab}{a+b}$. 15. $\dfrac{2ab}{a+b}$. 16. $ab-a-b$.
17. $\dfrac{1}{ab}$. 18. $\dfrac{a^2-b^2}{b-4a}$. 19. $\dfrac{ab}{a+b}$. 20. $\dfrac{a(c^2-b^2)}{a^2+b^2}$.
21. ab. 22. $\dfrac{a+b}{2}$. 23. $\dfrac{ab}{b+1}$. 24. $\dfrac{2ab}{a+b}$.

Section VII. Simultaneous Equations, p. 171.

1. $a=2\cdot2$, $b=0\cdot11$, $4\cdot4$. 2. $=243\cdot9$, $b=-26\cdot59$, $y=671\cdot9$.
3. $t=18\cdot385$, $p=8\cdot685$. 4. 4, 3. 5. $\frac{2}{3}$, 0. 6. 2, $2\frac{1}{2}$.
7. 10, 7. 8. $\frac{1}{2}$, 1. 9. $0\cdot02$, $1\cdot9$. 10. $\frac{3}{8}a$, $\frac{3}{16}a$, $-\frac{5}{16}a$.
11. $\frac{7}{3}$, $\frac{5}{3}$, $\frac{37}{3}$. 12. $a+b$, a. 13. 13, $\frac{1}{11}$. 14. 10, -7.

Section VIII. Problems, p. 172.

1. £1. 2s. 6d., £1. 16s. 0d., £1. 4s. 0d. 2. $76\frac{1}{2}$, $202\frac{1}{2}$.
3. 55. 4. £1. 6s. 8d., £1. 3s. 4d., £1. 8s. 4d. 5. $1\frac{1}{7}$.
6. 2 miles per hour. 8. 4 men, 5s.
9. $a=4\cdot284$, $b=\cdot000916$, $C=$£5$\cdot867$, 25 hours £146. 14s.
10. $45\cdot6$, $30\cdot4$. 11. 184, 161. 12. $7\cdot481$, $5\cdot059$.
13. 670800. 14. $44\cdot52$, $27\cdot84$. 15. 68 yds., 40 yds.
16. 63, 84. 17. 15 days. 18. 25, 24.

Section IX. Squared Paper, p. 174.

1. 0·195, 0·0895, 0·352, 2·34.   **3.** 16.   **4.** 8·6.

5. 470.   **6.** − 3·749, − 1·097, 1·559, $x=2·13$.

7. 0·87.   **8.** 1·645.   **9.** $a=18$, $b=0·26$.

10. 0·84, 1·65, 58°, 145°, 87°.   **11.** 0·174.

12. 2·34 or 0·452.   **13.** 0·428, 1·89.   **14.** − 2·2, 1·3.

15. £1100000.   **16.** 1350 ft., 1700.

17. $G=20P+230$; 230.   **18.** 118·9, 160·8, 213·3.

19. 13550, 14350, 14740; 14350 cub. ft.   **20.** 2·012.

22. $x=12·03$ in.   **23.** $n=\frac{5}{2}$, $c=2·86$, $Q=2·66H^{\frac{5}{2}}$; 19·09.

24. 6·005.   **25.** 790 sq. ft.   **26.** 2628000 cub. ft.

27. 0·1137, 12·4.   **28.** 12·32 cub. ft.

29. $x=1·51$.   **30.** 17·93.

Exercises XXIX., p. 181.

1. 0·3491, 0·4468, 0·6981, 0·7941, 1·0716, 1·2357, 1·4835, 1·5307

2. 10° 24′, 15° 30′, 32° 30′, 54° 18′, 70° 18′, 73° 42′, 89° 42′.

3. 8·069 ft.   **4.** 0·6528, 68·55 ft.   **5.** 38° 11 .

6. 1·967, 300·9 ft.   **7.** 30°, 68° 45′.   **8.** 47° 13'.   **9.** 57·3°.

10. 52·36.   **11.** 20·94, 1200.   **12.** 145·2 miles.   **13.** 78° 44′.

14. 865600 miles.   **15.** 2234 miles.

Exercises XXX., p. 186.

1. 0·9315, 0·3904.   **2.** 65° 10′, 0·9075, 0·1611.   **3.** 0·766, 0·6428, 1.

4. 0·9539, 0·3147.   **5.** 0·5572.   **6.** 64° 37′, 0·9035, 2·1076.

7. 32° 24′.   **8.** $A=17°\ 28′$, $B=81°\ 22′$, $C=60°\ 56′$.

9. y/x, 0·6687, 0·6691.   **10.** 0·82.   **11.** 119·8 sq. ft.   **12.** 27° 38′.

13. 41° 24′.   **14.** 34° 22′, 0·5645, 0·8254.   **15.** 0·5736, 0·8192, 0 7002.

16. 30°, 0·5774, 0·866.   **17.** 139·1 yds.   **18.** 75° 23′.

Exercises XXXI., p. 190.

1. 0·2924, 0·4695, 0·7314, 0·3355, 0·5553, 0·9679.

2. 0·8746, 0·7986, 0·7193, 0·6639, 0·4751, 0·2798.

3. 0·4663, 0·7265, 2·7475, 0·2648, 0·4571, 0·9152.

4. 33°, 0·5446, 0·6494.   **5.** $A=58°$, 0·8480, 0·5299.

6. 0·4667, $A=27°\ 49′$.   **7.** 0·8978, 26° 8′.

8. 0·4450.   **9.** 39·65 sq. in.

Exercises XXXII., p. 191.

1. 3·356 in., 6·71 sq. in. **2.** 5·782, 13·69, 25°, 35·85 sq. ft.

3. $A = 62°\ 45'$, $b = 2·06$ in., 4·124 sq. in.

4. 34°, 5·14 in., 3·467 in., 8·91 sq. in.

5. 41°, 1·64 ft., 1·887 ft., 1·547 sq. ft.

6. 62°, $a = 4·61$, $b = 8·67$, 1·998. **7.** 0·8066, 0·5911, 1·3646.

8. $b = 12·06$, $c = 6·745$. **9.** 41·13, 81° 42'.

10. 7·144 in. **11.** 16·07 miles, 19·15 miles. **12.** 17° 48'.

Exercises XXXIII., p. 194.

1. (i) 168·2 ft., (ii) 59·51 ft., (iii) 128·5 ft., (iv) 122·3 ft.

2. (i) 963·2 ft., 1025 ft. ; (ii) 866·2 ft., 1000 ft. ;
(iii) 63·84 ft., 163·4 ft. ; (iv) 119·3 ft., 141·3 ft.

3. 76·99 ft. **4.** 98·79, 24·4 ft. **5.** 151·5 ft. **6.** 61·48 yds.

7. 69·99 ft. **8.** 0·5 mls., 0·866 mls. **9.** 209·5 ft., 299·2 ft.

10. 923·2 ft. **11.** 59·4 ft. **12.** 1192 ft. **13.** 27·71 ft.

14. 121·24 ft. **15.** 136·7 ft. **16.** 1199 yds., 1055 yds., 931·7 yds.

17. 29·96 ft. **18.** 99·54 ft. **19.** 45 ft. **20.** 200·4 ft., 53° 10'.

Exercises XXXIV. p. 200.

1. (i) $A = 26°\ 23'$, $B = 36°\ 20'$, $C = 117°\ 17'$, 5·33 sq. ft. ;
(ii) 21° 46', 38° 12', 6·49 sq. ft. ;
(iii) $B = 27°\ 44'$, $C = 39°\ 12'$, 11·01 sq. ft. ;
(iv) 61° 24', 71° 50', 46° 46', 889·2 sq. ft. ;
(v) 53°, 39° 2', 87° 58', 121·7 sq. ft. ;
(vi) 81° 24', 57° 54', 40° 42', 313700 sq. ft.

2. (i) 47° 24', 58° 36', 74°, $c = 48·32$ ft., 762·8 sq. ft. ;
(ii) 47° 40', 80° 20', 52°, $c = 31·98$, 472·6 sq. ft. ;
(iii) $B = 80°\ 42'$, $C = 39°\ 18'$, $a = 71·1$ ft., 1824 sq. ft. ;
(iv) 88° 53', $B = 42°\ 55'$, $c = 67·87$ ft., 2101 sq. ft. ;
(v) 73° 44', 28° 56', $a = 125$ ft., 3719 sq. ft. ;
(vi) 92° 53', 49° 31', $c = 22·3$ ft., 309·5 sq. ft.

3. (i) 55° 18', $a = 12·65$ ft., $b = 15$ ft., 78 sq. ft. ;
(ii) $a = 15$ ft., $b = 16$ ft., 72 sq. ft. ;
(iii) $a = 2·99$, $c = 3·196$, $B = 80°\ 30'$, 4·712 sq. ft. ;
(iv) $B = 119°\ 59'$, $a = 2·996$, $c = 4·992$, 6·489 sq. ft.

4. 308·3 ft., 183·1 ft., £221. 2s. **5.** 9° 26'.

6. 178·1 yds., 291·8 yds., 167·4 yds. **7.** 898·8 yds.

8. 5·83, 5. **9.** 41° 24', 55° 48', 82° 48'.

10. $A = 36°\ 52'$, $B = 53°\ 8'$, 6 sq. in., 5 in. **11.** 34·01 yds.

12. 11196·3 ft.

INDEX

PRINTED IN GREAT BRITAIN BY ROBERT MACLEHOSE AND CO. LTD.
THE UNIVERSITY PRESS, GLASGOW.

Books for Engineering Students

LONDON : MACMILLAN AND CO., LTD

Books for Engineering Students

THEORETICAL AND PRACTICAL MECHANICS AND PHYSICS. By A. H. MACKENZIE, C.I.E., M.A., B.Sc. and A. FORSTER. 216 pages. 3s.

ENGINEERING SCIENCE. By H. B. BROWN, B.Sc., A.M.I.Mech.E. and A. J. BRYANT, B.Sc., A.M.I.Mech.E.

Vol. I. Applied Mechanics and Hydrostatics. 403 pages. 7s.

Vol. II. Heat and Heat Engines and Electrotechnics. 450 pages. 7s. 6d.

Vol. III. In the press.

APPLIED MECHANICS FOR BEGINNERS. By J. DUNCAN, M.I.Mech.E. 338 pages. 4s. 6d.

APPLIED MECHANICS FOR ENGINEERS. By J. DUNCAN, Wh. Ex., M.I.Mech.E. 718 pages. 15s. net.

PROPERTIES AND STRENGTH OF MATERIALS. An Elementary Text-Book for Students of Engineering. By J. A. CORMACK, B.Sc., and E. R. ANDREW, Assoc. M.C.T. 384 pages. 10s.

ALTERNATING CURRENT ELECTRICAL ENGINEERING. By PHILIP KEMP, M.Sc. Tech., M.I.E.E. Sixth Edition (1942). 611 pages. 18s. net.

AN INTRODUCTION TO THE PRACTICE OF CIVIL ENGINEERING. By E. E. MANN, M.Sc. 296 pages. 7s.

LONDON : MACMILLAN AND CO., LTD